THE RELIABILITY OF THE
NEW TESTAMENT

THE RELIABILITY OF THE
NEW TESTAMENT

BART D. EHRMAN & **DANIEL B. WALLACE** IN DIALOGUE

Robert B. Stewart, Editor

FORTRESS PRESS
Minneapolis

THE RELIABILITY OF THE NEW TESTAMENT
Bart D. Ehrman and Daniel B. Wallace in Dialogue

Cover art and design: Joe Vaughan
Book design: Christy J. P. Barker and Douglas Schmitz / Timothy W. Larson

Library of Congress Cataloging-in-Publication Data
The reliability of the New Testament / Bart D. Ehrman and Daniel B. Wallace in dialogue ; Robert B. Stewart, editor.
  p. cm.
  Includes bibliographical references and index.
  ISBN 978-0-8006-9773-0 (alk. paper)
  1. Bible—Evidences, authority, etc. I. Wallace, Daniel B. II. Stewart, Robert B. III. Title.
BS2332.E37 2011
225.1—dc22   2010049012

Manufactured in the U.S.A.

15   14   13   12   11   1   2   3   4   5   6   7   8   9   10

For Rhyne Putman

CONTENTS

CONTRIBUTORS

Bart D. Ehrman is the James A. Gray Distinguished Professor at the University of North Carolina at Chapel Hill, where he has served as both the Director of Graduate Studies and the Chair of the Department of Religious Studies. A graduate of Wheaton College, Professor Ehrman received both his M.Div. and Ph.D. from Princeton Theological Seminary, where his 1985 doctoral dissertation was awarded magna cum laude. Since then, he has published extensively in the fields of New Testament and Early Christianity, having written or edited twenty-one books, numerous scholarly articles, and dozens of book reviews. Among his most recent books are a Greek-English edition of the Apostolic Fathers for the Loeb Classical Library, an assessment of the newly discovered *Gospel of Judas*, and three *New York Times* best sellers: *Jesus Interrupted* (2010), on what scholars have long said but lay readers have not heard about the contradictions, discrepancies, and forgeries of the New Testament; *God's Problem* (2008), an assessment of the biblical views of suffering; and *Misquoting Jesus* (2007), an overview of the changes found in the surviving copies of the New Testament and of the scribes who produced them.

Craig A. Evans is the Payzant Distinguished Professor of New Testament at Acadia Divinity College in Wolfville, Nova Scotia, Canada. He received his Ph.D. from Claremont and his D.Habil. from Budapest.

Professor Evans is the author of several books, including *Jesus and His Contemporaries* (1995), *Jesus and the Ossuaries* (2003), and with N. T. Wright, *Jesus, the Final Days* (2009), as well as many articles and studies in scholarly journals such as *Biblica, Catholic Biblical Quarterly, Journal of Biblical Literature, New Testament Studies*, and *Novum Testamentum*. He also edited the *Dictionary of New Testament Background* (2000) and the *Encyclopedia of the Historical Jesus* (2008). Professor Evans has lectured at universities and museums around the world, including Cambridge, Durham, Oxford, Yale, and the Field Museum in Chicago. He has also appeared in several television documentaries concerned with the Bible and archaeology.

K. Martin Heide is Associate Professor for Semitic Languages at Philipps-Universität Marburg. He published the *editio princeps* of the Testaments of Isaac and Jacob (*Die Testamente Isaaks und Jakobs*, 2000), and just recently prepared a critical edition of the Arabic and Ethiopic texts of the Testament of Abraham (*Das Testament Abrahams*, 2011). He has published several Hebrew ostraca from the First Temple period and has written a book on New Testament textual criticism, *Der einzig wahre Bibeltext? Erasmus von Rotterdam und die Frage nach dem Urtext* [*The Only True Bible? Erasmus of Rotterdam and the Quest for the Original Greek*] (2006). He also collated the Ethiopic Bible for the *Editio Critica Maior* and edited and translated the Syriac citations for a new online Septuagint database.

Michael W. Holmes is University Professor of Biblical Studies and Early Christianity and Chair of the Department of Biblical and Theological Studies at Bethel University, St. Paul, Minnesota. He holds degrees from Trinity Evangelical Divinity School (M.A.), and Princeton Theological Seminary (Ph.D.). A specialist in New Testament textual criticism and the Apostolic Fathers, he has edited and translated *The Apostolic Fathers: Greek Texts and English Translations* (3rd edition, 2007), edited with Bart D. Ehrman *The Text of the New Testament in Contemporary Research: Essays on the Status Quaestionis* (1995), and co-authored with Bart D. Ehrman and Gordon Fee *The Text of the Fourth Gospel in the Writings of Origen, volume 1: Introduction, Text, and Apparatus* (1992). He is the author of *1 and 2 Thessalonians: The NIV Application Commentary* (1998) and editor of *The New Testament in the Greek Fathers*.

Dale B. Martin is Woolsey Professor of Religious Studies at Yale University. He specializes in New Testament and Christian origins, including attention to social and cultural history of the Greco-Roman world. He has also published on the politics and ideology of modern biblical interpretation, especially with regard to family, gender, and sexuality. His books include *Slavery as Salvation: The Metaphor of Slavery in Pauline Christianity* (1990); *The Corinthian Body* (1999); *Sex and the Single Savior: Gender and Sexuality in Biblical Interpretation* (2006); *Inventing Superstition: From the Hippocratics to the Christians* (2007); and *Pedagogy of the Bible: An Analysis and Proposal* (2008). He has edited several books, including (with Patricia Cox Miller) *The Cultural Turn in Late Ancient Studies: Gender, Asceticism, and Historiography* (2005). He was an associate editor for the revision and expansion of the *Encyclopedia of Religion*, published in 2005. He has held fellowships from the National Endowment for the Humanities, the Alexander von Humboldt Foundation (Germany), the Lilly Foundation, the Fulbright Commission (USA-Denmark), and the Wabash Center for Teaching and Learning in Theology and Religion. In 2009, Martin was elected to the American Academy of Arts and Sciences.

David Parker is Edward Cadbury Professor of Theology at the University of Birmingham, United Kingdom, and a director of the Institute for Textual Scholarship and Electronic Editing. His publications include *Codex Bezae: An Early Christian Manuscript and its Text* (1992); *The Living Text of the Gospels* (1997); *An Introduction to the New Testament Manuscripts and their Texts* (2008); *Manuscripts, Texts, Theology: Collected Papers, 1977–2007*; and *Codex Sinaiticus: The Story of the World's Oldest Bible* (2009). He is Executive Editor of the International Greek New Testament Project, making editions of John and the letters of Paul in the *Editio Critica Maior*, and has copublished editions of the papyri (1993) and majuscules (2007) and of the Byzantine text (2007). He is coeditor of Texts and Studies (third series) and *Arbeiten zur neutestamentlichen Textforschung*.

Sylvie T. Raquel is Associate Professor of New Testament at Trinity International University. Dr. Raquel, who received both her M.Div. and Ph.D. degrees from New Orleans Baptist Theological Seminary (NOBTS), combines her areas of specialization (textual criticism of the New Testament, the Synoptic Gospels, and Revelation) with her interest in apologetics. She has conducted research at the Center of New Testament Textual Studies in New Orleans. Her doctoral dissertation, "The Text of the Synoptic Gospels in the Writings of Origen," is in revision for publication. She has published book reviews and articles in several journals and has presented papers at colloquiums and professional meetings. She is a contributor to *Essays on Revelation: Appropriating Yesterday's Apocalypse in Today's World* (2010) and the revised *Quest Study Bible* (2011). She is also a member of the editorial board of the *Sacred Tribes* journal.

Robert B. Stewart is Associate Professor of Philosophy and Theology at New Orleans Baptist Theological Seminary, where he is Greer-Heard Professor of Faith and Culture. He received both his M.Div. and Ph.D. from Southwestern Baptist Theological Seminary. He is editor of *The Resurrection of Jesus: John Dominic Crossan and N. T. Wright in Dialogue* (2006); *Intelligent Design: William A. Dembski and Michael Ruse in Dialogue* (2007); and *The Future of Atheism: Alister McGrath and Daniel Dennett in Dialogue* (2008), all from Fortress Press. In addition, he is author of *The Quest of the Hermeneutical Jesus: The Impact of Hermeneutics on the Jesus Research of John Dominic Crossan and N. T. Wright* (2008). A contributor to the *Cambridge Dictionary of Christianity* and the *Revised Holman Bible Dictionary*, he has published articles and book reviews in numerous journals.

Daniel B. Wallace is Professor of New Testament Studies at Dallas Theological Seminary and Executive Director of the Center for the Study of New Testament Manuscripts. He received both his Th.M. and Ph.D. from Dallas Theological Seminary and has done postdoctoral studies at Tyndale House, Cambridge; the Institut für neutestamentliche Textforschung, Münster, Germany; and Universität Tübingen, Germany. He is a member of *Studiorum Novi Testamenti Societas, Institute for Biblical Research, Society of Biblical Literature, and the Evangelical Theological Society.* He has published dozens of articles in academic theological journals, and has authored, edited, or contributed to more than twenty books, including *Greek Grammar beyond the Basics: An Exegetical Syntax of the New Testament* (1996); *New English Translation/Novum Testamentum Graece* (2004); *Reinventing Jesus: How Contemporary Skeptics Miss* *the Real Jesus and Mislead Popular Culture* (2006); *Dethroning Jesus: Exposing Popular Culture's Quest to Unseat the Biblical Christ* (2007); *Granville Sharp's Canon and Its Kin: Semantics and Significance* (2009); and, forthcoming, *Revisiting the Corruption of the New Testament: Manuscript, Patristic, and Apocryphal Evidence* (2011).

William Warren is Professor of New Testament and Greek at New Orleans Baptist Theological Seminary, where he holds the Landrum P. Leavell II Chair of New Testament Studies. Professor Warren, who received both his M.Div. and Ph.D. degrees from New Orleans Baptist Theological Seminary, is the founding director of the H. Milton Haggard Center for New Testament Textual Studies. He is the editor of *La Teología de la liberación: una respuesta evangelica* [*Liberation Theology: An Evangelical Response*] (1990); translator of *Introducción a la crítica textual* [*Introduction to Textual Criticism*] (2004); author of *Luke: A Study Guide* (1997); and Senior Project Director and Editor for the CNTTS Textual Apparatus, an electronic textual apparatus for the Greek New Testament (2003 to present). A contributor to the *Revised Holman Bible Dictionary*, he has published articles and book reviews in numerous journals in both Spanish and English.

PREFACE

The purpose of the Greer-Heard Point-Counterpoint Forum in Faith and Culture is to provide a venue for fair-minded dialogue on subjects of importance in religion or culture. The intention is to have an evangelical Christian dialogue with a non-evangelical or non-Christian. The forum is intended to be a dialogue rather than a debate. As such, it is a bit more freewheeling than a traditional debate, and it is not scored. The goal is a respectful exchange of ideas without compromise. So often in our culture the sorts of issues that the forum addresses stoke the emotions and, consequently, the rhetoric is of such a nature as to ensure that communication does not take place. There may be a place and time for such preaching to the choir, but minds are rarely changed as a result of such activity—nor are better arguments forthcoming as a result of gaining a better understanding of positions with which one disagrees. The result often is that what passes for argument is really nothing more than a prolonged example of the straw man fallacy.

The subject of the 2008 Greer-Heard Point-Counterpoint Forum in Faith and Culture was "The Textual Reliability of the New Testament." The dialogue partners were Bart Ehrman of the University of North Carolina at Chapel Hill and Daniel B. Wallace of Dallas Theological Seminary. I would hope that every Bible reader has at least some interest in whether he or she is reading what the authors of the New Testament books actually wrote.

The dialogue took place April 4 and 5, 2008, in the Leavell Chapel on the campus of the host institution, New Orleans Baptist Theological Seminary. On that unusually fair April evening in New Orleans, nearly a thousand people filled the Leavell Chapel to hear the exchange. The audience was enthusiastic and appreciative. No doubt, the popularity of Ehrman's best-selling book *Misquoting Jesus: The Story behind Who Changed the Bible and Why* had much to do with the size of the audience and its evident enthusiasm for the topic. The discussion between Ehrman and Wallace was spirited and direct but respectful, punctuated with good-natured humor. It was obvious that both men believed passionately in their position and felt they had an important message to convey to those in attendance. One of the consistent fruits of the forum has been the realization that disagreement does not have to be shrill or heated; one does not have check one's convictions at the door in order for respectful dialogue to take place.

Along with my introductory chapter, this book includes a transcript of the April 4, 2008, dialogue between Ehrman and Wallace, as well as the papers presented the following day by Michael Holmes, Dale Martin, David Parker, and William Warren.

In addition to the essays presented at the Greer-Heard Forum, three other essays are included. The first author, K. Martin Heide, offers a Continental perspective on issues related to the New Testament text. Craig A. Evans writes of how his training in critical studies has affected his understanding of the New Testament text and what this means for his personal faith. Kim Haines-Eitzen also agreed to contribute a chapter for the book but, unfortunately, had to withdraw due to circumstances beyond her control. The final chapter is Sylvie Racquel's contribution discussing early Christian scribal practices.

While one could easily note issues that are not addressed in this volume or think of significant scholars who are not included, these chapters make for a fuller treatment of the issue. Readers will have to judge for themselves whether this is, in fact, the case.

I am grateful that Fortress Press has seen fit to allow us to present the fruit of the 2008 Greer-Heard Forum. I trust that you will read it with an open mind and carefully consider what each author has to say. You will be the richer for having done so.

ACKNOWLEDGMENTS

Thanking others in print always causes me a bit of anxiety because I fear that I will fail to recognize someone who truly deserves a word of appreciation. But many deserve to be publicly thanked, and even praised, so I must go on. First of all, I must thank Bill and Carolyn Heard for their passion to have a forum where leading scholars can dialogue about important issues in faith and culture in a collegial manner and on a balanced playing field—and their willingness to fund such a project. Without them, the Greer-Heard Point-Counterpoint Forum in Faith and Culture would be a dream rather than a reality. As always, I thank Dr. Chuck Kelley, President of New Orleans Baptist Theological Seminary, for his support and encouragement.

The event would never have come off successfully without the efforts of Craig Garrett and his staff at the Providence Learning Center. He endured countless meetings and thousands of questions while showing great flexibility throughout.

I also am grateful to Vanee Daure and her staff for the work they did in media support. James Walker and the staff of Watchman Fellowship must be thanked for audio CD reproduction, order fulfillment, and Web site management related to making the forum available to others via audio CDs and MP3 files. Sheila Taylor and the NOBTS cafeteria staff must be applauded for serving numerous meals of all varieties to large numbers. Lisa Joyner of Johnson Ferry Baptist

Church in Marietta, Georgia, deserves a word of recognition for her work in producing the programs and CD covers. Without the high-quality graphic art and public relations work of Boyd Guy and Gary Myers, the task would have proven too great.

Jeremy Evans must be thanked for organizing the Evangelical Philosophical Society (EPS) special-event program that took place in conjunction with the Greer-Heard Forum, as must the EPS executive committee for supporting the idea. I also thank Scott Smith for his efforts in publicizing the event, and Joe Gorra for providing EPS support materials. I am especially grateful to EPS president Paul Copan for speaking at the event.

Our conference speakers, Michael Holmes, Dale Martin, David Parker, and Bill Warren, must all be thanked. In addition, the contributions of our other authors, Craig A. Evans, K. Martin Heide, and Sylvie Raquel, are much appreciated. All are outstanding scholars.

I am grateful for NOBTS Provost Steve Lemke making it possible for Baptist College groups to attend the event. His efforts, along with those of Archie England and Page Brooks, and their respective staffs are much appreciated.

Brantley Scott and the staff at Lifeway Books deserve a word of thanks for working so hard at the book signing and for going the extra mile to ensure that all the books ordered actually arrived on time. This was a massive undertaking, but they never complained.

Michael West, Editor-in-Chief of Fortress Press, must be thanked for his enthusiasm for fair-minded, respectful dialogue on important issues and for choosing to publish the fruit of the Greer-Heard Forum. Michael's knowledge of contemporary theology coupled with his judicious recommendations significantly strengthened this book. Susan Johnson of Fortress Press also deserves a word of thanks. Her cheerful attitude, consummate professionalism, and eagerness to help in any way possible are much appreciated.

As always, my wife, Marilyn, and my children must be thanked. I suspect they enjoy the rush that accompanies an event like the forum, but they still make numerous sacrifices in order to make sure things come off without a hitch. By the time this book is released, Marilyn and I will be empty-nesters. I am grateful to my children for their patience through the years as these events have come and gone. I am more thankful that they all have a concern to read and understand the Bible.

My right-hand man for the past four years has been Rhyne Putman. He did everything he was asked to do and more—and all of it with a cheerful attitude. He was the webmaster for the conference Web site, as he has been for several years. He also produced the index, in addition to making numerous forays to various libraries to find resources I needed, as well as doing anything that didn't fall under somebody else's job description. His efforts have significantly strengthened this book. By the time this book is published, Rhyne will no longer be my teaching assistant but a colleague and fellow faculty member. I am very pleased to know this. It is to him that I gratefully dedicate this book.

Introduction

Why New Testament Textual Criticism Matters: A Non-Critic's Perspective

Robert B. Stewart

I thank God for text critics. Everyone who reads the New Testament owes them a debt. This is not merely an opinion, it is a fact—a fact of which many are blissfully unaware. The debt that readers of the New Testament who have no training in biblical languages owe translators is obvious. But even those who can read the Bible in its original languages owe a debt to text critics. When I read from a modern edition of the Greek New Testament, I am not reading *the* Greek New Testament but *a* Greek New Testament. In other words, I am reading an *edited* Greek New Testament, the product of multitudinous editorial decisions, all of which were made by New Testament textual critics.

Both Bart Ehrman and Daniel B. Wallace are well aware of this debt. In fact, as text critics, they occupy a privileged position from which to appreciate this fact and thus understand the issues involved in the thousands of decisions that text critics make. And make no mistake, New Testament text critics are faced with many more decisions than are critics of other ancient texts. This is because the New Testament is the best-attested book of antiquity—by far. This is good news

1

for those interested in knowing about Jesus and early Christianity. But this preponderance of evidence also complicates things. Simply put, the more manuscripts one has of any text, the more textual variants one is likely to encounter—and every textual variant demands a decision, a decision that will be made by a text critic.

As someone whose field is not New Testament textual criticism, I have tremendous respect for those who dedicate their lives to the sort of painstaking preparation and research that the field demands. A host of skills is required for this work. One not only needs to know several languages but also must be able to discern which words one is seeing on the page or digital copy of the page (to put it mildly, ancient copyists did not write as clearly as modern editions read—to say nothing of the difficulties that modern readers face when dealing with texts that have no breaks between words). One also has to learn how best to apply the general rules of textual criticism.[1] But at the end of the day, general rules are still only *general* rules, not hard-and-fast laws that can be applied in a one-size-fits-all manner and thus provide a guaranteed resolution to a problem. In other words, text critics must make judgment calls at times. New Testament textual criticism is as much an art as it is a science. Text critics thus have to combine the mind of a scientist with the heart of an artist.

Text critics are not always in agreement as to methodology. Although my look-around-town epistemology tells me that most of the leading text critics of our day would identify with reasoned eclecticism,[2] other approaches compete for the allegiance of text critics.[3] More significant still is the fact that, even among those who are agreed as to the overall method that should be used, there is a bewildering difference of opinion. It is probably best to say that at this time, text critics are broadly agreed but at numerous particular points have significant differences of opinions. These differences can only be resolved by experts.

There is still more reason to be thankful for New Testament textual critics. Not only do they play the role of nursemaids in delivering a single usable text to Bible translators, who then pass on the product of their work to ordinary Bible readers, the work of text critics can also provide a window through which to view at least a sliver of the past, even if only indirectly. In similar fashion to how physicists provide us a glimpse into how the universe came to be through the detailed analysis of fundamental particles of matter, text critics provide us a glimpse of the early church through the detailed analysis of manuscripts of the New Testament. Different scholars will disagree as to what the evidence they examine means or the degree to which we can gain insights from such investigation, but virtually all agree that, at least in theory, we can learn something about the early church in this way. For this we should be grateful.

In studying the manuscripts of the New Testament, text critics are confronted with some obvious challenges. For instance, not all New Testament manuscripts contain all the same books. Some contain books not retained in our "New Testament," while others lack certain books that are part of the New Testament as we recognize it today. Still others feature differences in order among the books of the New Testament. These differences allow scholars a glimpse into how the New Testament canon developed. So historians and theologians are also in debt to text critics.

Despite its importance, New Testament textual criticism is generally seen by those outside the field as being about as exciting as watching mold grow on old bread. The reason for this is that the work of textual criticism is quite complex and detailed, and therefore proceeds at a snail's pace. Most who study the New Testament, however, want to get on with the "real work" of exegesis, theology, preaching, and applied ministry, or at the very least devotional reading. But text critics do their work prior to the work of biblical studies or theology. Indeed, biblical studies and theology cannot be done apart from a biblical text, and in one very important sense, it is text critics who give—or at the very least deliver—the New Testament to us. Indeed, we mere mortals should be grateful for text critics every time we take up the New Testament.

Bart Ehrman is the rare writer who can make textual criticism interesting to the layperson. His *Misquoting Jesus* is a clear and provocative book that makes basic New Testament textual criticism understandable to the novice as it popularizes some of the major points in his earlier work *The Orthodox Corruption of Scripture*.[4] In the introduction to *Misquoting Jesus*, Ehrman shares some of his personal journey from fundamentalist Christianity, emphasizing the inerrancy of Scripture, to liberal Christianity.[5] To the best of my knowledge, *Misquoting Jesus* is the only book on New Testament textual criticism ever to be on the *New York Times* best-seller list. All New Testament textual critics should thank Ehrman for making their discipline relevant to the masses. In a very real sense, the dialogue and essays in this book result from the popularity of *Misquoting Jesus*. *Misquoting Jesus* has sold extremely well not only because it is very well written (although it certainly is) but also because it raises some fundamental questions as to the textual reliability of the New Testament and insists that these questions have significant ramifications for all of us.

One question that must be answered when considering the question of the textual reliability of the New Testament is this: What exactly does one mean in asking whether the New Testament is textually reliable? For instance, what does it mean to speak of the New Testament? Of what exactly does the New Testament consist? Does the New Testament contain the longer ending of Mark's Gospel? Does it contain the story of the woman taken in adultery? Does it contain 1 John 5:7 or Acts 8:37 as recorded in the King James Version?[6] These are only a few of the most obvious passages that are seriously questioned as to whether they actually are part of the New Testament.

Still, the fundamental question is not simply whether a given verse or pericope is included in the final edition but rather, "Is there any such text as the 'New Testament'?" In one sense, the answer is surely no. The New Testament is no single text but rather a *collection* of individual texts penned by ancient Christians. But for our purposes, let us say that the "New Testament" text refers to the New Testament that text critics provide for scholars to use in translation and critical research (including the critical apparatus).[7] Obviously, this is no single translation, nor any single ancient manuscript, but rather an edited text composed from numerous ancient manuscripts. It is from such a text that modern translations are derived. Still, this doesn't get us to one single text, because there are different edited Greek New Testaments still in use, as is clearly demonstrated by the fact that at least one modern edition of the Bible, the New King James Version, translates a different Greek text than most others. It is probably best to say that when text critics speak of the New Testament text, they generally refer to the latest edition of the Nestle-Aland *Greek New Testament*.[8]

What does it mean for a text to be textually "reliable"? Is textual reliability like balancing a checkbook (either it balances to the penny, or it does not)? Is anything less than 100 percent certainty deemed unreliable? Not unless we are prepared to consider virtually every extant Greco-Roman document unreliable and cease talking about what notable ancient authors, religious and secular, taught. For our purposes, I suggest that we think of textual reliability in terms of probability, or failing that, plausibility.[9] We simply cannot have certainty about historical texts whose originals are not available. But we can have confidence that the wording of contemporary critical New Testament texts reflects what the autograph most likely said, given the available evidence. Textual reliability is more like a legal verdict than it is like the balancing of a checkbook: given the available evidence, we can be confident beyond a reasonable doubt that this reading is most likely the original.

The answer, then, to the question of New Testament textual reliability depends, at least in part, on what one thinks of New Testament textual criticism. In other words, it seems that we are actually questioning how reasonable it is to believe that text critics, given the data and resources available to them coupled with their training and skill, can be trusted to deliver a reliable edition of the New Testament using the methodological procedures of the discipline. Make no mistake here: the critics are also on trial. On this point, Georg Luck comments, "Our critical texts are no better than our textual critics."[10] Some, no doubt, would have more serious questions about the state of the evidence—qualitatively or quantitatively, or both—while others would have concerns about the methods being used, or those evaluating the evidence. Still others are confident that the text of the New Testament is at least reliable, even if we don't know all the answers to all the questions that can be raised concerning it.

A debate is raging among New Testament textual critics at the present time. Traditionally, the task of New Testament textual criticism was conceived as one of recovery. Text critics have sought, at least since the days of Westcott and Hort, the architects of modern textual criticism, to recover the original wording of the New Testament. But some leading scholars are arguing that the task should be reconceived as *discovery of the earliest available text*, rather than recovery of the original text. Ehrman plainly believes that we cannot get back to the original (or autographic) text. Other critics agree that we cannot arrive at the original wording but hold that this inability is not too significant. David Parker, for instance, writes, "The recovery of a single original saying of Jesus is impossible."[11] The text is thus irretrievable. Yet he also insists, "But the question is not whether we *can* recover it, but why we want to."[12] Parker believes that instead of a single authoritative text, there are numerous, legitimate texts that represent the interpretations of differing Christian communities.[13] At the end of the day, in Parker's opinion, the manuscripts we have tell us about themselves and their communities, and he holds that seeing the primary purpose of New Testament textual criticism as one of arriving at the original reading is inconsistent with the nature of the texts with which the critic deals.[14]

Although Ehrman and Parker agree that we cannot recover the original wording of the text (for different reasons), they disagree as to the importance of this belief. For Ehrman, it matters a great deal; for Parker, not so much. Eldon Jay Epp follows Parker in holding that the role of the Spirit and the community take priority over a reliable text.[15] In effect, Ehrman, Parker, and Epp seem to hold that recovery of the original text is no longer to be seen as an end, or as the critic's primary point of focus; rather, the exploration of the manuscript tradition is to be used as a means, or as an instrument, through which one can see more clearly the early (and not so early) church as one seeks to understand how the text came to be as it is, rather than what the text says.

In contrast, Wallace and Moisés Silva reject this revisioning of the task of New Testament textual criticism. They grant that the text can reveal much about the early church—and that this is an important task that should be pursued. They do not, however, think recovering the original wording of the New Testament is in theory impossible or secondary in importance.[16] And like Ehrman, they believe it matters a great deal whether this in fact can be done.

Few evangelicals would argue that, ontologically speaking, the Spirit does not take priority over a text, even the biblical text. Clearly, the presence of the Spirit moving, guiding, filling, blessing, and empowering the community historically precedes the original text. Indeed, the text would never have come to be apart from the Spirit working among Christians. But the question at hand is not whether the Spirit and community are prior to or more fundamental than the text of the New Testament. The issue is what should the primary task of New Testament textual criticism be? It will certainly be interesting to see what direction the critical guild moves with regard to this issue.

As a philosopher, I find some areas especially interesting as I survey contemporary literature in New Testament textual criticism, particularly the work of Bart Ehrman. It is apparent that Ehrman is highly skeptical in some ways. Skepticism is generally a good thing for the scholar. (Please note that skepticism is not the same thing as cynicism. A skeptic insists upon evidence and/or reason for believing. A cynic will not believe in spite of evidence.) One thing that is abundantly clear to me is that New Testament textual criticism is an *evidential* discipline. Text critics critique the evidence they have—i.e., the available New Testament manuscripts.

Skepticism and its parent, empiricism, have a long and distinguished history in Western thought. But the line between proper skepticism and hyperskepticism is a fine one. Proper skepticism understands that evidence is required for one's beliefs about what is not the case, just as much as evidence is required for one's beliefs about what is the case. In other words, we must be as skeptical about our skepticism as we are of others' beliefs.

Bart Ehrman seems to hold that the New Testament that textual critics can deliver to us is unreliable because there are so many variant readings in the manuscripts and because our earliest manuscripts are copies of copies of copies, etc. But is this skepticism reasonable? Perhaps, but I have my doubts.

The problem with hyperskepticism is that it sets the bar for knowledge impossibly high. In chapter 2 of his classic work, *The Problems of Philosophy*, Bertrand Russell makes an important point. He takes up the question of whether there is in any sense an external world that we can know. He writes:

> This question is of the greatest importance. For if we cannot be sure of the independent existence of objects, we cannot be sure of the independent existence of other people's bodies, and therefore still less of other people's minds, since we have no grounds for believing in their minds except such as are derived from observing

their bodies. Thus if we cannot be sure of the independent existence of objects, we shall be left alone in a desert—it may be that the whole outer world is nothing but a dream, and that we alone exist. This is an uncomfortable possibility; but although it cannot be strictly *proved* to be false, there is not the slightest reason to suppose that it is true.[17]

There is not the slightest reason to suppose that it is true. Can the same be said of Ehrman's skepticism? Perhaps, but probably not—and the real issue is not whether or not there is the *slightest* reason to believe that we can't recover the original, but whether there is *sufficient* reason to do so. No doubt, Ehrman believes that he has at least 300,000 reasons to hold that we cannot know what the originals said. But is this reasoning justified?

Clearly, there is evidence of corruption among the manuscripts we have. This is indisputable. But what does this evidence prove? It seems to me that evidence has to be evidence *for* something. In the case of textual criticism, it has to be textual evidence for a particular reading. The very nature of New Testament textual criticism means that we will have evidence for a select number of possible readings, not evidence for an unlimited number of possible readings. Is it possible that the original reading of any verse of the New Testament is one that we have no evidence for at the moment? Of course it's possible. But where is the evidence for such a reading? We have none. Indeed, by definition, we can have none. If we had such a reading, it would not be a reading that we do not have.

I am not playing language games here but rather insisting that as scholars engaged in an evidential discipline, text critics always have before them a range of possible answers. They may select between two readings or twenty (or more), but they will not choose from an infinite number of readings. And I have confidence that most of the time, text critics will be able to put forward a reading that is quite reasonably believed—and quite probably correct or at least more likely to be correct than any other single reading. This does not in any sense mean I think they *will* always get it right. But they *can* get it right.[18] In fact, I have good reason to think that in many, if not most cases, text critics have gotten it right. How can I believe this? I believe this because

I believe in the rationality of the general rules of textual criticism and the integrity of text critics.

We must therefore insist not only that one must note *general* evidence *of* corruption over time but also that one's conclusions concerning any variant must be based upon *specific* evidence *for* a particular reading, rather than allowing evidence of alterations to lead one to a radically skeptical position with regard to the possibility of recovering the original wording. In other words, a variant creates a range of possibility—or, if one prefers, a degree of uncertainty—but we should not allow this degree of uncertainty to lead to unbridled skepticism. For the most part, we can certainly be confident of arriving at the point where we can responsibly say, "Given the available textual data and considering both internal and external factors, we may say that this reading is most likely to be the original." We should thus take Russell's words to heart and not be bothered by things we have no reason (i.e., evidence) to believe.

I am, however, more skeptical than Bart Ehrman on at least one point. My skepticism concerns what can be proven as to changes in the text. It is clear that there have been changes. Most of these changes are inconsequential and easily explained. Indeed, for most of the variants, there is near-universal agreement as to how they arose.

There are, however, a number of textual variants that are truly significant. There are plausible suppositions as to why these occurred, but that is what they are—plausible suppositions—and most of them subject to serious challenge. The critics who make these suppositions presume that one can identify which party corrupted the text and for what reason. This is a somewhat dubious assertion. The probability of correctly identifying the earlier reading is considerably higher than the probability of correctly inferring the identity of the corruptor and the theological reason or motivation behind the corruption. It is difficult to ascertain the theological motivation of an author who often can be placed within a particular context (time, locale, belief system, worldview). It is even more difficult to divine the theological motivation of an unknown copyist who generally cannot be placed with any degree of certainty in such a context.

Even if it is possible, this difficulty is further conditioned by the fact that we know that generally the non-orthodox were not intending to be heretical but in fact saw themselves as defenders of what they believed was orthodoxy. Their unorthodox beliefs were in fact overre-actions to beliefs that *they* deemed unorthodox (and which often were). The upshot is that in such a context, the "corruption" could have been a move away from what we now call orthodoxy rather than a move toward it, although it was clearly motivated by a concern for what the "corrupters" considered orthodox belief. In other words, it is likely that there was a whole lot of corrupting going on—and that those we today call orthodox were not the only corrupters.

Still, there is nothing that says that one *cannot* identify the theologi-cal reason behind a significant textual variant. I am proposing, how-ever, that one proceed with caution and a bit of reasoned skepticism on this point, recognizing that equally plausible alternative theories may arise. Indeed, fair-minded text critics and early church historians frequently interpret the same data in differing ways. Therefore, one should hold one's conclusions in this regard with a fair amount of epistemological humility.

This highlights the detective-like nature of the task. At the end of the day, the ultimate question in this regard is not only whether the explanation brought forward is plausible but also whether such an explanation is beyond a reasonable doubt.

In their masterful *The Text of the New Testament*, Bruce Metzger and Bart Ehrman cite the *Oxford Dictionary of National Biography* in referring to John W. Burgon, a nineteenth-century supporter of the Majority Text, as "a High-churchman of the old school," and as "a leading champion of lost causes and impossible beliefs."[19] Burgon "could not imagine that, if the words of Scripture had been dictated by the inspiration of the Holy Spirit, God would not have providentially pre-vented them from being seriously corrupted during the course of their transmission."[20] I find it interesting that Ehrman agrees with Burgon on this point. Ehrman writes, "For the only reason (I came to think) for God to inspire the Bible would be so that his people would have his actual words; but if he really wanted people to have his actual words, surely he would have miraculously preserved those words, just as he had miraculously inspired them in the first place."[21]

Apparently, Burgon would argue *modus ponens*:[22]

(1) If God inspired the New Testament autographs, then he would also prevent them from being seriously corrupted.

(2) God inspired the New Testament autographs.

(3) Therefore, God has also providentially prevented the New Testament manuscripts from being seriously corrupted.

Ehrman, in contrast, seems to be arguing *modus tollens*:[23]

(1) If God inspired the New Testament autographs, then he would also prevent them from being seriously corrupted.

(2) New Testament manuscripts show numerous signs of corruption.

(3) Therefore, God did not inspire the New Testament autographs.

Both are valid argument forms. The major premise (1) is the same in both. Some will reject (2) in one or both arguments. I have no interest in rejecting (2) in either argument. I affirm the inspiration of the autographs. I also accept the fact that there has been some significant corruption in the transmission of the New Testament text. Bracketing the question of what one means by "serious corruption," it appears then that the only issue is whether or not (1) is true.

I see no compelling reason to think that (1) is true. The Bible does not explicitly teach any such thing, although the Bible does affirm its own inspiration. (I am *not* arguing that the Bible is inspired because it says it is!) But more importantly, at least from a logical perspective, is the fact that the antecedent of (1), "If God inspired the New Testament autographs," does not entail its consequent, "then he would also prevent them from being seriously corrupted."[24] It is thus incumbent upon both Burgon and Ehrman to demonstrate the truthfulness of (1). I do not know upon what grounds they can do so if there is no biblical or logical warrant for believing (1).[25]

I suspect that (1) "seems" logical to both Burgon and Ehrman because that's what they would do if they were God. But *seeming* logical is not the same thing as *being* logical. To think that one is the same as the other is to mistake psychology for logic. Furthermore, understanding how *I would act* is not a sound theological method for discerning how *God must act*. Both Burgon and Ehrman are mistaken in their reasoning. It appears then that Ehrman, like Burgon, is a "High-churchman," so to speak: he just affirms a different creed.

So the question for now is this: How well have text critics done in delivering to us the Greek New Testament? Do we have good reason to believe that the fruit of their work is reliable—that is, close enough to what the original authors wrote to be trusted? Bart Ehrman and Dan Wallace disagree as to the reliability of the New Testament. Dan thinks it is reliable enough, although he grants that there are some viable variants that matter in terms of what the text means.[26] He holds that none of these variants, regardless of how one handles them, changes any cardinal doctrine of Christian faith. Therefore, modern Bible readers can trust that modern translations are generally based upon a reliable Greek text. Bart agrees that none of these variants changes any cardinal doctrine of Christian faith but does not think the issue is whether or not doctrine is affected.

In the dialogue that follows, Bart and Dan lay out their respective positions and then forcefully question each other. The discussion is lively, and the issues are important. I hope you benefit from reading it.

1

✛

The Textual Reliability of the New Testament: A Dialogue

Bart D. Ehrman and Daniel B. Wallace

OPENING REMARKS
Bart D. Ehrman

Thank you very much; it's a privilege to be with you. I teach at the University of North Carolina. I'm teaching a large undergraduate class this semester on the New Testament, and of course, most of my students are from the South; most of them have been raised in good Christian families. I've found over the years that they have a far greater commitment to the Bible than knowledge about it. So this last semester, I did something I don't normally do. I started off my class of 300 students by saying the first day, "How many of you in here would agree with the proposition that the Bible is the inspired word of God?" *Voom!* The entire room raises its hand. "Okay, that's great. Now how many of you have read *The Da Vinci Code*?" *Voom!* The entire room raises its hand. "How many of you have read the entire Bible?" Scattered hands. "Now, I'm not telling you that *I* think God wrote the Bible. You're telling me that *you* think God wrote the Bible. I can see why you'd want to read a book by Dan Brown. But if God wrote a book, wouldn't you want to see what he had to say?" So this is one of the mysteries of the universe.

The Bible is the most widely purchased, most thoroughly read, most broadly misunderstood book in the history of human civilization. One of the things that people misunderstand, of course—especially my nineteen-year-old students from North Carolina—is that when we're reading the Bible, we're not actually reading the words of Matthew, Mark, Luke, John, or Paul. We're reading translations of those words from the Greek of the New Testament. And something is always lost in translation. Not only that, we're not reading translations of the *originals* of Matthew, Mark, Luke, John, or Paul, because we don't have the originals of any of the books of the New Testament. What we have are copies made centuries later—in most instances, many centuries later. These thousands of copies that we have all differ from one another in lots of little ways, and sometimes in big ways. There are places where we don't know what the authors of the New Testament originally wrote. For some Christians, that's not a big problem because they don't have a high view of Scripture. For others, it's a big problem indeed. What does it mean to say that God inspired the words of the text if we don't have the words? Moreover, why should one think that God performed the miracle of inspiring the words in the first place if he didn't perform the miracle of preserving the words? If he meant to give us his very words, why didn't he make sure we received them?

The problem of not having the originals of the New Testament is a problem for everyone, not just for those who believe that the Bible was inspired by God. For all of us, the Bible is the most important book in the history of Western civilization. It continues to be cited in public debates over gay rights, abortion, over whether to go to war with foreign countries, over how to organize and run our society. But how do we interpret the New Testament? It's hard to know what the words of the New Testament mean if you don't know what the words were. And so [we have] the problem of textual criticism, the problem of trying to establish what the original authors wrote and trying to understand how these words got changed over time. The question is a simple one: "How did we get our New Testament?" I'll be spending my forty minutes trying to deal with that particular issue.

I'm going to start by giving an illustration of one of the books of the New Testament, the Gospel of Mark. Mark is our shortest Gospel. Many scholars think that Mark was the first Gospel to be written. We don't know *where* Mark was actually written. Scholars have different hypotheses about where it was written. Many scholars over the years have thought that maybe Mark was written in the city of Rome. Fair enough, let's say that the Gospel of Mark was written in the city of Rome. Somebody—we call him Mark, because we don't know his name and it doesn't make sense to call him Fred—sat down and wrote a Gospel. How did this Gospel get put in circulation? Well, it wasn't like it is today. Today, when an author writes a book, the book gets run off by electronic means and gets composed and produced and distributed so that you can pick up a copy of any book—*The Da Vinci Code*, for example—in a bookstore in New Orleans and another in California and another in New York, and it's going to be exactly the same book. Every word will be exactly the same because of our ways of producing books. But they didn't have these means of producing books in the ancient world. The only way to produce a book in the ancient world was to copy it by hand—one page, one sentence, one word, one letter at a time, by hand. Mass producing books in the ancient world meant some guy standing up in front dictating and three others writing down what he said. That was mass production, producing books three at a time. What happens when books are copied by hand? Try it sometime and you'll find out what happens: people make mistakes. Sometimes my students aren't convinced of this, so I tell them, "Go home and copy the Gospel of Matthew, and see how well you do." They're going to make mistakes.

So Mark's book gets copied by somebody in Rome who wants a copy. They don't want just one copy, they want another copy. So somebody makes a copy, and probably the person makes some mistakes. And then somebody copies the copy. Now, when you copy the copy, you don't know that the guy who copied it ahead of you made mistakes; you assume that he got it right. So when you copy his copy, you reproduce his mistakes—and you introduce your own mistakes. And then a third person comes along and copies the copy that you've made of a copy and reproduces the mistakes that you made and that your predecessor made, and he makes his own mistakes. And so it goes. Somebody eventually visits the city of Rome—somebody from Ephesus, say—and decides, "We want a copy of that." So he copies one of the copies. But he's copying a copy that has mistakes in it, and he takes it back to Ephesus, and there in Ephesus, somebody copies it. And then somebody from Smyrna shows up and decides they want a copy. Well they copy the copy of the copy of the copy, and then somebody decides they want a copy in Antioch. And so they come, and they make a copy. Copies get made and reproduced. As a result, you get not just copies of the original but copies of the copies of the copies of the original.

The only time mistakes get corrected is when somebody is copying a manuscript and they think that the copy they're copying has a mistake in it. And they try to correct the mistake. So they change the wording in order to make it correct. The problem is, there's no way to know whether somebody who's correcting a mistake has corrected it correctly. It's possible that the person saw there was a mistake and tried to correct it but corrected it incorrectly, which means that now you've got three states of the text: the original text, the mistake, and the mistaken correction of the mistake. And then somebody copies that copy, and so it goes on basically for year after year after year after year. Mistakes get made en route, mistakes get copied and recopied, mistakes get corrected, but sometimes incorrectly, and so it goes.

Now, if we had the original copy of Mark, it wouldn't matter, because we could look at the original and say, "Yeah, these guys made mistakes, but we've got the original." But we don't have the original. And we don't have the first copy, or the copy of the copy. We don't have copies of the copies of the copies of the copies. What do we have? We have copies that were made many, many years later.

The first copy of Mark that we have is called $\mathfrak{P}^{45}$. It's called $\mathfrak{P}^{45}$ because it was the forty-fifth papyrus manuscript discovered in the modern age and cataloged. Papyrus is an ancient writing material, kind of like paper today, only it was made out of reeds that grew in Egypt, and they made writing material out of it. The oldest manuscripts we have of the New Testament are all written on papyrus. $\mathfrak{P}^{45}$ dates from the third century, around the year 220 C.E. Mark probably wrote his Gospel around 60 or 70 C.E., so $\mathfrak{P}^{45}$ dates to about 150 years later—but it is the earliest copy we have. By the time $\mathfrak{P}^{45}$ was produced, people had been copying Mark year after year after year, making mistakes, reproducing mistakes, trying to correct mistakes, until we got our first copy. Our next copy doesn't come for years after that. Our first *complete* copy doesn't show up until around the year 350 C.E., 300 years after Mark was originally written. Starting with the fourth-century copies, we begin getting more copies. And there are, of course, lots of these later copies.

You hear sometimes that the New Testament is the best-attested book from the ancient world. That's absolutely right. We have more copies of the New Testament than we have of any other book from the ancient world. But you need to realize that the copies we have—by and large—are from later times, centuries after the copying process began. Now, you might say, "Well, look, you're talking about these mistakes and these copies, but God wouldn't let that happen." Well, there's only one way to check, to see whether it could happen, that mistakes would be made. And that is by comparing the copies that survive with one another. It's striking that when you do that, you don't find two copies that are exactly alike. People were changing these manuscripts.

What can we say about these surviving copies of the New Testament? Let me give you just some data, some basic information. First of all, how many do we have? Well, we don't need to be overly precise for now. Basically, we have something like 5,500 Greek manuscripts of the New Testament. As you know, the New Testament was originally written in Greek and was circulated in Greek. This is another thing I ask my students the first day of class. I give them this quiz the first day of class to see what their Bible knowledge is. The first question I ask is "How many books are there in the New Testament?" And that usually knocks off half the class right there. But then I ask what language it was written in, and about half of my students think the New Testament was written in Hebrew. Interesting. The other half thinks that it was written in English. So I think we're doing okay.

The New Testament was originally written in Greek. We have some 5,500 manuscripts in Greek from over the ages. When I say we have these manuscripts, I don't mean we have 5,500 *complete* manuscripts. Some are just little fragments, but if you have a little fragment, you count that as the manuscript. Some manuscripts are small fragments; some of them are enormous tomes that were produced in the Middle Ages and were found in libraries or monasteries. We have some 5,500 Greek manuscripts.

What are the dates of these manuscripts? Well, they range in dates from the second century up through the invention of printing. You would think that once Gutenberg had invented the printing press, people would stop writing things out by hand because now you can produce things with the printing press. As it turns out, even after the invention of the printing press, some people didn't think that was going to catch on. So they still copied things out by hand. Just like today, even though you have a computer, sometimes you use a number two pencil. Even after the invention of printing, there still was the copying of things by hand. So we actually have manuscripts that go down to the seventeenth and eighteenth centuries and even into the nineteenth century. So they span from the second century up to the nineteenth century.

The earliest manuscript we have of any kind is a manuscript called $\mathfrak{P}^{52}$. Again, it's on papyrus, that's why it's called $\mathfrak{P}$. It's 52 because it's the fifty-second papyrus manuscript discovered and cataloged. It measures 2.5 by 3.5 inches, about the size of a credit card. It's an interesting little piece. It was discovered by a scholar named C. H. Roberts, who was digging through the papyri collection at the John Rylands Library in Manchester, England.

Fig. 1.1: $\mathfrak{P}^{52}$.

Some of these libraries have these bushels or envelopes filled with papyri that have been discovered by archaeologists. These archaeologists find these little pieces of things in garbage dumps, and they don't know what texts they are. Sometimes they're too small to read, so they throw them in an envelope or put them in a bushel, and it goes to some museum. And then someone working through them will notice something. In the 1930s, C. H. Roberts pulled out a little triangular piece (since named $\mathfrak{P}^{52}$) and noticed that he could read some of the writing. For instance, the Greek word *oudena* (ουδενα), which means "no one," and *hina*, which means "in order that." He realized that it sounded like the trial of Jesus before Pilate in the Gospel of John, chapter 18. So you know that the people who do this kind of thing are pretty smart. This is what they do for a living. (Strangely enough, there's a living in it.) There's writing on the back of the piece as well, which is significant, because it shows that the piece isn't from a scroll, but from a book—a book like we think of books, written on both sides of the page and then sewn together at the binding. This came from a book, and since it is written on the front and the back, you can figure out—since you can see about how wide the letters are—that you've got a top margin here and a left margin here. You can figure how many letters you need to get to the end of this line [in order] to get to the beginning of the next line like that. So you can figure out how long the lines were. And since you have writing on the back, you can figure out how many lines this thing would have originally been, so when you turn it over, you can get to the top of the writing on the back. So just with this little writing, you can figure out how many pages were in this manuscript originally, just from this little 2.5-by 3.5-inch piece.

The way you date these things isn't by carbon-14 dating or something like that, but on the basis of handwriting analysis. The technical term is paleography (*paleo* meaning ancient, *graphe* meaning writing), a study of ancient writing. On the basis of paleography, scholars have dated this manuscript, $\mathfrak{P}^{52}$, sometime to the first part of the second century—say, the year 125 or 130, plus or minus twenty-five years. It's from the Gospel of John. John was probably written in the 90s, so this manuscript is only about thirty years away from the Gospel of John. It's just a little piece, but it's only thirty years away, which is pretty good. This is the oldest manuscript of the New Testament that we have. Would that we had more ancient manuscripts of this age! But we don't. This is the oldest. Most of the copies we have are written much later than this. Of our 5,500-some Greek manuscripts, over 94 percent were made after the eighth century. In other words, 94 percent of our surviving manuscripts were produced 700 years or more after the originals. So we have a lot of manuscripts, but most of them are not very close to the date of the originals. Most of them are from the Middle Ages.

How many mistakes are in these manuscripts? Scribes copied the books of the New Testament. Most tried to do a pretty good job of reproducing what they were copying. They didn't try to make mistakes, but sometimes mistakes happen. So how many mistakes are there in the 5,500 manuscripts we have? This did not seem to be a very big problem to scribes who were actually copying the texts in the Middle Ages. Some scribes knew there were mistakes, but I'm not sure they realized how big the problem was—that there were a lot of mistakes.

It wasn't until about 300 years ago that scholars starting realizing the enormity of the problem. There was a scholar named John Mill, who I believe is unrelated to the Victorian John Stuart Mill. John Mill was an Oxford scholar who in the year 1707—almost exactly 300 years ago—produced a printed edition of the Greek New Testament that he called the *Novum Testamentum Graece*, the Greek New Testament. This was an interesting book because of how it was constructed. Mill printed the lines of the Greek New Testament on the top of the page, and then on the bottom of the page, he indicated places where manuscripts that he examined had different readings for the verses that he cited at the top. Mill had access to about a hundred manuscripts, and he looked at how the church fathers had quoted the New Testament in places, and he looked at how different ancient versions of the New Testament—ancient translations into Latin, Syriac, and Coptic—presented the New Testament. He looked at all these materials—devoting thirty years of his life to this—and then produced his *Novum Testamentum Graece*, presenting the Greek text at the top and indicating some of the places where the manuscripts differed from one another at the bottom.

To the shock and dismay of many of his readers, John Mill's apparatus indicated 30,000 places of variation among the manuscripts he had discovered. Thirty thousand places where the manuscripts had differences! This upset a lot of John Mill's readers. Some of his detractors claimed that he was motivated by the devil to render the text of the New Testament uncertain. His supporters pointed out that he actually hadn't invented these 30,000 differences; he just noticed that they existed. He was just pointing out the facts that are there for anyone to see. Moreover, as it turns out, Mill did not cite everything that he found. He found far more variations than he cited in his apparatus.

So that was John Mill in 1707, 300 years ago, looking at a hundred manuscripts. What about today? What can we say about the number of differences in our manuscripts today? As it turns out, it is very hard to say exactly how many differences there are in our surviving manuscripts. We have far more manuscripts than Mill had. He had a hundred; we have 5,500. So we have fifty-five times as many manuscripts as he had. And this may seem a little weird, but in this field, the more evidence you have, the harder it is to figure out what you're doing, because the more evidence you have, the more manuscripts you have, the more differences you have. So, it turns out, half the time, evidence just complicates the picture. So we have 5,500 manuscripts. How many differences are there? The reality is, we don't know, because no one has been able to count them all, even with the development of computer technology. It is probably easiest simply to put it in comparative terms. There are more differences in our manuscripts than there are words in the New Testament. That's a lot. There are more differences in our manuscripts than there are words in the New Testament.

Some scholars will tell you there are 200,000 differences, some will tell you 300,000 differences, some say 400,000. I don't know. It's something like that; between 300,000 and 400,000 would be my guess. But what do we make of that fact?

But the first thing to say about these 300,000 or 400,000 differences is that most of them don't matter for anything. They are absolutely irrelevant, immaterial, unimportant, and a lot of them you can't even reproduce in English translations from the Greek. As it turns out, the majority of mistakes you find in manuscripts show us nothing more than that scribes in antiquity could spell no better than my students can today. The scribes can be excused on this; they didn't have spell-check. (I just don't understand students who have spell-check on their computer but have spelling mistakes in a paper. I mean the computer tells you! It's in red! This word is wrong!) If scribes had had spell-check, we might have 50,000 mistakes instead of 400,000, but scribes didn't have spell-check. And half the time, scribes frankly didn't care how they spelled things. We know that scribes often didn't care how they spelled things because sometimes the same word appears within a line or two, and the scribe spells it differently in the two places. It also turns out that scribes didn't have dictionaries. Spelling wasn't a big deal for most of these people. So that's one kind of mistake, which of course doesn't matter for anything. What other kinds of mistakes do you have?

Often scribes will leave out things, often by accident—not planning to leave something out. They just mess up because they miss something on the page. Sometimes they leave out a word, sometimes a sentence, and sometimes an entire page. Sometimes scribes were incompetent, sometimes they were sleepy, and sometimes they were bored.

You can see how it would happen with this illustration from Luke 12:8-10:

> And I tell you, everyone who acknowledges me before others,
> The Son of Man also will acknowledge before the angels of God;
> But whoever denies me before others will be denied before the
>   angels of God
> And everyone who speaks a word against the Son of Man . . .

And it goes on to say that blasphemy "against the Holy Spirit will not be forgiven." Notice that the second and third lines end in the same words, "before the angels of God." What scribes would sometimes do is copy the second line, "will acknowledge before the angels of God," they look at the page, and then they copy it. Then their eyes go back to the page and inadvertently go to the [end of the] *third* line, which ends the same way, "before the angels of God." The scribes think this was the line that they had just copied. So they keep copying with the following words, and the result of that is that they leave out the entire second line. So in some manuscripts, you have "will acknowledge before the angels of God," followed by "And everyone who speaks a word against the Son." They've left out the middle line. You see how that works? That kind of eye-skip goes under a technical name. An eye-skip is called parablepsis. Parablepsis happens because the words at the end of the line are the same. Lines ending with the same words is called homoeoteleuton. So, this kind of mistake, I try to teach my students, is parablepsis occasioned by homoeoteleuton.

This, then, is another accidental kind of mistake. Accidental mistakes are exceedingly common in our manuscripts, in part because some scribes were completely inept. My favorite example of an inept scribe was a fourteenth-century scribe of a manuscript that's called MS[109]. Now this example is a little bit complicated. MS[109] is copying the genealogy of Jesus in Luke. There are two genealogies of Jesus in the New Testament. Matthew has a genealogy that takes Jesus back to Abraham, the father of the Jews. And Luke has a genealogy that takes Jesus back to Adam, as in Adam and Eve. This is an amazing genealogy when you think about it. I have an aunt who is a genealogist, who has traced my family line back to the *Mayflower*. The *Mayflower*? Pfoo! Adam and Eve! We're talking serious genealogy here!

The genealogy begins with Joseph and works backward. Joseph is supposedly the father of Jesus, and Joseph is son of so-and-so, who is son of so-and-so, son of so-and-so, who is son of David, who is son of so-and-so, who is the son of so-and-so, who is the son of Abraham, who is the son of so-and-so who is the son of Adam, son of God. So it actually traces Jesus' genealogy back to God, which is even better than tracing back to Adam. It's an amazing genealogy.

The scribe of MS[109] in the fourteenth century was copying a manuscript that had Luke's genealogy in two columns, but the second column didn't go all the way down the page. And instead of copying the first column and then the second column, the scribe copied across the columns, leading to some very interesting results. In this genealogy, in MS[109], the father of the human race is not Adam, but some guy named Pherez, and as it turns out, God is the son of Aram. And so it goes.

There are all sorts of accidental mistakes in the manuscripts, and probably most of the mistakes we have in our manuscripts are accidental. In these cases, it is fairly easy to figure out what happened. Not a big problem. There are other mistakes in our manuscripts, though, that appear to be intentional. It's hard to say absolutely that a scribe intentionally changed the text because the scribe is not around for us to ask, "Did you do this on purpose?" But there are some changes that really look as though they had to be done on purpose. I'll give you a few examples of these because they tend to be rather important. These are the ones that most textual critics spend their time talking about. These big changes are the kind of things that if somebody has a New Testament class with me, they ought to know about by the time the semester is over. First is the story that is probably the favorite story among Bible readers and has been for many years, the story of Jesus and the woman taken in adultery. One of my reasons for thinking that this is people's favorite Bible story is because it's in every Hollywood movie about Jesus. You simply can't make a Jesus movie without this story. Even Mel Gibson, wanting to do a movie about Jesus' last hours, had to sneak this scene in as a flashback. So you're familiar with the story: The Jewish leaders drag this woman before Jesus and say, "She has been caught in the act of adultery, and according to the Law of Moses, we're supposed to stone her to death. What do you say we should do?" This is setting up a trap for Jesus, because if Jesus says, "Well, yeah, stone her to death," he's breaking his teachings of love and mercy. If he says, "No, forgive her," then he's breaking the Law of Moses. So what's he going to do? Well, Jesus, as you know, has a way of getting out of these traps in the New Testament. In this instance, he stoops down and starts writing on the ground. He then looks up and says, "Let the one without sin among you be the first to cast a stone at her." He stoops down again and continues writing, and one by one, the Jewish leaders start feeling guilty for their own sins, and they leave until Jesus looks up, and it's just the woman there. And he says to her, "Woman, is there no one left here to condemn you?" And she says, "No, Lord, no one." And Jesus says, "Neither do I condemn you; go and sin no more."

This is a beautiful story, and it's rightly one of the favorite stories of readers of the Gospels of the New Testament—filled with pathos, teaching a very powerful lesson about the need for forgiveness and about not casting the first stone. The difficulty, as many of you know, is that this story, in fact, was not originally in the Bible. It is now found in John 7–8 (part of the end of chapter 7 and the beginning of chapter 8), but it's not found in our oldest and best manuscripts of the Gospel of John. And the vocabulary used in this story is unlike what you find elsewhere in the Gospel of John, and when you actually look at this story in its context, it seems to be badly placed in its context. It interrupts the flow of the context.

Scholars for centuries have realized that this story does not belong in the Gospel of John, and it is not found in any other Gospel. You'll still find it in a lot of your English Bibles, but in most English Bibles, the editors will put brackets around it to tell you that it may be a really old and popular story, but it wasn't originally part of the Gospel. That's a pretty big change of the text. My assumption is that however that story got in there, it wasn't by pure accident. It might have been an accident, but I think somebody came up with a story and put in there. My hunch actually is that somebody found it in the margin of a manuscript. A scribe was copying his manuscript of John, and knowing the story, he decided to write it out in the margin. The next scribe came along and saw the story in the margin and thought that the scribe before him had inadvertently left out a story, so this second scribe put the story in the text itself. And the next scribe came along and copied that manuscript and left it in. Pretty soon, the story was propagated as being part of the Gospel of John, even though it originally was not part of the Gospel of John. That's a pretty big change, and I assume it is probably in some sense intentional.

Another example, a big example, is the last twelve verses of Mark. Mark, as I was saying earlier, is the shortest Gospel. It is probably my favorite Gospel. Mark doesn't beat you over the head with his theology. Mark is very subtle, and for that reason, I really like it. One of the best parts of Mark is how it ends. Jesus has been condemned to death, he's been crucified, he's been buried. On the third day, the women go to the tomb to anoint his body, but when they arrive, Jesus is not in the tomb. There's a young man there who tells the women that Jesus has been raised and that the women are to go tell Peter and the disciples that Jesus will precede them and meet them in Galilee. And then the text says, "But the women fled from the tomb and didn't say anything to anyone, for they were afraid." Period. That's it! That's where it ends.

You say, "Ai, yai, yai! How can it end there? Doesn't Jesus show up? Don't the disciples go to Galilee? Don't they see him?" You're left hanging. Well, scribes got to this passage that they were copying out, and they got to chapter 16:8, and it said, "The women fled from the tomb and didn't say anything to anyone, for they were afraid." And the scribes said, "Ai, yai, yai! How can it end there?" So the scribes added an ending. In your Bibles today, you'll find an additional twelve verses in which the women *do* go tell the disciples. The disciples do go to Galilee. Jesus does meet them there, and Jesus tells the disciples that they are to go out and make converts. And he tells them those who believe in him will be able to handle snakes and that they'll be able to drink deadly poison, and it won't harm them. And then Jesus ascends to heaven. So now the Gospel has an ending that's more familiar. This ending, by the way, is used in my part of the world. We have these Appalachian snake handlers that base their theology on these last twelve verses. I've always thought that somebody in the ambulance on the way to the hospital ought to maybe tell one of these guys, "You know, actually those verses weren't originally in there."

The verses are not found in our two best and oldest manuscripts of Mark. The writing style of these verses is different from the rest of Mark. When you read it in Greek, there's a rough transition between that story and the preceding story. Most scholars, then, are pretty convinced that either Mark ended with verse 8 or the ending of Mark got lost—that we lost the last page. I personally think that it ended with verse 16:8—that the women didn't tell anybody. The reason is that throughout Mark's Gospel, unlike the other Gospels, the disciples never can figure out who Jesus is. Jesus is always frustrated with his disciples in Mark's Gospel. He keeps asking, "Don't you understand? Don't you get it?" At the end, they still don't get it. They're never told.

Moreover, it's interesting that in Mark's Gospel, whenever Jesus performs a miracle, he tells people, "Don't tell anybody." Or he'll heal somebody and say, "Don't tell anybody." Or he'll cast out demons, and he'll tell them, "Don't say anything." And then at the end, when somebody is told to say something, they don't say anything. When they're told not to say anything, they do say things. So I think Mark is interesting and it ended with 16:8.

I'll give you another example of a major change. Jesus heals a leper in Mark 1. The leper comes up to him, asks to be healed, and Jesus says, "I am willing." The text says, "Filled with compassion, Jesus reached out his hand and touched the man. 'I am willing,' he said. 'Be clean!'" (Mk. 1:41, NIV) In some of our earlier manuscripts, though, instead of saying, "feeling compassion for the man," it says "Jesus got angry" and reached out his hand and touched him and healed him. He got angry? That's a big difference.

Well, which did the text originally say? Did it say that Jesus felt compassion or that he got angry? Now, you have to imagine that you're a scribe copying this text. If you're a scribe copying it, and you have the word in front of you that Jesus "felt compassion," are you likely to change it to say that he "got angry"? On the other hand, if you came across the word saying Jesus "got angry," would you be likely to change it to say that "he felt compassion"? If you put it that way, the latter is the more likely possibility, which is why a lot of scholars think, in fact, that originally this text said that Jesus got angry and that scribes changed it to say he felt compassion. But what did he get angry at? That's the big question. But my point is that you can't interpret what the words *mean* if you don't know what the words *are*. Textual critics try to figure out what the words are.

Is the text of the New Testament reliable? The reality is there is no way to know. If we had the originals, we could tell you. If we had the first copies, we could tell you. If we had copies of the copies, we could tell you. We don't have copies in many instances for hundreds of years after the originals. There are places where scholars continue to debate what the original text said, and there are places where we will probably never know.

Thank you very much.

OPENING REMARKS
Daniel B. Wallace

Bart, as I expected, your presentation was energetic, informative, and entertaining. It was vintage Bart Ehrman. What many folks here probably don't realize is that you and I have known each other for more than twenty-five years. Our academic paths, in fact, have been remarkably similar. I met you when you were just starting out in your doctoral program at Princeton. Six months later, you were *cruising* through the program while I was *driving* a truck to make ends meet. Similar activities. The year you completed your doctorate, I was just starting mine. Seven years later, in 1993, when you wrote your magnum opus, *The Orthodox Corruption of Scripture*, I began thinking about my dissertation, which should soon be published. But by the time you wrote your fifteenth book, I had already finished my fifteenth article. And when you were nominated to be Man of the Year for *Time* magazine, after writing *Misquoting Jesus*—when the name Bart Ehrman became a household word—most of my students knew my name. Yes, we have a lot in common.

Seriously, it's an honor for me to share the stage with Bart Ehrman. He's the only scholar I know who has been featured on NPR, BAR, SBL, CBS, NBC, and ABC. Not only this, but he's been on Jon Stewart's *Daily Show*—twice. And he's the only biblical scholar I know whom Stephen Colbert dissed with a classic line, which I can't repeat in mixed company.

I've tried to keep up with Bart's voluminous output, but it hasn't been easy. Normally, he writes in a clear, forceful style and punctuates his writing with provocative one-liners and a good measure of wit. I must confess, however, that his *Misquoting Jesus* left me more perplexed than ever. I wasn't sure exactly what he was saying. Reading it one way contradicted what he had written elsewhere, while reading it another way was hardly controversial—and certainly not the sort of book that would warrant being a blockbuster on the *New York Times* best-sellers list.

So, at the outset of my lecture, I acknowledge that I'm not sure what all the points of disagreement between us are. But I do know some.

I think that it would be good if I began by speaking about what we agree on. There is often a gulf between those "inside" a particular scholarly discipline and those on the outside. And when outsiders hear what insiders are talking about, sometimes they can get quite alarmed. Bart says in the appendix to *Misquoting Jesus*, "The facts that I explain about the New Testament in *Misquoting Jesus* are not at all 'news' to biblical scholars. They are what scholars have known, and said, for many, many years."[1] He's right. So at the outset, I want to discuss our common ground. There are basically five things that we agree on:

1. The handwritten copies of the New Testament contain a lot of differences. We're not sure exactly what the number is, but the best estimate is somewhere between 300,000 and 400,000 variants. And this means, as Bart is fond of saying, that there are more variants in the manuscripts than there are words in the New Testament.

2. The vast bulk of these differences affect virtually nothing.

3. We agree on what we think the wording of the original text was almost all the time.[2]

4. Our agreement is even over several well-known or controversial passages:

• In Mark 16:9-20, Jesus tells his disciples that they can drink
poison and handle snakes and not get hurt. If you are from West
Virginia, I'm sorry to disappoint you, but both Bart and I agree
that this passage is not part of the original text of Mark.

• We both agree that the story of the woman caught in adultery
(Jn. 7:53—8:11) was not part of the original text of John. It's my
favorite passage that's *not* in the Bible.

• 1 John 5:7 says, "For there are three that bear record in heaven,
the Father, the Word, and the Holy Ghost: and these three are
one" (KJV). This would be the most explicit statement about the
Trinity in the Bible, but it's definitely not part of the original text.
And this fact has been known for more than half a millennium.

• As for Mark 1:41, although most manuscripts say that Jesus was
moved with compassion when he healed a leper, we both agree
that the original text probably said he was angry when he did so.

5. We both agree that the orthodox scribes occasionally
changed the New Testament text to bring it more into con-
formity with their views.

All these agreements raise a fundamental point: even though we
are looking at the same textual problems and arriving at the same
answers most of the time, conservatives are still conservative, and lib-
erals are still liberal.

What's the issue then? The *text* is not the basic area of our disagreement; the *interpretation* of the text is. And even here, it's not so much the
interpretation of the text as it is the interpretation of how the textual variants arose, and how significant those variants are. That's where our differences lie. Bart puts a certain spin on the data. If you've read *Misquoting
Jesus*, you may have come away with an impression of the book that is far
more cynical than what Bart is explicitly saying. Whether that impression
accurately reflects Bart's views is more difficult to assess. But one thing is
clear: Bart sees in the textual variants something more pernicious, more
sinister, more conspiratorial and therefore more controlled than I do.

My job is to paint a different picture than what one sees in *Misquoting Jesus*; my job is to tell you the rest of the story.

In the time allotted, I won't even try to discuss the many passages that Bart has brought up in his lecture, let alone his book. I will touch on one or two, but for the most part, I want to put the textual variants in their historical framework.

To begin with, there are two attitudes that I try to avoid: absolute certainty and total despair. On the one side are King James Only advocates: they are absolutely certain that the KJV, in every place, exactly represents the original text. To be frank, the quest for certainty often overshadows the quest for truth in conservative theological circles. And that's a temptation we need to resist. It is fundamentally the temptation of modernism. And to our shame, all too often evangelicals have been more concerned to protect our presuppositions than to pursue truth at all costs.

On the other side are a few radical scholars who are so skeptical that no piece of data, no hard fact is safe in their hands. It all turns to putty because *all views are created equal.* If everything is equally possible, then no view is more probable than any other view. In Starbucks and on the street, in college classrooms and on the airwaves, you can hear the line, "We really don't know what the New Testament originally said, since we no longer possess the originals and since there could have been tremendous tampering with the text before our existing copies were produced."

But are any biblical scholars this skeptical? Robert Funk, the head of the Jesus Seminar, seemed to be. In *The Five Gospels,* he said:

> Even careful copyists make mistakes, as every proofreader knows. So we will never be able to claim certain knowledge of exactly what the original text of *any* biblical writing was.
>
> The temporal gap that separates Jesus from the first surviving copies of the gospels—about one hundred and seventy-five years—corresponds to the lapse in time from 1776—the writing of the Declaration of Independence—to 1950. What if the oldest copies of the founding document dated only from 1950?[3]

Funk's attitude is easy to see: rampant skepticism over recovering the original wording of any part of the New Testament. This is the temptation of postmodernism.[4] The only certainty is uncertainty itself. It's the one absolute that denies all the others. Concomitant with this is an intellectual pride—pride that one "knows" enough to be skeptical about all positions.

Where does Bart stand on this spectrum? I don't know. On the one hand, he has made statements like these:

> If the primary purpose of this discipline is to get back to the original text, we may as well admit either defeat or victory, depending on how one chooses to look at it, because we're not going to *get* much closer to the original text than we already are. . . . At this stage, our work on the *original* amounts to little more than tinkering. There's something about historical scholarship that refuses to concede that a major task has been accomplished, but there it is.[5]

> In spite of these remarkable [textual] differences, scholars are convinced that we can reconstruct the original words of the New Testament with reasonable (although probably not 100 percent) accuracy.[6]

The first two statements were made at the Society of Biblical Literature, in an address to text-critical scholars. The third statement is in a college textbook. All of this sounds as if Bart would align himself more with those who are fairly sure about what the wording of the text is.

But here's what Bart wrote in his immensely popular book, *Misquoting Jesus*:

> Not only do we not have the originals, we don't have the first copies of the originals. We don't even have copies of the copies of the originals, or copies of the copies of the copies of the originals. What we have are copies made later—much later. . . . And these copies all differ from one another, in many thousands of places . . . these copies differ from one another in so many places that we don't even known how many differences there are.[7]

> We could go on nearly forever talking about specific places in which the texts of the New Testament came to be changed, either accidentally or intentionally. . . . The examples are not just in the hundreds but in the thousands.[8]

And here's what he wrote in another popular book, *Lost Christianities*:

> The fact that we have thousands of New Testament manuscripts does not in itself mean that we can rest assured that we know what

the original text said. If we have very few early copies—in fact, scarcely any—how can we know that the text was not changed significantly *before* the New Testament began to be reproduced in such large quantities?[9]

The cumulative effect of these latter statements seems to be that not only can we have no certainty about the wording of the original, but that, even where we are sure of the wording, the core theology is not nearly as "orthodox" as we had thought. The message of whole books has been corrupted in the hands of the scribes, and the church, in later centuries, adopted the doctrine of the winners—those who corrupted the text and conformed it to *their* notion of orthodoxy.

So you can see my dilemma. I'm not sure what Bart believes. Is the task done? Have we essentially recovered the wording of the original text? Or should we be hyperskeptical about the whole enterprise? It seems that Bart puts a far more skeptical spin on things when speaking in the public square than he does when speaking to professional colleagues. I am hoping that he can clarify his position for us this evening.

These two attitudes—total despair and absolute certainty—are the Scylla and Charybdis that we must steer between. There are three other questions that we need to answer.

1. The number of variants—how many scribal changes are there?

2. The nature of variants—what kinds of textual variations are there?

3. What theological issues are at stake?

Let's begin with a definition of a textual variant: any place among the manuscripts in which there is variation in wording, including word order, omission or addition of words, even spelling differences. The most trivial changes count, and even when all the manuscripts except one say one thing, that lone manuscript's reading counts as a textual variant. The best estimate is that there are between 300,000 and 400,000 textual variants among the manuscripts. Yet there are only about 140,000 words in the New Testament. That means that on average for every word in the Greek New Testament, there are between two and three variants. If this were the only piece of data we had, it would discourage anyone from attempting to recover the wording of the original. But there's more to this story.

Two points to ponder: First, the reason we have a lot of variants is that we have a lot of manuscripts. It's simple, really. No classical Greek or Latin text has nearly as many variants, because they don't have nearly as many manuscripts. With virtually every new manuscript discovery, new variants are found.[10] If there was only one copy of the New Testament in existence, it would have zero variants.[11] Yet several ancient authors have only one copy of their writings in existence. And sometimes that lone copy is not produced for a millennium. But a lone, late manuscript would hardly give us confidence that that single manuscript duplicated the wording of the original in every respect. To speak about the number of variants without also speaking about the number of manuscripts is simply an appeal to sensationalism.[12]

Second, as Samuel Clemens said, "There are lies, damn lies, and statistics." A little probing into these 400,000 variants puts these statistics in a context.

In Greek alone, we have more than 5,500 manuscripts today. Many of these are fragmentary, of course, especially the older ones, but the average Greek New Testament manuscript is well over 400 pages long. Altogether, there are more than 2.5 million pages of texts, leaving hundreds of witnesses for every book of the New Testament.

It's not just the Greek manuscripts that count, either. The New Testament was early on translated into a variety of languages—Latin, Coptic, Syriac, Georgian, Gothic, Ethiopic, Armenian. There are more than 10,000 Latin manuscripts alone. No one really knows the total number of all these ancient versions, but the best estimates are close to 5,000—plus the 10,000 in Latin. It would be safe to say that altogether we have about 20,000 handwritten manuscripts of the New Testament in various languages.

Now, if you were to destroy all those manuscripts, we would not be left without a witness. That's because the ancient Christian leaders known as church fathers wrote commentaries on the New Testament. To date, more than one million quotations of the New Testament by the church fathers have been recorded. "If all other sources for our knowledge of the text of the New Testament were destroyed, [the patristic quotations] would be sufficient alone for the reconstruction of practically the entire New Testament,"[13] said Bruce Metzger and Bart Ehrman.

These numbers are breathtaking! But they also, if left by themselves, would resemble Samuel Clemens's quip about statistics. I'm tempted to say that these numbers are reminiscent of membership rolls at a Southern Baptist church, but I dare not use such an analogy in this company.

Far more important than the numbers are the dates of the manuscripts. How many manuscripts do we have in the first century after the completion of the New Testament, how many in the second century, the third? Although the numbers are significantly lower, they are still rather impressive. We have today as many as a dozen manuscripts from the second century, sixty-four from the third, and forty-eight from the fourth. That's a total of 124 manuscripts within 300 years of the composition of the New Testament. Most of these are fragmentary, but collectively, the whole New Testament text is found in them multiple times.

How does the average classical Greek or Latin author stack up? If we are comparing the same time period—300 years after composition—the average classical author has no literary remains. Zip, nada, nothing. But if we compare all the manuscripts of a particular classical author, regardless of when they were written, the total would still average less than twenty, and probably less than a dozen—and they would all be coming much more than three centuries later. In terms of extant manuscripts, the New Testament textual critic is confronted with an embarrassment of riches. If we have doubts about what the original New Testament said, those doubts would have to be multiplied a hundred-fold for the average classical author. And when we compare the New Testament manuscripts with the very best that the classical world has to offer, it still stands head and shoulders above the rest. The New Testament is far and away the best-attested work of Greek or Latin literature from the ancient world.

There's another way to look at this. If all of the New Testament manuscripts of the second century are fragmentary (and they are), how fragmentary are they? We can measure this in several different ways. First, three out of four Gospels are attested in the manuscripts, as well as nine of Paul's letters, Acts, Hebrews, and Revelation—in other words, most of the New Testament books. Another way to look at this is that over 40 percent of all the verses in the New Testament are already found in manuscripts within a hundred years of the completion of the New Testament.[14]

Now, Bart in one place seems to say that we don't have *any* second-century manuscripts.[15] In an interview in the *Charlotte Observer*, he declared, "If we don't have the original texts of the New Testament—or even copies of the copies of the copies of the originals—what do we have?" His response is illuminating: "We have copies that were made *hundreds* of years later—in most cases, many hundreds of years later. And these copies are all different from one another."[16] He is saying that we don't have *any* manuscripts of the New Testament until hundreds of years after the New Testament was completed. He even repeated this statement again tonight. But that is not the case. The impression Bart sometimes gives throughout the book—but especially repeats in interviews—is that of wholesale uncertainty about the original wording, a view that is far more radical than he actually embraces.

In light of comments such as these, the impression that many readers get from *Misquoting Jesus* is that the transmission of the New Testament resembles the telephone game. This is a game every child knows. It involves a line of people, with the first one whispering some story into the ear of the second person. That person then whispers the story to the next person in line, and that person whispers it to the next, and so on down the line. As the tale goes from person to person, it gets terribly garbled. The whole point of the telephone game, in fact, is to see how garbled it can get. There is no motivation to get it right. By the time it gets to the last person, who repeats it out loud for the whole group, everyone has a good laugh.

But the copying of New Testament manuscripts is hardly like this parlor game:

• The message is passed on in writing, not orally. That would make for a pretty boring telephone game!

• Rather than one line or stream of transmission, there are multiple lines.

- Textual critics don't rely on just the last person in each line, but can interrogate several folks who are closer to the original source.

- Patristic writers are commenting on the text as it is going through its transmissional history. And when there are chronological gaps among the manuscripts, these writers often fill in those gaps by telling us what the text said in that place in their day.

- In the telephone game, once the story is told by one person, that individual has nothing else to do with the story. It's out of his or her hands. But the original New Testament books were most likely copied more than once, and may have been consulted even after a few generations of copies had already been produced.

- There was at least one very carefully produced stream of transmission for the New Testament manuscripts. And there is sufficient evidence to show that even a particular fourth-century manuscript in this line is usually more accurate than *any* second-century manuscript.

We can illustrate this [last point] with two manuscripts that Bart and I would both agree are two of the most accurate manuscripts of the New Testament, if not *the* two most accurate. I am referring to Papyrus 75 ($\mathfrak{P}^{75}$) and Codex Vaticanus (B). These two manuscripts have an incredibly strong agreement. Their agreement is higher than the agreement of any other two early manuscripts. $\mathfrak{P}^{75}$ is 100 to 150 years older than B, yet it is not an ancestor of B. Instead, B copied from an earlier common ancestor that both B and $\mathfrak{P}^{75}$ were related to.[17] The combination of both of these manuscripts in a particular reading goes back to early in the second century.

Bart has asserted, "If we have very few early copies—in fact, scarcely any—how can we know that the text was not changed significantly *before* the New Testament began to be reproduced in such large quantities?"[18] I'm not sure what large quantities he's speaking about, since there are more manuscripts from the third century than there are from the fourth or fifth century.

But how can we know? It's a legitimate question. There is a way to be relatively confident that the text of the fourth century looked remarkably like the earliest form of the text. $\mathfrak{P}^{75}$ has large portions of Luke and John in it—and nothing else. Codex B has most of the New Testament in it. If B and $\mathfrak{P}^{75}$ are very close to each other yet B often has the earlier reading, we can extrapolate that the text of B is pretty decent for the rest of the New Testament. And when it agrees with a manuscript such as Codex Sinaiticus, which it usually does, that combined reading almost surely goes back to a common archetype from deep in the second century.[19]

Nevertheless, Bart has carefully and ably described the transmission of the text. He has detailed how the winners succeeded in conquering all with their views and emerged as the group we might call "orthodox." What he has said is fairly accurate overall. The only problem is, this is the right analysis, but the wrong religion. Bart's basic argument about theological motives describes Islam far more than Christianity. Recent work on the transmissional history of both the New Testament and the Qur'an shows this clearly.

Within just a few decades of the writing of the Qur'an, it underwent a strongly controlled, heavy-handed editing geared toward "orthodoxy" that weeded out variants that did not conform. But the New Testament, as even Bart argues, did not suffer this sort of control early on. Instead, Bart has often suggested that the earliest decades were marked by free, even wild copying.[20] You can't have it both ways. You can't have wild copying by untrained scribes *and* a proto-orthodox conspiracy simultaneously producing the same variants. Conspiracy implies control, and wild copying is anything but controlled.

On the one hand, there *was* uncontrolled copying of manuscripts in the earliest period. But this was largely restricted to the Western text-form.[21] On the other hand, there was a strand of early copying that may appear to be controlled. This is the Alexandrian family of manuscripts. Yet the reason that manuscripts of this text-form look so much like each other is largely that they were in a relatively pure line of transmission.[22] There was no conspiracy, just good practices. What Westcott said over a century ago is relevant to this discussion:

> When the Caliph Othman fixed a text of the Koran and destroyed all the old copies which differed from his standard, he provided

for the uniformity of subsequent manuscripts at the cost of their historical foundation. *A classical text which rests finally on a single archetype is that which is open to the most serious suspicions.*[23]

What we see in the New Testament copies is absolutely nothing like this. Bart tries to make out a case for significant theological alterations to the text of the New Testament *by a group that did not have control over the text from the beginning*, but the historical ingredients for his hypothesis are missing. It's like trying to bake a cake with romaine lettuce and ranch dressing.

In another respect, when Ehrman discusses whether God has preserved the text of the New Testament, he places on the New Testament transmissional process some rather unrealistic demands—demands that Islam traditionally claims for itself with respect to the Qur'an but that no bona fide theologian or Christian scholar would ever claim was true of the New Testament manuscripts. As is well known, most Muslims claim that the Qur'an has been transmitted perfectly, that all copies are exactly alike. This is what Ehrman demands of the New Testament text *if* God has inspired it. Methodologically, he did not abandon the evangelical faith; he abandoned a faith that in its bibliological constructs is what most Muslims claim for their sacred text.

Let's sum up the evidence from the number of variants: There are a lot of variants because there are a lot of manuscripts. And even in the early centuries, the text of the New Testament is found in a sufficient number of manuscripts, versions, and fathers to give us the essentials of the original text.

How many differences affect the meaning of the text? How many of them are plausible or viable—that is, found in manuscripts with a sufficient pedigree that they have some likelihood of reflecting the original wording? The variants can be broken down into the following four categories:

1. Spelling differences and nonsense errors

2. Minor differences that do not affect translation or that involve synonyms

3. Differences that affect the meaning of the text but are not viable

4. Differences that both affect the meaning of the text and
are viable

Of the hundreds of thousands of textual variants in New Testament manuscripts, the great majority are spelling differences that have no bearing on the meaning of the text.[24] The most common textual variant involves what is called a movable *nu*. The Greek letter *nu* (ν) can occur at the end of certain words when they precede a word that starts with a vowel. This is similar to the two forms of the indefinite article in English: a book, an apple. But whether the nu appears in these words or not, there is absolutely no difference in meaning.

Several of the spelling differences are nonsense readings. These occur when a scribe is fatigued, inattentive, or perhaps does not know Greek very well. For example, in 1 Thess. 2:7, the manuscripts are divided over a very difficult textual problem. Paul is describing how he and Silas acted among the new converts in their visit to Thessalonica. Some manuscripts read, "We were gentle among you," while others say, "We were little children among you." The difference between the two variants is a single letter in Greek: *nēpioi* vs. *ēpioi* (νήπιοι vs. ἤπιοι). A lone medieval scribe changed the text to "We were horses among you"! The word *horses* in Greek *hippoi* (ἵπποι) is similar to these other two words.

After spelling differences, the next largest category of variants are those that involve synonyms or do not affect translation. They are wordings other than mere spelling changes, but they do not alter the way the text is translated, or at least understood. A very common variant involves the use of the definite article with proper names. Greek can say "the Mary" or "the Joseph" (as in Luke 2:16), while English usage requires the dropping of the article. So whether the Greek text has "the Mary" or simply "Mary," English will always translate this as "Mary."

Another common variant is when words in Greek are transposed. Unlike English, Greek word order is used more for emphasis than for basic meaning. That's because Greek is a highly inflected language, with a myriad of suffixes on nouns and verbs, as well as prefixes and even infixes on verbs. You can tell where the subject is by its ending, regardless of where it stands in the sentence. Take, for example, the sentence, "Jesus loves John." In Greek, that statement can be expressed in a minimum of sixteen different ways, though every time, the translation would be the same in English. And once we factor in different verbs for "love" in Greek, the presence or absence of little particles that often go untranslated, and spelling differences, the possibilities run into the hundreds. Yet all of them would be translated simply as "Jesus loves John." There may be a slight difference in emphasis, but the basic meaning is not disturbed.

Now, if a three-word sentence like this could potentially be expressed by hundreds of Greek constructions, how should we view the number of *actual* textual variants in the New Testament manuscripts? That there are only three variants for every word in the New Testament when the potential is almost infinitely greater seems trivial—especially when we consider how many thousands of manuscripts there are.

The third largest category [of variants] involves wording that is meaningful but not viable. These are variants found in a single manuscript or group of manuscripts that, by themselves, have little likelihood of reflecting the wording of the original text. In 1 Thess. 2:9, one late medieval manuscript speaks of "the gospel of Christ" instead of "the gospel of God," while almost all the other manuscripts have the latter. Here, "the gospel of Christ" is a meaningful variant, but it is not viable because there is little chance that one medieval scribe somehow retained the wording of the original text while all other scribes for centuries before him missed it.

The final, and by far the smallest, category of textual variants involves those that are both meaningful and viable. Less than 1 percent of all textual variants belong to this group. But even saying this may be misleading. By "meaningful," we mean that the variant changes the meaning of the text to some degree. It may not be terribly significant, but if the reading impacts our understanding of the passage, then it is meaningful.

For example, consider a textual problem in Rev. 13:18, "Let the one who has insight calculate the beast's number, for it is the number of a man, and his number is 666." A few years ago, a scrap of papyrus was found at Oxford University's Ashmolean Museum. It gave the beast's number as 616. And it just happens to be the oldest manuscript of Revelation 13 now extant. This was just the second manuscript to do so. (This manuscript, not quite so early, is a very important witness to the text of the Apocalypse and is known as Codex Ephraimi Rescriptus.) Most scholars think 666 is the number of the beast and 616 is the neighbor of the beast. It's possible that his number is really 616. But what is the significance of this, really? I know of no church, no Bible college, no theological seminary that has a doctrinal statement that says, "We believe in the deity of Christ, we believe in the virgin birth of Christ, we believe in the bodily resurrection of Christ, and we believe that the number of the beast is 666." This textual variant does not change any cardinal belief of Christians—but, if original, it would send about seven tons of dispensational literature to the flames.

Although the quantity of textual variants among the New Testament manuscripts numbers in the hundreds of thousands, those that change the meaning pale in comparison. Less than 1 percent of the differences are both meaningful and viable. There are still hundreds of texts that are in dispute. I don't want to give the impression that textual criticism is merely a mopping up job nowadays, that all but a handful of problems have been resolved. That is not the case. But the nature of the remaining problems and their interpretive significance is probably far less monumental than many readers of *Misquoting Jesus* have come to believe.

Finally, we need to ask, "What theological issues are involved in these textual variants?" Bart argues that the major changes that have been made to the text of the New Testament have been produced by "orthodox" scribes; they have tampered with the text in hundreds of places, with the result that the basic teachings of the New Testament have been drastically altered. Before we look at his evidence, I should point out that his basic thesis that orthodox scribes have altered the New Testament text for their own purposes is one that is certainly true. And this occurs in hundreds of places. Ehrman has done the academic community a great service by systematically highlighting so many of these alterations in his *Orthodox Corruption of Scripture*. However, the extent to which these scribes altered these various passages and whether such alterations have buried forever the original wording of the New Testament are a different matter. Indeed, the very fact that Ehrman and other textual critics can place these textual variants in history and can determine what the original text was that they corrupted presupposes that the authentic wording has hardly been lost.[25]

In the concluding chapter of *Misquoting Jesus*, Bart summarizes his findings as follows:

> It would be wrong . . . to say—as people sometimes do—that the changes in our text have no real bearing on what the texts mean or on the theological conclusions that one draws from them. . . . In some instances, the very meaning of the text is at stake, depending on how one resolves a textual problem: Was Jesus an angry man [Mark 1:41]? Was he completely distraught in the face of death [Hebrews 2:9]? Did he tell his disciples that they could drink poison without being harmed [Mark 16:9-20]? Did he let an adulteress off the hook with nothing but a mild warning [John 7:53–8:11]? Is the doctrine of the Trinity explicitly taught in the New Testament [1 John 5:7-8]? Is Jesus actually called the "unique God" there [John 1:18]? Does the New Testament indicate that even the Son of God himself does not know when the end will come [Matthew 24:36]? The questions go on and on, and all of them are related to how one resolves difficulties in the manuscript tradition as it has come down to us.[26]

I have dealt with these passages in detail in my essay "The Gospel according to Bart," published in the *Journal of the Evangelical Theological Society*.[27] What I will present here will be much briefer and more selective.

This summary paragraph gives us seven passages to consider:

• Mark 16:9-20
• John 7:53—8:11
• 1 John 5:7 (in the KJV)
• Mark 1:41
• Hebrews 2:9
• John 1:18
• Matthew 24:36

The first three passages have been considered inauthentic by most New Testament scholars—including most evangelical New Testament scholars—for well over a century. The presence or absence of these passages changes no fundamental doctrine, no core belief, in spite of the fact that there is much emotional baggage attached to them. In the next three passages, Bart adopts readings that most textual critics would consider spurious. I think he's right in one of them (Mk. 1:41) but probably not in the other two. Nevertheless, even if his text-critical decisions are correct in all three passages, the theological reasons he gives for the changes are probably overdone. But because of time, I will focus only on the last passage, Matthew 24:36.

In Matthew's version of the Olivet Discourse, we read, "But about that day and hour no one knows, neither the angels of heaven, nor the Son, but only the Father" (NRSV). The words "nor the Son," however, are not found in all the manuscripts. And this raises a significant issue: Did some scribes omit these words from the text of Matthew, or did other scribes add these words? Bart is firmly convinced that the words were expunged by proto-orthodox scribes who bristled at the idea of the Son of God's ignorance.

Bart often refers to this passage. He discusses it explicitly at least half a dozen times in *Misquoting Jesus*.[28] And in an academic publication, he calls it "the most famous instance" of doctrinal alteration.[29] In *Misquoting Jesus*, he argues, "The reason [for the omission] is not hard to postulate; if Jesus does not know the future, the Christian claim that he is a divine being is more than a little compromised."[30] Bart does not qualify his words here; he does not say that *some* Christians would have a problem with Jesus' ignorance. No, he says that *the* Christian claim would have a problem with it. Now, if he does not mean this, then he is writing more provocatively than is necessary, and he's misleading his readers. And if he does mean it, he has overstated his case.

Bart suggests that the omission would have arisen in the late second century, as a proto-orthodox response to the Adoptionist heresy.[31] This is possible, but there are three problems with this hypothesis:

1. It is somewhat startling that no church father seems to have any problem with the words "nor the Son" until the fourth century,[32] yet several comment on this very passage. Irenaeus (late second century), Tertullian (late second, early third century), and Origen (early third century) all embraced

the deity of Christ, yet none of them felt that this passage caused any theological problems.[33] Irenaeus goes so far as to use Christ's ignorance as a model of humility for Christians.[34] If the scribes were simply following the leads of their theological mentors, then the lack of any tension over this passage by second- and third-century fathers suggests that the omission of "nor the Son" either was not a reaction to Adoptionism or was not created in the late second century.

2. If the omission was created intentionally by proto-orthodox scribes in the late second century, then it most likely would have been created by scribes who followed Irenaeus's view that the four Gospels were the only authoritative books on the life of Jesus.[35] But the parallel passage in Mark 13:32 definitely has the words "nor the Son." (We know of almost no manuscripts that omit the phrase there.) And even though Mark was not copied as frequently as Matthew in the early centuries of the Christian faith, by the end of the second century, the proto-orthodox would have regarded it as scripture. The question is, Why didn't they strike the offensive words from Mark?

3. If the scribes had no qualms about deleting "nor the Son," why did they leave the word "alone" alone? Without "nor the Son," the passage still implies that the Son of God does not know the date of his return: "But as for that day and hour no one knows it—not even the angels in heaven—except the Father *alone*." Since the Father is specified as the only person who intimately knows the eschatological calendar, it is difficult to argue that the Son is included in that knowledge.[36]

This point is not trivial. It cuts to the heart of Bart's entire method. In *Orthodox Corruption*, he argues that the reason the same manuscript can vacillate in the kinds of theological changes it makes is "the individuality of the scribes, who, under their own unique circumstances, may have felt inclined to emphasize one component of Christology over another."[37] But he immediately adds, "It strikes me as equally likely, however . . . , that the same scribe may have seen different kinds of problems in different texts and made the requisite changes depending on his perceptions and moods at the moment of transcription."[38] If this kind of logic is applied to Matthew 24:36, we would have to say that the scribe had a major mood swing, because just four words after he deleted "nor the Son," he couldn't bring himself to drop the "alone."

A recent critique of Bart's overarching method at this juncture did not mince words:

> If this view is accurate, then how can we have any possibility of determining the theological motivations involved in textual changes? With statements such as these, it becomes nearly impossible to falsify any hypothesis regarding theological tendencies. . . . Rather than verify his conclusions through the rigorous work of evaluating individual manuscripts, the major prerequisite in Ehrman's methodology is the alignment of a favorable theological heresy with particularly intriguing variants.[39]

Another reviewer complained about the wax nose on Bart's pronouncements over theological *Tendenz* of the orthodox scribes with these words:

> No matter what textual problem one finds which relates to the central theme and soul of the Bible (i.e., the Trinitarian God), one can always postulate a motivation for an orthodox corruption, whether or not it is probable. This disingenuous method can be applied because no matter whether an article is left off or added, a word slightly shifted or removed, due to orthographic errors or any other unintentional type, it often changes the meaning just enough that there is bound to be a heresy which would benefit from the change. If an article is missing, it may seem that the unity of the Godhead is in danger. If the article is present, it may appear to threaten their distinct personalities. If a phrase exemplifying Jesus' humanity is removed, it was obviously to combat the heresy of Adoptionism. If it is added, it was obviously to combat the heresy of Sabellianism.[40]

My point on Matthew 24:36 is not that Bart's argument about the omission of "nor the Son" is entirely faulty, just that it's not the only option and doesn't tell the whole story. In fact, several aspects of the problem have apparently not been considered by him, yet this is his prime example of orthodox corruption. It strikes me that Bart is often certain in the very places where he needs to be tentative, and he is tentative where he should have much greater certainty. He's more certain about what the corruptions are than what the original wording is, but his certitude about the corruptions presupposes, as Moisés Silva has eloquently pointed out, a good grasp of the original wording.[41]

To sum up, although Bart's reconstructions of the reasons for certain textual corruptions are *possible*, they often reveal more about Bart's ingenuity than the scribes' intentions. Or, as Gordon Fee said, "Unfortunately, Ehrman too often turns mere *possibility* into *probability*, and probability into *certainty*, where other equally viable reasons for corruption exist."[42]

It would have been an impossible task for me to try to address all the passages that Bart puts forth as examples of early orthodox corruption of the text. But I have tried to raise some questions about his method, his assumptions, and his conclusions. I do not believe that the orthodox corruptions are nearly as pervasive or as significant as Bart does. And I have tried to show that there is no ground for wholesale skepticism about the wording of the original text, and even that Bart is far less skeptical than the impression he gives in the public square.[43]

So, is what we have now what they wrote then? Exactly? No. But in all essentials? Yes.

QUESTIONS AND ANSWERS

Question: You said that the Bible is the most accurate of all the documents in antiquity but we still can't know what it originally said, then how can we determine what actually happened in any part of antiquity?

Ehrman: Well, I don't actually think that I said the Bible was the most accurate book from antiquity. I said that we have more manuscripts of the Bible than any other book in the ancient world. Then I said that we have difficulty determining what the New Testament authors originally said. The question is then how can we decide what anybody in the ancient world said. We can't. We wish we could. It would be nice if we could. You would like to think that because you can go to the store and buy an edition of Plato that you are actually reading Plato, but the problem is that we just do not have the kind of evidence that we need in order to establish what ancient authors actually wrote. In some cases, we have all these data, and sometimes we have just one manuscript. Sometimes we have a manuscript that was written two-thousand years later, and that's it! So, as much as we would like to be able to say that we know what ancient authors actually wrote, we often just do not know.

Question: Dan, I have a question. If scholars who are believers have known about the things that Bart writes about for a long time, why do so many in churches have to wait until someone like Bart comes along to tell them?

Ehrman: Yeah, I want this answer too.

Audience erupts in laughter.

Wallace: I think that what Bart has done for the Christian community is a great service. I said so in my review of his *Misquoting Jesus* in the *Journal of the Evangelical Theological Society* (*JETS*), with the wonderful title "The Gospel According to Bart." At least *I* thought it was a good title. In his book, in his interviews, and in his talk tonight Bart has used as a first example the story of the woman caught in adultery. I think he has done that calculatingly as a shock value for people, but I think on the other side of it that most Christian leaders will not address that. You might hear a pastor on Sunday say that he does not believe the story to be literarily authentic—that is, the evangelist did not write this story—but that he believes it to be historically authentic. Now Bart and I both agree that it is probably not entirely historically authentic either. The article Bart wrote in *New Testament Studies*[49] was a great piece that demonstrated to me that this story was a conflation between two different stories. I think what has happened is that there has been a tradition of timidity among evangelical scholars for many years. Several years ago, a Bible put the story of the woman caught in adultery at the end of John's Gospel rather than its normal place. They just weren't selling enough of those Bibles, and so they decided to put it back in its normal place with one marginal note: "the oldest manuscripts don't have this." I think one of the things Bart has done is to demonstrate that people are not reading those marginal notes because they are shocked when they hear that this is probably not authentic. And so what I suggested in the *JETS* article is that it is time to quit following this tradition of timidity. Let's get out there and say what we believe, which is that the story of the woman caught in adultery—as fascinating as it is, as interesting as it is—is not part of John's Gospel. I would propose putting it in the footnotes. Now, it's not in the footnotes of evangelical Bibles. It's not even in the footnotes of broader theological spectrum Bibles like the New Revised Standard Version (NRSV). But I think that's where it belongs—in the footnotes. When we did the New English Translation (net) Bible (I'm the senior New Testament editor for the NET Bible) we wrestled with this at first, and we finally settled on a compromise. The compromise was to put it in brackets, to have a lengthy discussion about why we don't think it is authentic, and to reduce the font size by two points so that it could not easily be read from the pulpit.

Question: Dr. Ehrman, you kept talking about the limits of our knowledge, saying, "We don't know, we don't know." It seems like there are some philosophical presuppositions that are going into your evaluation of the evidence that we have. There seems to be a lot of evidence that suggests we could know something even if it is not with absolute certainty. Is there something in your personal life or in your philosophical reading outside of New Testament studies that has led you to say that "I really can't know what the New Testament says with any sort of reliability just because it's just not the evidence that I want"? Is there something that has pointed you in that direction that you can't move past?

Ehrman: That's a good question. The short answer is no. We can know some things with relative certainty. We can know what Bibles looked like in the twelfth century. We can know what Christians churches in the twelfth century read—what their Bibles looked like. We can know what Bibles look like in some areas in the seventh century. We can know what one community's Bible looked like in the fourth century. The farther you go back, the less you can know. So, it isn't that my mother deprived me of something when I was a child and that I'm just working this out now. It's the nature of historical evidence that you have. You have to go with the evidence. If you're going to be a historian, you can't fill in the gaps when you don't have evidence. And so, we have the problem: in the early period, we have very few manuscripts. But not only that: the other striking phenomenon is that the manuscripts we do have vary from one another far more often in the earlier period than in the later period. The variation is immense, and there just aren't very many manuscripts! So, the historical result, whether we like it or not, is that we just can't know.

Question: Multi-spectral photography and imaging seems to be turning up some interesting things in ancient documents. I have a question about that. I hope I'm not propagating an urban legend here, but on the internet someone suggested that in Codex B where Mark ends there's a blank spot and then maybe somebody pumiced it out. That would be the first question; is that an urban legend or not? If multi-spectral imaging can potentially reveal things not visible to the naked eye, would the ending of Mark in Codex B be something worth testing with multi-spectral imaging (MSI)? If not, are there any manuscripts you would like to try multi-spectral imaging on?

Wallace: Great question. Let me explain real quickly what multi-spectral imaging, or MSI, is to everybody. It is camera technology that was developed for NASA so they could examine camouflaged military

installations from outer space. Later, it was applied to ancient manuscripts. A few years ago in Europe there was a group known as Rinasci-
mento virtuale that conducted a three-year study involving twenty-six
nations doing multi-spectral imaging on ancient manuscripts. They
were trying to read what is known as a palimpsest. The study of palimp-
sests is where the real value of MSI is in the study of manuscripts. A
palimpsest is simply a manuscript that was scraped over again and
reused by someone else, typically centuries after it was originally used.
Imagine a writer getting to the last two leaves of his book and he runs
out of parchment. He has to make a decision between killing a goat
and making a couple more leaves or ripping leaves out of a an older
book—certainly a cheaper solution. So, he reuses those leaves in his
book. In one of the manuscripts we discovered in Constantinople, the
last two leaves were a palimpsest and it may well be the second manuscript of Mark recovered from the third century. I don't know yet; I
suspect not. Just two leaves. I doubt that. It's probably fifth century.
We'll find out one of these days.

   Now as far as using MSI for Codex B and the ending of Mark's
Gospel, first of all, I would say it's absolutely impossible that the scribe
of Codex B at the end of Mark's Gospel would have put in the twelve
verses and then erased them. The reason I say this is because there's
not enough room in that place in Codex B to put those twelve verses in.
The Codex has three columns, and at the bottom the second column,
there's a gap of about three or four lines. Then in the third column,
there is not nearly enough room to put those twelve verses. Several
people have tested it. It couldn't be done. What is interesting about
Codex B along these lines is that there are three other places in the
manuscript where it has a gap at the end of the book, and they're all
in the Old Testament. And that gap appears each time because we're
shifting genres from historical documents to prophetic or something
like that or something along those lines. And what may well be the
case—this is something that Dr. J. K. Elliot suggested to me—is that
the original form of the Gospels—when they were collected into one
piece—may have been in what's called the Western order of Matthew,
John, Luke, and Mark. Now, if that's the case, and Mark was the last
of those Gospels, I suspect that what we have in Codex B is a very
early form of the text that the scribe is copying—a form of the text

where it had been in the Western order. He could simply be retaining the gap at the end of Mark, even though he had changed the order (or someone before him had changed it), and it no longer made any sense there. So, it seems to me that there's a lot of evidence that suggests that he is going back very close to the original with that change; even the order of the material suggests that with the gaps that are in there.

Question: Dr. Ehrman: You said you were a historian, and I was just wondering if you put the same emphasis on other texts, such as Plato, as you do the New Testament, and if so, can you prove to me that all those texts are correctly written and that you can interpret that?

Ehrman: I don't personally study these. I'm not a classicist. I'm a scholar of the New Testament, and so the texts I work on are the New Testament. So the answer would be no. I can't show you that Plato is accurately transmitted any better than the New T.estament. In fact, it's probably transmitted worse. So it is harder actually to know the words of Plato than it is Paul.

Question: This question is for Dr. Wallace. This relates to a question or actually a comment made by Dr. Ehrman about the preservation of the text. If God has given his word to man, how can he not preserve it faithfully so that we can know it with close to one hundred-percent certainty? Given that you have denied a doctrine of preservation yourself, Dr. Wallace, how would you respond to that? How would you recommend the church deal with this?

Wallace: First of all, let me explain why I don't believe in a doctrine of preservation. There are two fundamental reasons why I do not. There are typically five passages used to argue that the text has been preserved. For example, in Matthew's Gospel, we have the Lord saying that not "one jot or tittle" is going to pass from the law until all is fulfilled (Mt. 5:18). And "heaven and earth may pass away but my words will not pass away" (Mt. 24:35). Well, when you read the end of John's Gospel it says that if the evangelist recorded everything Jesus did, and presumably for some of those things he did he actually spoke in those contexts, it would fill all the libraries of the world. It's a bit hyperbolic I suspect, but nevertheless what we've got is John telling us that there's a whole lot more he could tell you about what Jesus said. Consequently, we have not preserved all of his words. So, however we are going to take that kind of text, like those from Matthew, we need to recognize that it is not talking about the preservation of the words of Jesus in our Gospels. If you read through the Gospels at a reverential pace, just the words of Jesus—get an old King James, a red-letter edition; they're easier to find this way—you can get through everything Jesus said in about two hours. I highly suspect he spoke more than two hours worth in his whole life! So, it's rather doubtful that these texts mean what people want them to mean.

The second reason I would argue against the doctrine of preservation, which, by the way, is not an ancient doctrine (the first time it is mentioned is in the Westminster Confession in the seventeenth century!), is that it does not work for the Old Testament. There are places in the Old Testament where we simply do not know what the original wording was, and we have to move to conjecture without any textual basis to say, "We think it said this here, but we're just not sure." Before the Dead Sea Scrolls were discovered, there were several places that were the product of conjecture and many of them were cleared up once the scrolls were discovered. But there are still several places left in the Old Testament. I don't want to be bibliologically Marcionite and claim that the New Testament is more inspired than the Old or that the New Testament was inspired while the Old was not. I think that's schizophrenic.

Here are two points I'd raise concerning the doctrine of preservation. First of all, what I think Dr. Ehrman has said, when he mentioned in his presentation tonight, is: If God inspired the text, why didn't he preserve the text? That's the very kind of question that Muslims have asked, and they have answered it by arguing that God has preserved the text. But I know of no *bona fide* Christian theologian who has ever said that God has preserved the text exactly as the original. The only people I know that claim that are *Textus Receptus* people—King James Only-type folks—and we know that they're just a little bit weird. So we probably don't give them much credibility.

I would suggest one other thing. C. S. Lewis made the interesting argument about miracles that when Jesus Christ changed the water into

wine, immediately it had alcohol in it.[50] Oh, I'm sorry, this is a Southern Baptist seminary! (*Audience laughs*) I'm sorry, I agree with Lewis on
that point! Well, it seems to me what Lewis is saying is that when Jesus
makes the wine it's going to become alcoholic. When you raise Lazarus
from the dead, he's still going to die. When miracles are done, after the
miracle is done, then natural processes take over. And if the Bible is
originally inspired, the natural processes due to humans rewriting this
text, copying it, or whatever, are going to take over. I think I can argue
for a general preseveration of the Scripture based on the historical evidence, but I cannot do so on the basis of any doctrine.

Question: This question is for Dr. Ehrman. You asked the question
why study variants if they don't make a significant difference. But since
many people abandon their faith because they don't believe the truths
taught by Scripture can be relied on, wouldn't one of the most important reasons for Christians to study textual criticism be to defend its
integrity against people like you?

Ehrman: Good luck.

Audience roars with laughter.

Ehrman: My personal belief about this is, as I said before, that given
the kind of evidence we have, I don't think that there's any hope of getting closer to an original text. So, there's going to be no defense against
people who say we don't know what the original is because we don't
know what the original is. Ten or fifteen years ago my interests in textual criticism shifted away from trying to figure out what the original
is to trying to figure out *why* the text got changed. For me, this a very
interesting question. Why did scribes change the text? And that's why
I wrote *The Orthodox Corruption of Scripture*, to show why it was, in some
instances, that scribes felt motivated to change the text. At least one of
the other presenters has been quite outspoken in his writings in saying
we should give up talking about the original text. I don't know if he'll
be saying that in his lecture, but he should! So, I think there are lots of
reasons to study the text other than trying to establish the original to
protect the text against skeptics, because I think that if that's the goal,

it's really going to run into roadblocks. I think there are other good reasons for doing textual criticism.

Question: My question is going toward intentional changes in texts. In comparison to Thomas Jefferson's Bible—where he leaves Christ in the grave—have either one of you found any texts that leave Christ in the grave?

Wallace: I suppose you could almost argue that for Mark 16, except for the fact that even if it ends at verse 8, you still have the angelic announcement that Jesus is risen. You don't have any human witnesses to it. He may have still stayed in the grave. The problem that we've got with that is that three times in Mark's Gospel Jesus prophesied that he will suffer and that he will rise again from the grave. And it seems to me, and I think Bart would agree with me on this, that the abrupt ending you have to Mark's Gospel is really profound. [This tactic] wasn't used in ancient literature that often, but it was used. Basically, the tactic was to stop the text right in mid-sentence and have somebody keep reading, although there's nothing to look at. The [text says the] women were afraid, and it ends. Period. Consequently, it is moving the reader into the place of the disciples. What Mark's Gospel is trying to do is to get these readers to answer the question, "What are you going to do with Jesus?" The fulcrum of Mark's Gospel is in Mark 8, where Peter makes his confession that Jesus is the Christ. When he does so, Jesus then says, "Do you know that the Son of Man is going to suffer and die?" And Peter pulls him aside and rebukes him. *Now, look Peter, if you know he's the Christ, why are you doing this?* Whatever Peter's thinking, it's not on the level of what we think of when we think of Jesus as the Christ. I think he was thinking of a military conqueror who was going to kick some Roman butt back in Jerusalem. The point is that Peter doesn't have a good grasp on what it means for Jesus to be Messiah. *He wants Jesus in his glory but will not accept him in his suffering.* So, all the way through the rest of Mark, we see Jesus as the suffering servant of Isaiah. He's the one who's going to come and die for us. And the question ultimately gets asked at the end of Mark 16: Okay, did you accept Jesus in his suffering? If you did, you will see him in his glory. If you didn't, you won't.

So, that's the closest we have of any text that might even suggest that he wasn't raised from the dead, but it doesn't even come close to even suggesting that.

Question: When the church considers the New Testamnet text, how should we approach it? Are they the exact divine words of God, are they the words of followers of Jesus inspired by God or the closest we have to that, or are they simply brilliant ideas for teaching and encouraging a good life? Simply put, what is a righteous and scholarly responsible way to approach the New Testament text?

Wallace: This may surprise you, but the basic view that I would give has to do with my bibliology—my doctrine of the Bible. I have a three-tiered bibliology. The foundational tier is that the Bible tells us of the great acts of God in history. The second level is that the Bible is normative for faith and practice, what is sometimes called infallibility. The top level is that the Bible is true in what it teaches, and I would call that inerrancy. Most evangelicals today, I'm afraid, flip that pyramid on its head, and then it can come crashing down if someone finds what they think is a mistake in the Bible. I don't think that is the proper way for us to view this. I think a righteous—and I'm not sure I would use that term—or better, a more orthodox scholarly approach to it would be to recognize that we are dealing with something that has been considered to be the word of God throughout the history of the church. But even then, the way I approach my own method in dealing with the text is this: I hold in limbo my own theological views about the text as I work through it; it makes for an interesting time! In one respect I have an existential crisis every time I come to the text, and that's fine because the core of my theology is not the Bible, it's Christ. Now you say, how can you have Christ without the Bible? I'd say, how can they have Christ in the first century without the New Testament? But they did. The way I approach this is to recognize the primacy of Christ as Lord of my life, as sovereign master of the universe. And, as I look at the Scriptures, they first and foremost have to be those documents that I regard as relatively trustworthy to guide us as to what Christ did and what God has done in history. On that basis, on that foundation, I begin to look at it in more ways than that.

Question: Dr. Ehrman, at this point in scholarship, does the earliest reconstructible form of the text portray an orthodox understanding of the resurrection and the deity of Christ?

Ehrman: I'm not sure what the orthodox understanding of resurrection is. You mean that Jesus is bodily resurrected from the dead?

Question: Yeah, that Jesus was bodily resurrected from the dead and that he's both God and man.

Ehrman: I don't think that the texts affect those views one way or another. My own view is that the biblical authors thought Jesus was physically resurrected from the dead but that most of the biblical authors did not think Jesus was God. The Gospel of John does. I think Matthew, Mark, and Luke do not think Jesus was God. It is hard to know what Paul's view about Jesus' divinity is, in my opinion. So, I think different authors had different opinions, but I don't think in most cases that is affected by textual variation.

Question: Dr. Ehrman, I was just wondering if you ascribed to a particular theory [of New Testament textual criticism], such as reasoned eclecticism, because I don't see a consistency in how you are dealing with issues methodologically.

Ehrman: The reason you don't see a consistency is because usually the way I argue is I figure out what I think is right and then I argue for it. (*Audience erupts in laughter.*) Actually, I would call myself a reasoned eclectic. But that's why you don't see a consistency, because that's the way reasoned eclecticism works. (Sorry if this is coded language for the rest of you!) You look at the external evidence. You look at what kind of manuscripts support a particular reading. You look for the earliest manuscripts. You look for the best quality manuscripts. But you also look at intrinsic probabilities and you look at transcriptional probabilities. The reason you don't detect a certain method in my argumentation is because for every variant you have to argue all the best arguments. For some variants, the transcriptional argument is going to be superior to the manuscript argument. And in other variants, the manuscript argument is going to be superior to the intrinsic evidence. You have to argue it out in every instance and come up with the most convincing argument. If I were just sticking with transcriptional probability the whole time, then you would see that kind of consistency, but precisely because I'm a reasoned eclectic, you don't see it. Whereas with David [Parker], for example, you would clearly see a genealogical method and probably transcriptional probability but he would never use intrinsic probability. Is that right?

Ehrman: They're just not reasoned enough. It's not the method, though. I learned my method from Bruce Metzger, who is completely a reasoned eclectic. I put more weight on intrinsic probability and transcriptional probability than Metzger did. As years have gone by, I've placed less weight on manuscripts for precisely the reasons I've laid out for you. The manuscripts generally are many hundreds of years later than the original and they are not very useful for what the earliest form of the text is.

Question: Dan, I have some questions about the story of the woman caught in adultery.

Wallace: I've heard of that story.

Question: We've heard of it several times this weekend, and it made me think: Do textual critics have any idea when this story was inserted into the Gospel of John? Do you have any idea of the possible authenticity of this story? Is there any possible connection to a genuine story from the ministry of Jesus or is it just creative writing? And, I think probably the most important question concerning how to apply textual criticism to what we do every day as ministers is: If you were preaching a series of sermons through the Gospel of John and came to this story, would you preach a sermon on this text as if it has authority for the Christian life?

Wallace: Those are great and very practical questions that Bart can answer far better than I, so I'll turn it over to him.

Ehrman: No, I would not preach on that.

Audience roars with laughter.

Wallace: Bart has actually done some of the very best work on the pericope of the woman caught in adultery. I am relatively convinced not only that the story is not literarily authentic, but also that it is not entirely historical. Bruce Metzger thought that it had all the earmarks of historicity. The way that I've been looking at it is that it seems that it was a conflation of two different stories that finally coalesced in the third century. I've been very impressed, frankly, with Ehrman's academic work on this subject in his very fine article in *New Testament Studies*.[51] It's hard to read because it's so detailed, but it has some really good information. One of the things that I've wrestled with on the *Pericope Adulterae* is that it looks to me as if there are an awful lot of Lukanisms in it. It looks far more Lukan or Matthean than it does Johannine in terms of its style of writing, the language, the vocabulary, and so forth. And there is a group of manuscripts that has this story after Luke 21:38. It seems to me that if we have a historical kernel to this story it would have gone after Luke 21:38. That seems to be a likely place for it. There is some work that has been done on the style and grammar of Luke. Working with this, what I've been wanting to do— it's one of those backburner projects—is to take this story and look at it through Luke's syntax and style and reduce it down to what it would have looked like if Luke had access to this or had actually written the story. Then I would ask the question, why didn't he put it down in his Gospel? At least at this stage, my guess—and that's all it is, it's not even on the level of a hypothesis—is that he probably had access to a story like this but much shorter. I rather doubt that the Pharisees peeled out from the oldest to the youngest. That looks like a later accretion. I think what Luke had was a shorter form that ended up being a little bit too bland. There's a little more work that needs to be done on this.

Now as far as the major question you're asking, should we preach this? I would personally say no. When I get to this place when I am working through John, I have taken an entire Sunday, or sometimes two, to talk about whether we should preach this passage. Is it authentic? Prepare people to think about this. One of the deep concerns I have for the church today is that there is such a huge difference between the pulpit and the pew and between the pulpit and professors. We need to educate our people and let them know that these are the issues that are going on. So, when I did this one year, I went through and talked about the passage, talked about textual criticism for two weeks, and when we got to the text I said, "It's probably not authentic, let's go on." Nobody had a problem. But if you just walk in there and say that this passage is not authentic; if you do not prepare people to think about that, they're just going to think that the sky has fallen and that you've picked and chosen which passages you didn't want to be original.

Question: Dr. Ehrman, my question is regarding John 1:1 and the reading "and the Word was God." I was curious as to what your view is on that textually. You've mentioned it in the footnote of one of your books. And I was curious what your opinion was on that with regard to the new information that has come to light based on W^{Sup} and the presence of the article before *theos.* It seemed to support your view and I was hoping you could tell me what you think the original reading is there.

Ehrman: I wish I could remember what I said in my footnote. Remind me. What did I say?

Question: I think you were making the case that the reading *ho theos ēn ho logos* was original.

Ehrman: Wow! Really?

Wallace: I think it was Codex L he was talking about, not W^{Sup},[52] though.

Question: It was an eighth-century manuscript that you were talking about.

Ehrman: I said that was the original reading?

Question: No. I don't know what you were saying, that's why I am asking.

Ehrman: Oh. It sounded like a brilliant insight.

Wallace: It's in *The Orthodox Corruption of Scripture.*[53]

Ehrman: I have no recollection. [Bart laughs.] I don't think it had the article, no. How's it go? *Theos ēn ho logos,* right? Is that how it goes? I think it still means the "Word was God," capital G. I think the Gospel of John understands that Jesus is the Word of God that has become incarnate, and as the Word of God he is in some sense God. At the end of the Gospel in John 20:28, Thomas says "My Lord and My God." Jesus is identified as divine at the beginning and at the end of the Gospel and so the Gospel of John understands that in some sense—not in a Nicene sense or a full trinitarian sense—Jesus is God. Am I answering the question?

Question: Yeah, so you think the original is anarthrous there?

Ehrman: Yes, I think it is originally anarthrous there. I'm sorry, for the rest of us mortals what we're saying is that there was not a definite article there. The issue is that normally when you talk about God, capital G in Greek, you say *ho theos*–literally "the God." But in John 1:1 it just says *theos* without the *ho.* There are grammatical reasons for it doing that, but I think that it means capital G, God. It's not surprising to me that scribes on occasion would stick an article in there to make sure you understood that in fact this isn't small-g gods or divine but it actually means God.

Stewart: Our time has come to an end. Let's thank our speakers for great presentations and great answers to good questions.

2

✛

Text and Transmission in the Second Century

Michael W. Holmes

t is widely acknowledged that the text of the documents comprising the New Testament, preserved today in thousands of manuscripts, is better attested than any other text from the ancient world. Yet as true as that statement is, it is potentially misleading, in that the bare statement does not reveal the circumstance that approximately 85 percent of those manuscripts were copied in the eleventh century or later—over a millennium after the writing of the New Testament. With regard to the 15 percent or so of manuscripts that do date from the first millennium of the text's existence, the closer one gets in time to the origins of the New Testament, the more scarce the manuscript evidence becomes. Indeed, for the first century or more after its composition—from, roughly, the late first century to the beginning of the third—we have very little manuscript evidence for any of the New Testament documents, and for some books the gap extends toward two centuries or more.[1]

To put the matter a bit differently, we have—beginning about 200 C.E. for some books, such as the Gospel of John ($\mathfrak{P}^{66}$, $\mathfrak{P}^{75}$), the Gospel of Luke ($\mathfrak{P}^{75}$), and the Pauline corpus ($\mathfrak{P}^{46}$), but not until 300 C.E. or later for others, such as the Gospel of Mark or some of the Catholic letters—

substantial hard evidence for what each book of the New Testament looks like, in general and in detail: its overall structure and arrangement, the order of the paragraphs, the sequence of sentences, and the wording of a very large percentage of its text. This is not at all to say that the text is without variation, but the overall shape of the document is stable and recognizable with regard to both its form and its content, and, with a very few notable exceptions, such as John 7:53—8:11, the sixteenth chapter of Mark, and the ending of Romans, remains stable at all levels above that of the sentence right up until today.

Prior to that 200 to 300 C.E. time frame, however, we have very little evidence for any of these books, only some small fragments preserving a few verses each. (These fragments do document a book's existence, but preserve very little of its contents.) It is widely recognized that in the ancient world the first century or so of a document's existence was a critical period for the transmission of its text, a time when alterations or disruptions, if they were to occur, were most likely to occur, and for this crucial period in the history of the transmission of the New Testament we know relatively little.[2]

So, given these circumstances—that the first century of a text's existence was the critical period, and that we have almost no manuscript evidence from that time—the question arises: *how well does the text of the New Testament as we have it in the late second/early third century reflect the state of the text in the late first century?* (Using "in the late first century" as shorthand for "the time when the various documents that now comprise the New Testament began to be copied and circulated," whenever and in whatever form that was for a particular document.)[3] This is the question I wish to investigate.

How might we begin to answer this question? I propose that we first examine three rather different claims or hypotheses about the transmission of the New Testament text in the second century, each of which, in my estimation, is incorrect. In showing why each is incorrect, we will be putting on the table, as it were, critical information that will be useful to have in hand if we are to begin to reach an answer to our question.

Trobisch

The first proposal is that of David Trobisch, in his book *The First Edition of the New Testament.*[4] His thesis "is that the New Testament, in the form that achieved canonical status, is not the result of a lengthy and complicated collecting process that lasted for several centuries." Instead, "the history of the New Testament is the history of an edition, a book that has been published and edited by a specific group of editors, at a specific place, and at a specific time,"[5] the middle of the second century. Moreover, this "first edition," which included the Septuagint as well, arranged the books that now comprise the LXX and the canonical New Testament into a specific order and arrangement.[6]

Turning specifically to the matter of the New Testament text, according to Trobisch the goal of "modern textual criticism" ought to be "to produce an edition of the Greek text that closely represents the *editio princeps* of the Canonical Edition," which he considers to be the archetype of virtually all extant New Testament manuscripts.[7] In making this claim that the text of the various New Testament documents as we see them from ca. 200 C.E. on have all derived directly from this "canonical edition," he appears to imply that in general we have no access to textual forms or traditions that predate this canonical edition.

If so, then we may infer a response to my "framing question" (*how well does the text of the New Testament as we have it in the late second/early third century reflect the state of the text in the late first century?*). Trobisch's implied answer seems to be this: the text as we have it in the third century reflects the text established by the editors of the "canonical edition" in the mid-second century. In short, we do not have access to the text as it left its author's control, but only as it was later fixed by the editor(s) of the "canonical edition."

Analysis: Trobisch

While this is an interesting hypothesis, it is not at all persuasive. Trobisch's claim is that this "first edition" established a standard order and arrangement of the New Testament documents and of the books of the LXX. If such an event had occurred, one would expect to find far more regularity and similarity among the surviving manuscripts of the New Testament and LXX—which, on Trobisch's hypothesis, all descend from this single edition—than is evident in the surviving manuscripts. With regard to the LXX, for example, our three earliest full copies are the famous codices Vaticanus, Sinaiticus, and Alexandrinus, from the fourth and fifty centuries C.E. The variation between these three with regard to the number and arrangement of books is striking. First, each contains a different number of books—forty-five, forty-seven, and fifty, respectively. Second, there are substantial differences in the order in which the books are presented, involving both the order of the sub-collections (cf. table 2.1) and the arrangement of books within each subcollection (cf. tables 2.2, 2.3, and 2.4).

In addition, while Vaticanus and Sinaiticus place *1-2 Esdras* after Chronicles, Alexandrinus places it among the "extras."

Vaticanus	Sinaiticus	Alexandrinus
Genesis—2 Chronicles	Genesis—2 Chronicles	Genesis—2 Chronicles
Writings	"Extras"	Prophets
"Extras"	Prophets	"Extras"
Prophets	Writings	Writings

Table 2.1: Order of Sub-Collections

Vaticanus	Sinaiticus	Alexandrinus
Psalms	Psalms	Psalms
Proverbs	Proverbs	Job
Ecclesiastes	Ecclesiastes	Proverbs
Song of Songs	Song of Songs	Ecclesiastes
Job	Wisdom of Solomon	Song of Songs
Wisdom of Solomon	Sirach	Wisdom of Solomon
Sirach	Job	Sirach
		Psalms of Solomon

Table 2.2: Order of the "Writings"

Vaticanus	Sinaiticus	Alexandrinus
Esther	Esther	Esther
Judith	Tobit	Tobit
Tobit	Judith	Judith
	1 Maccabees	1-2 Esdras
	4 Maccabees	1-4 Maccabees

Table 2.3: Order of the "Septuagintal Extras"

Vaticanus	Sinaiticus	Alexandrinus
the Twelve	Isaiah	the Twelve
Isaiah	Jeremiah	Isaiah
Jeremiah	Lamentations	Jeremiah
Baruch	Baruch	Baruch
Lamentations	Letter of Jeremiah	Lamentations
Letter of Jeremiah	Ezekiel	Letter of Jeremiah
Ezekiel	Daniel	Ezekiel
Daniel	the Twelve	Daniel

Table 2.4: Order of the Prophets

In all, the significant differences in both content and arrangement so evident in Vaticanus, Sinaiticus, and Alexandrinus constitute strong evidence against Trobisch's hypothesis that the mid-second century editors of what he terms a "Canonical Edition" standardized features of the LXX and placed the books in a specific order.[8]

The situation is not much different with regard to the New Testament. The Gospels generally come first in manuscripts containing more than just one segment of the New Testament, but not always,[9] and the order of the gospels themselves can vary considerably: in fact, nine different sequences are found among the extant manuscripts. After the Gospels (in whatever order they fall), Acts and the Catholic letters generally precede (but occasionally follow) the Pauline letters. Finally, while Revelation (in those manuscripts that include it) generally comes at the end, not even its position is without variation. Within the Catholic letters at least seven different arrangements occur, and within the Pauline letters, at least seventeen different sequences are known.[10]

Finally, if there had been a "canonical edition" in the mid-second century, it seems inexplicable that discussions about the limits of the New Testament canon did in fact continue for another two centuries or more.[11] In short, Trobisch's view, while engaging and provocative, is simply not persuasive, and we may set it aside.

Alands

A rather different proposal is offered by Kurt and Barbara Aland in their famous handbook *The Text of the New Testament*.[12] In it they spell out explicitly a view of textual transmission that is, I think, often taken for granted by most textual critics. If there is a default view among New Testament textual critics, this is probably it. The Alands stand out from their colleagues in that they clearly state what many of their colleagues silently assume.

According to the Alands, "The transmission of the New Testament textual tradition is characterized by an extremely impressive degree of tenacity. Once a reading occurs it will persist with obstinacy." This means that "we can be certain" that somewhere among the many surviving witnesses to the New Testament text "there is still a group of witnesses [that] preserve the original form of the text, despite the pervasive authority of ecclesiastical tradition and the prestige of the later text."[13] In short, "the element of tenacity in the New Testament textual tradition not only permits but demands that we proceed on the premise that in every instance of textual variation it is possible to determine the form of the original text, i.e., the form in which each individual document passed into the realm of published literature by means of copying and formal distribution."[14]

Lest we miss the point, they reiterate: "every reading ever occurring in the New Testament textual tradition is stubbornly preserved . . . any reading ever occurring in the New Testament textual tradition, from the original reading onward, has been preserved in the tradition and needs only to be identified." In addition, "Any interference with the regular process of transmission . . . is signaled by a profusion of variants. This leads to a further conclusion, which we believe to be both logical and compelling, that where such a profusion of readings does *not* exist the text has not been disturbed."[15]

In short, according to the Alands, in every instance of variation that occurs in the manuscripts of the New Testament, the original reading has been preserved somewhere among the surviving evidence, and needs only to be identified; once that identification has been made—that is, once the earliest recoverable text has been determined—then the original has been determined.

So with respect to my framing question (*how well does the text of the New Testament as we have it in the late second/early third century reflect the state of the text in the late first century?*), the Alands' answer seems clear: the "earliest recoverable text" and the "original text" are effectively identical;

the text as we have it in the third century is essentially the same as what the author published.

Analysis: Alands

This claim—that the original reading has always been preserved some-where among the more than 5,000 manuscripts of the New Testament—may be generally true, but cannot be sustained in detail. I offer some examples of evidence to the contrary.

- At Acts 16:12, the United Bible Societies Editorial Com-mittee, "dissatisfied for various reasons with all" the variant readings of the Greek manuscripts, adopted as the text a conjectural restoration, a reading not found in any extant manuscript of Acts.[16]
- At Acts 16:13, the Committee described "the difficulties presented by this verse" as "well-nigh baffling," and in the end adopted what it termed "the least unsatisfactory read-ing" as the text.[17]
- At 1 Cor. 6:5, the text as found in all extant Greek manu-scripts reads *diakrinai ana meson tou autou*, "to judge between his brother," an impossible phrase in Greek[18] that makes no more sense than it does in English to speak of "traveling between Minneapolis." It is, as Zuntz notes, the result of a homoeoteleuton error in the archetype from which all surviv-ing manuscripts descend.[19]
- In discussing the problematic variants in Acts 12:25, Metzger observed "that more than once K. Lake's frank admission of despair reflected [the Committee's] mood: 'Which is the true text? no one knows. . . .'" Eventually, "after long and repeated deliberation," the Committee printed what it described as "the least unsatisfactory" reading.[20]
- At 1 Cor. 8:2-3, Zuntz and Gordon Fee make a persuasive case that of all extant manuscripts, $\mathfrak{P}^{46}$ alone preserves the original text of these verses.[21] The point to note is this: prior to the acquisition of $\mathfrak{P}^{46}$ in the early 1930s, the original read-ing was not extant among the known evidence prior to that

time. Apart from the serendipitous survival and discovery of the Beatty papyri, it would still not be known.

• The same point may be made regarding the Freer logion, that expanded form of the longer ending of Mark. Jerome in the fourth century reports that this form of the ending of Mark could be found "in some exemplars and especially in Greek manuscripts of Mark,"[22] but today this form of the longer ending is found in only a single manuscript, codex Washingtonianus, acquired by Charles Freer in 1906. Once again, only a single recently discovered manuscript preserves a reading once more-widely known.

The last two examples are a bit different. They illustrate that the manuscript evidence as we know it today is sometimes rather different than it appeared in antiquity.

• At Rom. 3:9, the reading that Arethas of Caesarea (tenth century) says was the text of the oldest and most accurate manuscripts in his day (*katechomen perisson*) is today found only in two late manuscripts.[23]
• At Heb. 2:9 the variant *chōris theou* occurs in numerous early fathers, both eastern and western, indicating that it once was widely known, but today it is found in only a few manuscripts.

In summary, the Alands' claim that "we can be *certain*" that somewhere among the many surviving witnesses to the New Testament text "there is still a group of witnesses [that] preserve the original form of the text"[24] is not supported by the surviving manuscript evidence. For most of the New Testament there is little doubt that the original reading survives, and for much of the rest it is highly probable that it does, but in light of the examples given and the implications we may draw from them, we cannot be certain that it does in every case.

Petersen

The third perspective I wish to notice falls at the other end of a spectrum from the Alands. It is a perspective that proposes that the text of

the various New Testament documents as we know them from ca. 200
c.e. or so is *not* representative of the earliest form of the New Testament text. Among its more vocal proponents was William E. Petersen,
who in a series of essays set out a clear thesis regarding the early transmission of the text.[25] In a survey of the New Testament in the Apostolic Fathers, for example, Petersen offers this claim:

> *In the overwhelming majority of cases, those passages in the Apostolic Fathers
> which offer recognizable parallels with our present-day New Testament
> display a text that is very different from what we now find in our modern
> critical editions of the New Testament.*[26]

Or, as he writes in an essay on the origins of the gospels:

> To be brutally frank, we know next to nothing about the shape
> of the "autograph" gospels; indeed, it is questionable if one
> can even speak of such a thing. This leads to the inescapable
> conclusion that the text in our critical editions today is actually
> a text which dates from no earlier tha[n] about 180 c.e., at the
> earliest. Our critical editions do not present us with the text that
> was current in 150, 120 or 100—much less in 80 c.e.[27]

So with respect to my framing question (*how well does the text of the New
Testament as we have it in the late second/early third century reflect the state of the
text in the late first century?*), Petersen's answer seems clear: not very well
at all.

Analysis: Petersen

In analyzing these claims, we may begin with a general observation:
Petersen at times confuses the question of determining the earliest
form of a gospel tradition with the question of determining the earliest text of a specific gospel. For example, in summarizing his observations about early second-century writers, Petersen observes:

> Extra-canonical material is prominent, and mixed up with what
> we now regard as canonical material. There seems to have been
> no clear demarcation between traditions that were "proto-
> canonical" and those that were "proto-extra-canonical." While
> this is not surprising, given the fact that such distinctions are

anachronistic during this period, it nevertheless highlights the flexibility and unsettledness of textual traditions in general.[28]

Notice the leap in his argument: the use of extra-canonical *material* alongside "proto-canonical" material somehow highlights the "unsettledness" of *textual* traditions. But he has shown no such thing. All he has shown is that multiple gospel traditions were being used, and he has not even addressed the question of whether they were written and not oral. So his conclusion about *textual* "unsettledness" has no foundation.

Second, we may notice Petersen's persistent tendency to assert rather than argue the source of a gospel citation. Identifying the source of a patristic citation of gospel material can be a difficult (and sometimes impossible) challenge, as Petersen well knows. He includes in one essay a fine discussion of the methodological problems involved,[29] but in practice he regularly ignores his own guidelines. Two examples will illustrate the problem.

The first involves a gospel citation in Justin Martyr (*Dialogue* 101.2) that has parallels in Matthew, Mark, and Luke, which read as follows:

> Mt. 19:17: "Teacher . . . | . . . "Why do you ask me about what is good? *There is only one who is good.*"
> Mk. 10:18: "Good teacher . . . | . . . Why do you call me good? No one is good but God alone."
> Lk. 18:19: "Good teacher . . . | . . . Why do you call me good? No one is good but God alone."

The text of Justin Martyr runs like this:

> "Good teacher . . . | . . . Why do you call me good? *There is one who is good,* **my father in heaven**."

Even though Justin never identifies his source(s), Petersen declares that the similarity of Justin's "there is one who is good" to the text of Matthew "shows that it is the Matthean version which is being cited," and therefore Justin preserves the earliest version of Matthew 19:17, one that includes the phrase "my father in heaven"—proof, he says, that our critical text of the gospels does not correspond to the early second-century text of that gospel.[30]

But Petersen's identification of this as a citation of Matthew is surely debatable. The *two* preceding phrases, "good teacher" and "why do you call me good," reflect Mark and/or Luke, not Matthew. Furthermore, Justin is known to have used a harmonized collection of sayings of Jesus, one that was based on multiple sources in addition to Matthew, Mark, and Luke.[31] How does Petersen know that the phrase "my father in heaven" comes from Matthew and not one of Justin's other sources? He doesn't, but he makes an identification anyway.[32]

The second example involves a citation from Ignatius of Antioch (*Smyrn.* 3.2), which Petersen claims "is clearly the most ancient extant version of Luke 24:39."[33] The two passages read:

Ignatius, *Smyrn.* 3.2	Luke 24:37-42
[2] and when he came to Peter and those with him, he said to them: "Take hold of me; touch me and see that I am not a disembodied demon." And immediately they touched him and believed, being closely united with his flesh and blood.	[36]Jesus himself stood among them. [37]But they were startled and terrified, thinking they saw a spirit. [38]Then he said to them, "Why are you frightened, and why do doubts arise in your hearts? [39]See my hands and my feet; it is I myself! Touch me and see that a spirit does not have flesh and bones like you see I have." [40]When he had said this, he showed them his hands and his feet. [41]And while they still could not believe it (because of their joy) and were amazed, he said to them, "Do you have anything here to eat?"

Petersen bases his claim on the fact that the two passages share five identical words (*psēlaphēsate me kai idete hoti . . .*, "touch me and see that"). But in this case, the differences are more significant than the similarities. First, note the sharp difference between the immediately following phrase in each (Ignatius, "I am not a disembodied demon," vs. Luke, "a spirit does not have flesh and bones like you see I have"). Second, observe how what Ignatius says next ("and immediately [*kai euthys*] they touched him and believed") contradicts what Luke says in verse 41 (they were still *not* believing, *eti de apistountōn autōn*). It seems far more likely that Ignatius is working with a parallel or similar tradition than that he is citing Luke 24:39.[34]

These two examples are typical of Petersen's procedure throughout: he repeatedly asserts what needs to be demonstrated. The persistent failure to demonstrate that the early anonymous citations of gospel tradition that he discusses are in fact citations of a specific gospel undercuts his case and leaves it without a foundation upon which to build.

A third shortcoming is an inattentiveness to ancient citation techniques and their implications for how authors in antiquity handled texts and citations. One recent investigation summarized the matter this way:

> The changes brought by an author to the cited passage vary substantially. They generally consist in the omission or addition of words, in grammatical changes, in the combination of citations, and in the modification of the primary meaning of the quotation. These changes may be deliberate, which means that they are made by the citing author specifically in order to appropriate the content of the citation. They may also be accidental. If deliberate, the changes result from the author's wish to adjust the citation to his own purposes, to "modernize" the stylistic expression of a more ancient writer, or to adapt the grammar of the cited text to that of the citing text. It may be noted that deliberate changes do not always stem from the citing author's eagerness to tamper with the primary meaning of a passage, as modern scholars often suspect.[35]

Furthermore, some of the changes to a cited text may have occurred when and as it was excerpted from its source—a point of particular relevance for Justin Martyr, who indeed appears to have utilized collections of excerpts gathered from authoritative sources.[36]

Also to be noted is Justin's particular style and method of using authoritative texts in his arguments. In discussing the fulfillment of biblical prophecies, for example, Justin often harmonizes the gospel narratives to conform to the wording of the prophecies. As Skarsaune observes, in Justin's discussions of prophecy and fulfillment, "The report of the fulfillment gets words from the prophecy inserted into it," an example of what Skarsaune considers to be "postcanonical modifications of Gospel material."[37]

None of these factors receives attention in Petersen's analysis of early citations of gospel material.[38] This is particularly surprising with regard to Justin Martyr, given the major role that citations from Justin play in Petersen's arguments.

Finally, the logic of Petersen's argumentation is often unpersuasive. In a quotation cited earlier, for example, Petersen claims that "we know next to nothing about the shape" of the earliest stage of the gospel texts; he then contends that "this leads to an inescapable conclusion . . . Our critical editions do not present us with the text that was current in 150, 120 or 100—much less in 80 C.E."[39] But the conclusion does not follow: if we know nothing about the early shape of the gospels, then how can we know that they don't match our critical texts? The only way we can know that "our critical editions" do not match the early text is if we know what the early text looked like—but according to Petersen, that is precisely what we do not know.

To summarize, Petersen's claims about the lack of congruence between the early texts and our earliest MSS have no foundation. Petersen has shown that early Christian writers utilized a wide range of diverse gospel *traditions* in their work—some that would later become canonized, and others that would not—and he is quite right to observe that some of these gospel traditions—which may have been in either written or oral form—were sometimes rather different than the *texts* of Matthew, Mark, Luke, and John as we know them c. 180 or so. But Petersen definitely has *not* shown that the *text* of Matthew, Mark, Luke and/or John in the late first century was different from the text of those same gospels as we know it c. 180 and later. His case simply does not hold water.

Parker

So far, we have examined (and set aside) three very different answers to our framing question (*how well does the text of the New Testament as we have it in the late second/early third century reflect the state of the text in the late first century?*). There is also a fourth answer that we might look at briefly, and it is one given—or at least implied—by some of the recent contributions by David Parker.[40] If I read him correctly, his response to my question might well be, "why should it matter?"

I base this conclusion in part on Parker's declaration that pursuit of an "original text" (however one might define it) is neither appropriate nor possible.[41] One may demur, however. We may not have as much evidence as we might wish, but that in itself is no reason not to try. Nor is frustration with what theologians may or may not do with our work[42] sufficient reason not to pursue a goal. And pursue it we should: not as the only goal, nor as an attempt to convert a movie to a snapshot, to borrow Parker's metaphor, but rather to recover the missing opening scenes of that movie, in light of which the rest of it will make more sense.

Toward a More Adequate Answer

Keeping that objective in view, we may ask: have we found out anything that might get us started toward a more adequate answer? Permit me to offer an observation arising out of the analysis of Petersen's discussion of patristic citations.

We have seen in the case of Justin Martyr that his practice (a) of generally not identifying his sources and (b) of using a broad range of sources means that it is difficult (and often impossible) to identify the specific source of a given reading. Because Justin used a wide range of sources, we cannot simply assume that a reading that parallels Matthew, for example, or Luke or Mark is from that gospel; positive evidence is required in order to make an identification. The same circumstances hold true for Polycarp of Smyrna;[43] indeed, I believe that the same conditions hold true for every Christian document we know of prior to the time of Irenaeus, regardless of its theological orientation.[44]

This leaves us in an ironic position: about the only time early patristic citations can count as evidence for the text of a New Testament document is when their text agrees with that of a manuscript of that document (which is not when or where help is needed). In any other case, we can never be sure what source is being used, because an author typically doesn't identify it.

One result, therefore, of our investigation thus far is a restriction rather than an expansion of our range of possible sources of information about the early shape of the text. Evidence regarding what the text of the gospels looked like in the first half of the second century that we might have expected the early Christian writers to provide is simply not forthcoming.[45] This means that for the earliest stages of transmission, almost our only evidence will have to be whatever information we can tease out of our later manuscripts.

How might we proceed in such a situation? Petersen, in one of his essays, suggests a possible way forward: to take what we know about trends, patterns, and tendencies from a later period for which we have evidence, project them back into the earlier period for which we lack evidence, and see what they might suggest.[46] So permit me to sketch some observations and then see what they might suggest.

A) It would appear that a substantial percentage of the really interesting or more deviant readings that investigators such as Petersen have called to our attention are to be found in early Christian writings rather than in manuscripts of the New Testament documents. An obvious conclusion to be drawn from this observation is that copying is an inherently more conservative activity than composition.[47] As Kim Haines-Eitzen has argued:

> The scribes who copied Christian literature during the second and third centuries were not "uncontrolled" nor were the texts that they (re)produced marked by "wildness." Rather, the (re)production of texts by early Christian scribes was bounded and constrained by the multifaceted and multilayered discursive practices of the second- and third-century church.[48]

This would suggest that the textual tradition itself is not as "wild" or "unstable" as is sometimes claimed.[49]

B) While gospel traditions about Jesus appear to have been rather fluid up through the mid-second century and even later, actual documents, once created, appear to have been relatively stable. That is, existing documents appear to have been utilized as sources for new documents rather than revised and then circulated under the same name. An example (assuming for the sake of the argument a common solution to the Synoptic problem) would be the way that the authors of Matthew and Luke made heavy use of the gospel of Mark to create new documents with different titles, rather than a revised form of Mark that continued to use the existing title (whatever that may have been).[50]

The two obvious exceptions would be Marcion's treatment of Luke,[51] and the *Shepherd of Hermas* (which apparently circulated in two or more forms at one point in its history).[52] But the kind of evidence that makes these two stand out is precisely what is lacking in the case of other documents.[53] Once created, a document tended to be stable rather than fluid.

C) The range and extent of textual variation evident in the extant late second early third century manuscripts is such that we cannot assume that every original reading has survived (the evidence presented earlier in fact points in the other direction). Our earliest evidence, *1 Clement* at the end of the first century, for example, reveals already the presence of variant forms of the textual tradition.[54] With due allowance for some hyperbole, an observation by Origen offers a perspective on the state of affairs during the early third century: "It is evident that the differences between the manuscripts have become numerous, due either to the negligence of some copyists, or to the perverse audacity of others; either not caring about the correction (*diorthōseōs*) of what they have copied, or in the process of correction (*en tē diorthōsei*) making additions or deletions as they see fit."[55] What this observation testifies to is a relative increase in the amount of variation; what it does not indicate, however, is how much variation there was at that time: "numerous" compared to what? How much is "numerous"?

D) The kind of activity described by Origen correlates well with some of the scribal habits and patterns observable in the early papyri.[56] Observable patterns of behavior cover a wide spectrum: some copyists were relatively careless or cared more for the general sense than the precise wording,[57] while others were very careful and accurate; the scribe of $\mathfrak{P}^{75}$ in particular comes to mind at this point, "a disciplined scribe who writes with the intention of being careful and accurate."[58] In fact, one of the key reasons we are able to spotlight the rather free habits of some scribes is precisely because some of their colleagues copied their texts so carefully. But even the best copyist is not perfect, and so it is no surprise to find evidence of correction in many manuscripts. The extent and effect of correction (*diorthosis*)[59] could vary widely: (a) it could involve as little as correcting a copy against its exemplar. (b) It could also involve the correction by a reader or scribe of (what were perceived as) copyist's mistakes without reference to the manuscript's exemplar. (c) It could involve the correction of a copy by means of a different exemplar (as in, for example, $\mathfrak{P}^{66}$), in which case it could, in the next generation of copies made from the corrected manuscript, result in substantial alteration to the character of the copy being transmitted.[60]

It should be remembered, however, that the copyists are not the only actors in the mix: in light of what is known about the literary culture of antiquity, many of the non-accidental alterations made to the text during the early centuries will have been the work of users or readers of the text, rather than copyists.[61]

E) There is little evidence (if any) of "recensional" activity, in the sense of a deliberate, thoroughgoing, and authoritative editorial revision by scholars, affecting on any widespread scale the text of the New Testament.[62]

F) There is some evidence in the earliest papyri of efforts to preserve an early text. Zuntz's detailed analysis of $\mathfrak{P}^{46}$, the earliest copy of the Pauline letters, revealed evidence of a conscious concern to preserve an accurate text that he thought could be traced back as early as the beginning of the second century.[63] The work of Birdsall, Martini, and Fee on $\mathfrak{P}^{75}$ indicates that it "is a relatively careful exemplar of a sound and faithful philological tradition," a text that preserves many idiosyncratic features of Johannine style and diction no longer found in other witnesses.[64]

G) Wisse observes that "the strongest argument" against viewing the early history of the text as similar to that of later periods is the considerable length of time it took the New Testament writings to reach canonical status. "This has led to the assumption that Christian scribes would have been very reluctant to tamper with the text of a canonical writing, but would have felt free to introduce changes before a text was recognized as apostolic and authoritative. There are, however, good reasons to challenge this assumption," including the observation that texts whose canonical status remained in question longer show less, rather than more, textual corruption, and that "if we judge by the interpolations for which there is textual evidence then it appears that the numbers increase rather than decrease after the second century." In short, "it is indeed possible that in the pre-canonical period scribes were less hesitant to take liberties with the text, but at the same time there would have been less urgency to change or adapt the theology of these writings."[65]

H) Finally, the social context of the early Christian movement, specifically, its use and reading of early Christian texts in the context of worship, for example, almost certainly was an important factor toward stabilization in the transmission of early Christian texts.[66]

CONCLUSION

So, if we take these trends, patterns, and tendencies from a later period for which we have evidence, and project them back into the earlier period for which we lack evidence, what might the results look like? What might they suggest as an answer to our framing question: *how well does the text of the New Testament as we have it in the late second/early third century reflect the state of the text in the late first century?*[67]

First, it is evident that we are dealing with a situation that involves a mixture of both fluidity and stability; a key issue is the relationship between the two. On the one hand, there is evidence of variation (sometimes substantial) in the process of scribal transmission; on the other hand, there are also evident factors favoring the stability of the textual transmission. Second, with the possible exception of the gospel of Luke and of Acts (where the differences between the "Alexandrian" and "Western" textual traditions are considerably greater than they are elsewhere in the New Testament), there is little if any evidence of any major disruption to the text. Third, apart from the endings of Mark and of Romans,[68] nearly all variation during the time period in view affects a verse or less of the text.[69] In short, we appear to be dealing with a situation characterized by macro-level stability and micro-level fluidity.

This state of affairs leads me to conclude that the later texts represent the earlier stages "well enough," well enough to encourage us to seek to recover the earlier texts from which our extant copies appear to have descended, well enough to give us good grounds to be reasonably optimistic about the possibility of recovering earlier forms of the text on the basis of our extant witnesses. While not wishing to overstate the possibilities (as I think Aland does), neither should we overstate the difficulties (as I think Petersen does).[70] While it is true, as we noted in the introduction, that we have very little physical evidence prior to approximately the end of the second century, nonetheless it provides, as E. J. Epp observes, a "close continuity with the remote past" that "is unusual in ancient text transmission,"[71] which is an important point that ought not to be forgotten in the midst of all our legitimate interest in the later history of the text and its variations. That we don't have as much as evidence as we might wish should not prevent us from doing all we can with the evidence we do have. Indeed, to do anything less would be to squander the resources and evidence entrusted to us by the accidents of history, resources and evidence that will, if judiciously employed, enable us to move beyond the limits of the extant manuscripts to recover the earlier forms from which they themselves have descended.

3

The Necessity of a Theology of Scripture

Dale B. Martin

grew up in a very "Bible centered" church (okay, it was fundamentalist) and was taught a lot of Bible.[1] Even now, I need only hear the beginning words of certain verses, especially in the King James Version, and I will finish them automatically. And I don't mean just the "big ones," such as John 3:16, recognized by any decent football fan who watches television. We also memorized more obscure passages. Decades later, I can still finish: "Study to show thyself approved unto God . . ." (2 Tim. 2:15); "Repent and be baptized every one of you . . ." (Acts 2:38); and many more.

Some of us former fundamentalist kids remember "sword drills," popular sometimes in Sunday schools but especially as a competition at Bible camp. We would stand at attention with our Bibles held stiffly at our sides, like clumsy Revolutionary War muskets. The teacher would shout, in her best marine sargeant voice, "Presennnt arms!" and we would snap to attention with our Bibles, our "swords," ready in front of us (". . . and the sword of the Spirit, which is the word of God . . ." Eph. 6:17). The teacher would call out a Bible book, chapter, and verse ("Jeremiah 21:8!"), and we would race to get there first. The first student who found the passage was supposed to plant a finger on the verse and read it out loudly. "And unto this people thou shalt say, Thus saith the Lord; Behold I set before you the way of life, and the way of death" (Jer. 21:8, KJV).

Long before I ever attended seminary, I may not have known much about sophisticated modern methods of interpreting scripture, but I at least had much of it in my head. And I was not the only one. Not so long ago—recently enough that older professors can remember it well—faculty teaching in seminaries and divinity schools could assume that their beginning students mostly knew their Bibles. Students may not already have been educated in the critical study of scripture, but they could be expected to recognize basic stories, characters, and phrases from the Bible. Authors could expect most of their readers to know that *East of Eden*, *The Power and the Glory*, or *The Grapes of Wrath* were quotations of scripture. Political speeches could be sprinkled with biblical quotations and allusions with the expectation that many if not all the hearers would not only recognize them as being from the Bible but might even be able to tell where to find them.

No more. If you ask professors now teaching in theological schools, they will tell you that the level of basic knowledge of *what's in* the Bible is generally low. They will say that they feel at a disadvantage because they must teach not only how to *interpret* the Bible, but also basic Bible knowledge, knowledge that in previous generations, at least according to their perceptions, was carried as cultural equipage by any generally educated citizen, not to mention regular churchgoers.

In spite of the truth of this observation about "biblical illiteracy" among most people, even Christians, and even many Christians training for the ministry, I want to argue that a greater crisis for churches is caused by a lack of education in theological reasoning and theological interpretation of scripture. Even when students know *what's in* the Bible, I have come to believe that they do not know, and are generally not being instructed, how to interpret scripture with sufficient theological sophistication.

For years I have suspected that most theological schools, seminaries and divinity schools connected to universities, were teaching their students mainly the use of historical criticism when approaching the interpretation of the Bible. By "historical criticism" I mean a set of practices and skills designed mainly in the modern world that attempt to reconstruct the likely intentions of the ancient human author of the text or what ancient readers, who occupied the same cultural milieu as the author, would have taken the text to mean. Historical criticism, developed mainly in Germany in the nineteenth century, came to dominate instruction in biblical interpretation in the United States in the twentieth century, in "conservative" as well as "liberal" schools.

In order to test this suspicion of mine, I traveled around the United States, visiting ten different theological schools; I surveyed published materials designed for instructing theological students in the study of the Old and New Testaments; and I made use also of the Internet to survey instructional materials, such as syllabuses, made available by various sources there. Funded by a generous grant from the Wabash Center for Teaching and Learning in Theology and Religion, I spent a year researching pedagogical materials and practices for teaching theological students to interpret the Bible. I found that though many instructors and schools make some attempt to teach theological interpretation of the Bible, few are doing a good job teaching theologies of scripture or adequate skills for theological interpretation. In most schools, in spite of faculty perceptions to the contrary, historical criticism dominates the curriculum in biblical studies, and, in my view, theological reasoning is not adequately taught.[2]

The first step in learning how to interpret the Bible theologically is to make explicit what one thinks scripture *is*. How one interprets scripture depends a great deal on what one thinks the Bible is. Most people, entirely nonreligious people as well as Christians, are tacitly working with implicit, almost never explicit, "models" of scripture.

In the church of my youth, the Church of Christ in Texas, we were commonly taught that the Bible, or more particularly the New Testament, was a "blueprint" for the church. The church's organizational structure (Who were its leaders? How was the church supposed to be governed? What should be the relationships among different congregations?) was supposed to be "read off" the New Testament as a builder would "read off" the way to construct a house by studying and rechecking the architect's blueprints. So, congregations were governed by a plurality of "elders," all male, who were assisted by a plurality of "deacons," also male, all on the basis of 1 and 2 Timothy and Titus.

This practice extended even to forbidding instrumental music in worship because the New Testament contained "commandments" to "sing" (Eph. 5:19; Col. 3:16) but nowhere contained any "commandments" to play musical instruments in worship. It was unimportant that the New Testament contained no *prohibition against* instrumental music. It was enough that singing was commanded and instrumental music was not. God had indicated his desire (and of course we all assumed God was male) *for* a cappella music in church by putting that in the "blueprint." He no more needed to forbid instruments explicitly than an architect should need to write in his blueprints something like, "*Don't* use any of the following materials in constructing the roof." The architect needed only to designate that the roof was supposed to be built from wood shingles, and that should be taken to *exclude* the use of slate. So, the fact that some author in the New Testament said "sing" and none said "play an organ" was taken to indicate that God wanted singing and not organs.

I remember a preacher insisting that since God had instructed Noah to build the ark out of gopher wood (Gen. 6:14, KJV), God did not need to state explicitly that Noah was *not* to use pine, or oak, or cedar. Had Noah substituted other wood for gopher wood, or even supplemented the gopher wood with pine or oak, Noah would have been disobeying God. And the ark would have sunk. Just as Noah had a blueprint for building the ark, so we Christians had in the New Testament a blueprint for the organization and practices of the church.

Now this *is* a rational way of thinking about the nature of scripture, but it led to real problems, problems I remember thinking about even as a young teenager. There is no mention of Sunday schools in the New Testament, so some churches in my denomination split off in order to avoid offending God by the existence in the church of Sunday schools. There is no mention of missionary societies or orphanages or other "metachurch" organizations in the New Testament, so other churches split off in order to avoid participating with other congregations in supporting such organizations. I know of no churches that split off in order to avoid using microphones, hymnals, or printed educational materials in worship, but people did debate the issues. In any case, it is obvious that *the way* people were *reading* the New Testament was heavily influenced by what sort of thing they took scripture to *be*.

It is easy to see how the model of scripture I have just described was produced on the nineteenth- and twentieth-century American frontier.[3] The "American experiment" was an attempt to come up with new ways of being a nation as a constitutional republic. "Traditional" sources of "authority" and their institutions were rejected in favor of a textual source available to everyone. In the confusion of the growing religious pluralism of nineteenth-century America, with a rising cacophony of different and new ways of being Christian—several established denominations of Protestants, new churches, experimental sects, the rise of the Mormons and other new religious movements, all living cheek to jowl in new communities in what was then the West, and what is now the Midwest and South—a remedy for plurality and confusion was sought in an agreed-upon constitution. Some Christians, therefore, took the Bible, or particularly the New Testament, as just that constitution: the Christian version of the United States Constitution that founded and guided the young republic.

It is thus also no surprise that the modern world, mainly in the early twentieth century, produced a quintessentially "modernist" form of Christianity: fundamentalism, with its view that the Bible is historically and scientifically inerrant or infallible. Just as science had come to see itself as producing knowledge about reality by carefully and objectively observing the "facts" of "nature," so many Christians, using that same model of knowledge, saw themselves as looking to the Bible for certain "facts" about reality, including of course the nature of God, but also morality, history, and nature itself. The first chapters of Genesis were seen as offering an alternative, even "scientific," account of the history of nature and humankind, an alternative that could allow—or demand—the rejection of evolution or, as fundamentalists call it, "Darwinism." Fundamentalists, though, came to recognize that reading the Bible was a rather complicated activity. They knew that there were many different English translations possible. So they came to believe that the different *versions* or *translations* of the Bible were not infallible or inerrant; the texts which *really* were the inerrant or infallible word of God were those of the original Hebrew and Greek documents.

This is where Bart Ehrman's book, *Misquoting Jesus*, comes into my story. As you no doubt by now know, Ehrman was taught in his youth group and later at Moody Bible Institute that the Bible was verbally inspired and inerrant, not in any particular modern English translation, but in the original "autographs" (the physical documents penned by the historical authors). He decided that if the only completely accurate inspired text was the original text, he wanted to become an expert in the discipline that used the appropriate linguistic and historical tools to "discover" what that original wording was.

During graduate study at Princeton Seminary and afterwards, Ehrman came to realize just how many thousands upon thousands of textual variants there were in the many extant Greek manuscripts of the documents of the New Testament. He came to believe that all our editions of the Greek New Testament were in fact constructions of modern scholarship and that we never could really have any certainty about the original wording of the original texts of the New Testament. This came as a severe blow to his faith, precisely because he had been converted from a rather "social" Episcopalian background to a rigorous form of evangelical Christianity that stressed the absolute verbal inspiration and inerrancy of the original words of the Bible. As Ehrman put it, "What good is it to say that the autographs (i.e., the originals) were inspired? We don't *have* the originals! We have only error-ridden copies, and the vast majority of these are centuries removed from the originals and different from them, evidently, in thousands of ways."[4] Such realizations led Ehrman to abandon his evangelical faith in scripture.

Ehrman is quite right to insist that we do not have and cannot discover the "original text" of the New Testament (much less the entire Bible). And it is understandable if he assumed, in his "fundamentalist" period, that the view of scripture he entertained at that time could hardly stand up to the recognition that we *have no access* to the "original text" of the Bible. *If* one takes "scripture," that is, *to be* only the original autographs of the manuscripts that came to make up our Bible, *then* the radical inaccessibility of the wording of those autographs constitutes a challenge to faith in scripture. But this is true *only if* that is in fact what "scripture" is.

In fact, the view that various manuscript versions of the Greek New Testament, and indeed various translations of the New Testament, pose a challenge to Christian faith has been understandable—even possible—only in the modern world, to be exact since the dominance of the printing press in the production of modern "textuality." The church more generally, and educated Christians more especially, have never identified "scripture" with any particular physical embodiment of the text of the Bible, or with any particular manuscript.[5] Ancient and medieval theologians and scribes knew full well that there were many differences in the wording of the Greek of different manuscripts. Every time they picked up a different copy of "scripture," they were picking up manuscripts that contained different "readings" of the "text." They knew that sometimes the differences were minor, and sometimes major. They certainly at times saw that as a problem that deserved an attempt at a remedy, or an attempt at the "best" reading or perhaps a "unitary" recension. But they accepted the variation in the wording of different manuscripts of scripture as a fact of life, not an insurmountable challenge to faith.

In the modern world since the dominance of the printing press, we are used to thinking that there is one right edition of every document, and that in most cases we (or at least the experts) can produce it. Realizing that Christian scripture cannot be so published—that no editor or group of editors can deliver "the" right version, edition, or translation—may surprise modern people, but that is a reflection of the confusion about texts and textuality befogging modern people. It is also a result of the fact that most modern people, including most Christians, are living with what is an immature and untrained *theology* of scripture.

More sophisticated Christian theologians insist that no physical embodiment of "scripture" can be identified *as* "scripture" itself, the "word of God." The Bible isn't scripture simply in and of itself. It is scripture, the word of God, when it is read in faith by the leading of the Holy Spirit. Christians have traditionally believed, it is true, that scripture mediates truths that are essential for faith. But this is itself a matter of faith. The Christian view (properly) is that scripture is sufficient, that scripture supplies us with what we need for salvation, that scripture will not itself mislead us to destruction. But this means that the literal sense of scripture is necessarily true only to the extension of the essentials of faith. The Christian idea is that we have *enough* of the real words of scripture to be faithful people. But that belief cannot be verified in the public square of secular empiricism. It is itself a stance of faith.

The points I am making may be illustrated by comparing the relationship in Christian theology between the church universal (the "body of Christ") and particular, social manifestations of "church." We all feel we can recognize local, socially delineable congregations, and we with all correctness also call these "churches." It is much harder to point out the boundaries of *the* church, meaning the entire Christian community. Many Christians regularly confess, especially when they recite the Apostles' Creed, to believe in "the communion of saints," again referring to all members of the body of Christ no matter where they live in the world, and including all those Christians who have ever lived. But no one can point out the physical boundaries of that body. The Christian belief—properly speaking—is that the body of Christ, the church universal, is never *identical* with any physical social group.[6] It is a mystery of faith that the church does exist visibly and in reality, but we cannot delineate it by the normal means of social boundary-making. The body of Christ, though visible and real, must not be *identified* (made commensurate) with any particular human social group or organization. It is "the *mystical* body of Christ."[7]

We may therefore propose an analogy: just as the church is embodied in particular, visible, physical groups of people but must not be *identified* with any of those groups or even with all those groups gathered together, so scripture is embodied in particular texts, manuscripts, editions, and translations but cannot be *identified* with any of them, including the imagined "original autographs."[8] The acceptance of a text as scripture is no less a matter of faith in God than is the acceptance that a particular congregation is one instance of the body of Christ.

I offer the analogy not to move into a discussion of the church, but to illustrate the theological poverty reflected in the fear that ignorance about the "original wording" of the text of scripture may disrupt faith in God or confidence in scripture. The idea that the instability of the Greek wording of the New Testament throws up an insurmountable obstacle to faith in the sufficiency of scripture for salvation is the product of a particular modern view of books and textuality. I offer this discussion as part of my larger point that there are many different ideas about what scripture *is*. There are many different assumptions, often not self-consciously considered, about "what sort of thing scripture is or is like." People work with different "models" of scripture. And *how* they interpret the Bible depends greatly on what sort of thing they take scripture to be.

Many people, for example, especially in American Protestantism, think about the Bible as a rule book. We should go to it to see what it says about homosexuality, or divorce, or family, or abortion. In the past few decades, many Christians can be heard talking about the Bible as an owner's manual. Just as we should consult the owner's manual for our car in order to know how properly to maintain the vehicle, or for suggestions for what to do in case something goes wrong, so we should read the Bible to see how to run our lives according to the intentions and advice of the maker. Both these metaphors are very popular ways of conceiving what sort of thing scripture is among, especially, evangelical and conservative Christians.

There are obvious problems. If the Bible is a rule book, it is an awfully confusing and incomplete one. In spite of references to the Bible in the abortion debate, for instance, there is nowhere in the Bible any clear rule-like instruction about abortion, even though abortion was available in the ancient world also. If the Bible is an owner's manual, it needed a better author and editors. Unlike really useful owner's manuals, our Bible came to us without illustrations. People in debates about sexuality and Christianity might like to have a few pictures making it clear which "tab A" goes into which "slot B," but they will look in vain in our Bible for them.

Another common way Christians speak of scripture is to call it an "authority." Some Christians regularly challenge other Christians by implying that they are not sufficiently submitting to the authority of scripture. In my view, though, calling scripture an authority doesn't give us much because it doesn't tell us, without much more elaboration, what kind of thing is here meant by "authority." Is it like a government agency that sets rules for labor disputes? Is it like a scientific expert who may point out evidence but who has no real power to force us to act according to his advice? Is it like a television chef who can make gentle suggestions about improving a dish? The term *authority*, though bandied around much in Christian discussions and debates about scripture, is too variable, and indeed vacuous, to be of much use here unless it is stipulated what precisely is meant by authority and what sort of authority.

A more promising and fruitful model of scripture is the proposal of several theologians of the past few decades that we think of scripture as providing, more than any other one thing, narrative or a story. Though scripture contains many other literary forms that aren't really narratives—there are laws, poems, songs, gnomic sayings, and many other genres—these theologians of narrative insist that those other parts of scripture have still traditionally been taken by Christians as existing within the grander narrative of what God has done in and for Israel and in Jesus Christ for the entire world.[9] Again, one will interpret scripture in different ways if one takes it to be more like a story than a list of rules or a blueprint.

I have experimented with thinking of scripture as a space we enter, rather than a bookish source for knowledge. We should imagine scripture, in my suggestions, as something like a museum or a sanctuary, perhaps a cathedral. Just as we enter a museum and experience both its building and its art as communicating to us—yet without any explicit rules or propositions being heard in the air—so we should imagine that when we enter the space of scripture by reading it either alone or hearing it read in church we are entering a space where our Christian imaginations may be informed, reshaped, even surprised by the place scripture becomes for us. As is already apparent, imagining scripture as holy space we enter, rather than as a rule book or blueprint, will significantly affect how we interpret it. There is much more that could be said about scripture as sanctuary space, and I have indeed said more elsewhere, but this is enough to offer it as an example of a different model of "what scripture is."[10] The education of people in the theological interpretation of scripture should begin, I urge, with teaching them to think critically, self-consciously, and creatively about what sort of thing scripture is—in their own assumptions and in the history and practices of their communities.

So Bart Ehrman and most American evangelicals are both wrong. And they are both wrong because they ignore just how varied and ubiquitous is the necessity of interpretation.[11] The text of the Bible does not "say" anything. It must be interpreted. And how a Christian interprets scripture may legitimately differ from the way a text critic or a historian interprets the text of the Bible. After all, even taking the text of the Greek New Testament published in the Nestle-Aland edition, if that text is read rigorously and historically, with a view to establishing the meaning of the text as it likely would have been understood in its first or second century context, we must admit that the text so construed and interpreted will not support all sorts of orthodox Christian doctrines. Read historically, there is no doctrine of the Trinity in the New Testament. Paul's Christology is clearly subordinationist and would have been heretical by later standards of Christian orthodoxy. Many other issues of doctrine would be raised, including Adoptionism, the denial of a resurrection of the flesh, mistakes about the imminence of the parousia of Jesus, the teaching of the Gospel of Matthew that all followers of Jesus must obey the Jewish law, and on and on. Even if you gave evangelicals whatever Greek Testament they liked, you would still not be certain of a fully orthodox New Testament interpreted historically. In order to end up with a New Testament that renders properly orthodox Christian doctrine, you have to interpret the text "orthodoxly." It will not do so on its own.

The people who understood this correctly were the early Anglican divines and theologians, as demonstrated in a recent book by Rowan Greer, *Anglican Approaches to Scripture.* The Anglican theologians were willing to agree with their more radical reforming Puritan neighbors even to the point of confessing that scripture is "infallible," by which they meant that scripture would not lead Christians to perdition and damnable error. But they immediately added that all *interpretations* of scripture, done after all by fallible human beings, were themselves eminently "fallible." As John Locke insisted, while being willing to call scripture "infallible," "the reader may be, nay cannot choose but to be very fallible in the understanding of it."[12] Since we human beings have no access to the meaning of scripture apart from interpretation of scripture, which is fallible, we have no immediate and infallible access to the meaning of scripture. So no Christian may use his or her interpretation of scripture as if it were an infallible statement of scripture that can be used to beat other Christians over the head or slam dunk a theological or ethical debate.

The debate about whether textual criticism is unable to deliver a text of the Bible that will in itself "save us" is misguided on both of its sides. Bart Ehrman is correct to insist that we will never have substantiated confidence that we have found, or even approximated, the "original text" of the Bible. It simply can't be proven. And, in spite of the insistence of more conservative Christians, there are significant, doctrinal issues involved. But Ehrman is wrong in implying that such a realization need have any negative impact on Christian faith in scripture. The text of the Bible—whether in the original autographs, any manuscript, any edition, or any translation—is not simplistically in itself scripture. Scripture is the Bible, in whatever form a Christian holds it, read in faith and by the leading of the Holy Spirit.

Evangelicals, though, are also wrong on their side in believing that they can base their doctrine and ethics on a simple "hearing" of the text of the Bible. No responsible and rigorous historical-critical con-struction of the ancient meaning of the text of the Bible will render the Christian meaning of scripture. What is needed is a Christian theo-logical interpretation of the text guided by the traditions and teachings of the church, listening to the interpretations of our fellow Christians and others, and seeking to interpret the Bible in a way that, as Augus-tine insisted, builds up the love of God and the love of our neighbor.[13] Any other interpretation of that text, no matter how rigorously histori-cal or philological, will not be a Christian interpretation of scripture.

I believe that textual criticism is still an important and interesting topic that should be taught in theological education, but not because we need it in order to find the "original text" of scripture that will somehow save us. The text won't save us. God will save us. I believe textual criticism should be taught, rather, as part of the history of the interpretation of scripture itself. As Ehrman has shown in his book *The Orthodox Corruption of Scripture*, the history of the transmission of the text is part of the history of the interpretation of scripture itself and may render social, historical, and theological observations.[14] But if people think that by learning textual criticism they may secure the original text that will then ensure their own salvation, such people have put their faith in the wrong place. Elizabeth Johnson, a professor of New Testament at Columbia Theological Seminary, once said to me that the problem with evangelicals is that they don't have enough faith in God. If people put their faith in either a text or in a particu-lar, modern method of reading a text, their faith is misplaced. People should be better educated theologically to realize that the Christian reading of scripture must be learned and practiced as an activity of faith in God, with assurance that the Holy Spirit will not lead us to per-dition if we read in faith and with love as our guide and goal. Ehrman allowed textual criticism to destroy his faith in scripture because he had an inadequate theology of scripture. Most evangelicals mistakenly insist on the reliability of the historically constructed text of the Bible also because they have an inadequate theology of scripture. What is needed for American Christians is not better history or textual criti-cism, but better theological education, which must include a better theological understanding of what scripture is and how it may be interpreted Christianly.

4

✜

What Is the Text of the New Testament?

David Parker

The difficulties of resolving variations in the New Testament text were first brought home to me fully when I spent some hours studying a variant reading in Matthew 15:30-31. It may have escaped the reader's attention, so let me present the evidence. Jesus sits upon a mountain by the Sea of Galilee, and crowds of people bring to him people in need of healing. Of what ailments are they in need of healing? According to different witnesses, they are:

1. lame	blind	deformed	dumb
2. lame	deformed	blind	dumb
3. lame	blind	dumb	deformed
4. lame	dumb	blind	deformed
5. dumb	blind	lame	deformed
6. blind	lame	deformed	dumb

In verse 31, the crowd wonders at seeing:

the dumb speaking   the deformed whole   the lame walking
the blind seeing

Some manuscripts replace the first phrase with "the deaf hearing," according to the two possible meanings of the word *kōphos* (κωψός). Others read "the deaf hearing, the dumb speaking," possibly under the influence of Mark 7:37. I have listed six variations in verse 30, not counting versions with only three items, and I am confident in stating that there are likely to be more not listed in the editions I consulted.

How do we reconstruct the textual history of this phrase? That is to say, can we decide which of these versions is most likely to have given rise to those which were formed later, and in what order these others arose? Is there any way of deciding what is more likely? It would be nice to be able to argue that an author might be more likely to keep the order between verses 30 and 31 so that the sequence which corresponded to verse 31 was correct. Unfortunately, I have not found such a sequence, either forwards or backwards, in the forms of text I noted. Davies and Alison in their ICC commentary believe that such a chiastic structure is desirable, and conflate two versions—first half of (6) and first half of (1)—in order to achieve it.[1] So they think that even six possible orders is an insufficient number, and make a new one of their own. Or should one look for a parallel with similar Matthaean lists? The blind are mentioned before the lame in some manuscripts at 12:22 and 21:14 (but others reverse the order!). Or should one look for a neat balance within the list—the two referring to injury to limbs outside the two referring to sight and speech? Or could such a tidy list be more plausibly ascribed to later users who were as perplexed by us at the differences? One searches in vain for any principle which could lead one to a solution. As an editor, one would be reduced to the following options in making a critical text at this passage:

1. to follow the manuscript or manuscripts which one believed were more often reliable in places where a more informed judgment was possible.

2. to follow the editor or editors one found most consistently sensible.

3. to follow the most popular text—probably either the Byzantine or the Nestle text.

At this point, I hear you asking "Does it matter?" And this is precisely why I chose this variant to begin with. It serves another useful purpose, namely that a number of possible orders emerged in the course of the text's transmission. The examples used by Ehrman and Wallace in their presentations are rather strikingly of the either-or variety. This is convenient for the purposes of debate, but probably not a standard situation. I have no statistics to back me up, but I suspect that variants where there are three or more readings may be more usual.

The question "Does it matter?" is worth asking in several contexts. First, did it matter to ancient readers and copyists of the text? Or were they simply aware that there were four items, and put them down in whatever order they happened to remember them, sometimes corresponding to what they read in their exemplar (the manuscript from which they were copying), sometimes in a more or less random order? And would the author of Matthew's Gospel have been worried about a change to the order of his words? That is to say, are these four items set down for rhetorical effect, the precise details being more or less irrelevant? And if the precise wording did not matter either to the author of the Gospel or to the thousands of people who made copies of it, are we applying the wrong tools in trying to find a rational way of accounting for the differences?

Second, does the sequence of this text matter to us? There are several possible answers to this. It may matter to the textual scholar, who is looking for evidence in every atom of the text.[2] And it may matter to the exegete, who wants to be precise about the text requiring comment. And it may matter to someone who discovers a solution to the problem that nobody else has thought. But it is also likely to matter to several other groups. One of these consists of any person who believes that every word of the biblical text that they know is divine in origin. Another is a theological viewpoint—and I am thinking of self-styled radical orthodoxy—which claims adherence to the final canonical form of the text (whatever that may be). In my view it is quite impossible to claim any kind of priority for any single form of text where we have a number of forms, none of which we can reasonably claim to be older than the others.[3]

It is worth putting the debate which is the topic of this book into a wider context. Christian denominations do not all use the same forms of text. This is certainly more marked with regard to the Old Testament, Orthodoxy adhering to the Septuagint and versions derived from it, while Western Christianity generally prefers versions translated directly from the Hebrew Massoretic Text.[4] In the New Testament, Orthodoxy traditionally prefers forms of the Byzantine Text, since it was that which it received from the tradition, while Western denominations have adopted the critical text as its standard.[5] Syrian Christianity has inherited the text and canon of the Peshitta (lacking the Minor Catholic Epistles).[6]

Let us return to Matthew 15:30. This variant matters, precisely because it probably makes no ultimate difference to the sense. The critical editor and the believer in a single form of inspired text are in fact in a rather similar situation: in order for the text to make any sense, something must be read—but what? The one has to print, the other to accept, a single form of the text where there is nothing to choose between multiple forms. That is to say, we find that a particular *a priori* opinion or methodology turns out not to fit every situation as well as one might wish.

I can therefore already offer a provisional answer with regard to the textual reliability of the New Testament. This variant indicates the impossibility of believing every word of the text to be reliable. So, even though the different forms of the text do not seem to affect the sense, we may see that once we get into the study of textual variation, there is no solid foundation from which to survey anything. In this detail, the text is not reliable. It is no good replying that there is no difference to the sense, and therefore it does not matter. Either the text is reliable or it isn't. And if we can agree that there is no justification for preferring one form rather than another here, we should be able to agree, at least hypothetically, that there are also significant places where this holds true. There are several important consequences of this, of which I select one. If there is no way of selecting an oldest form of the text, then what we assume to be the task of the editor, namely constructing something called the original or the best form of text has to be abandoned. In fact, I suggest that this is really the situation with regard to every unit of variation.

Let me illustrate this with a hypothetical situation. Suppose that we are the first people ever to study a particular text. In quite remarkable circumstances, we have come across thirty manuscript copies of a previously unknown text, and discover quite quickly that they are all unique. They regularly attest half a dozen different forms of wordings: omissions, additions, transpositions and substitutions: each manuscript agrees sometimes with one manuscript, sometimes with another, and sometimes is unique. How do we decide which form at every variation is the oldest surviving? Remember, we do not have any tradition to build on, no "received text" to help us. The answer is that at every place we will have to make use of logical principles, common sense, and a developing experience of this particular text painstakingly to build up a picture of the character of each manuscript, the relationships between them, and the ways in which the text changed and developed. Only after careful study will we be able to establish a text which we can defend as most probably that which gave rise to every other form. At that point, we may be able to say how reliable we think the text is at each point of variation. The decision then as to how reliable it is will depend upon how good we are as editors, how useful our thirty copies happen to be, and in fact how much we manage to convince the rest of the world that we are right. For reliability is a comparative and not an absolute quality. Remember, to start with, no form of text has any claim over any other. Such claims only arise when a text has been passed on over a lengthy period of time, so that people have the opportunity to adopt particular versions of the text and to reject other forms. At the beginning of the process, in our hypothetical example, no form of the text should be rejected. Nor should it be rejected during the process. And when does the process end? For an individual scholar, it may end when the edition is complete. For the user of that edition, it will only end when they either throw the book away or forget what was in it. For the next editor, it will be a stepping stone to something different. In fact, the process never ends, for every editor will, by selecting a particular set out of all the possible variant readings, create a new form of the whole text which has probably never before existed.

Such situations as my hypothetical one are rare but not uncommon. A striking example is one of the texts from Qumran, which has turned up in a number of manuscripts. Initially scholars thought that these were all copies of varying quality of a single basic form of text. But the more convincing view which has subsequently emerged is that the manuscripts should be regarded as representing a number of different versions, each of which casts light on a particular phase in the development of the community using the text.[7]

But the New Testament is not at all like my hypothetical example. It has been passed down for twenty centuries in a continuous process of receiving it and passing it on. We have received multiple forms of it.[8] And these multiple forms are a permanent feature. Even when editors change the text and pronounce that the earliest form of text is something different, the other forms never go away. I have made this point elsewhere using the example of the story of Jesus and the woman accused of adultery, found in many manuscripts at John 7:53—8:11.[9] Critical editors since Lachmann in the first part of the nineteenth century have removed it from their reconstruction of the text. But it doesn't go away: everyone knows the story; in fact it remains one of the best-known stories about Jesus. It remains a part of the stream of tradition, even if it is no longer a part of the text. And within this story are further variations which are not found in all witnesses. These include a statement of what Jesus wrote on the ground. Another is that the accusers went away one by one. These are embellishments. But they remain a part of the tradition of the story. Mark 1:41 is similar. According to some witnesses Jesus felt pity; according to others he was angry. It is arguable that the harder reading—namely that he felt anger—is to be preferred. But the other does not go away. Readers may associate both emotions with their picture of Jesus in this story.[10]

One may take a further step from this recognition, and consider the role of textual variation in Christian tradition. Before I do so, I wish to make three further points. The first is that there is good evidence that the most significant variation in the text of the New Testament books had happened by about the year 200 C.E. Of course other changes took place thereafter, and as I have said the process continues. But it is reasonable to argue that for these books, as for most other texts, it was the earliest stage at which they were most likely to be altered. I have argued that in this early period the Gospels were a living text, altered freely—sometimes very freely—by those who read and passed on the text to bring out the meaning which they believed it to possess. Sometimes this adaptation was radical: Marcion produced what he believed to be a pure Pauline Gospel, namely his own version of Luke, and also his own edition of Paul's letters; at about the same time (third quarter of the second century) Tatian produced his *Diatessaron*, a working of the four Gospels into one Gospel in which nothing was lost. We see also other trends, including stylistic influences such as Atticising (the process of improving the Greek of the New Testament) and other adaptations to current language. We see too the influence of theological debate, extending into later centuries. From this period, we have virtually no direct evidence. Our oldest extensive copies of Luke and John date from around the year 200, while we have to wait until the middle of the fourth century for our oldest complete or even extensive copies of Matthew and Mark. Yet, even if one does not take such a radical attitude as W. Petersen, who argued that there are second-century traces of a text of Matthew that is both older and more in tune with the Jewish Christianity than the Hellenising version known to us from the manuscripts, the evidence of those who cited forms of the text during this period provides evidence that they knew and used manuscripts which differed from those later copies which happen to survive.

My second point is that it is mistaken to talk in a single way about "the text of the New Testament." The reason is that the New Testament consists of a number of collections of texts and single books:

1. Four Gospels, made into a collection at some point, probably in the second century. They are characterized by

   - a tendency to harmonize their versions
   - greater variation in the sayings of Jesus than in narrative sections

2. Fourteen or so letters attributed to Paul, based on one of what appear to be a number of second-century collections, the earliest probably in groups of seven and not including the Pastorals or Hebrews. They are characterized by editorial interference in various places, possibly solving problems of uncertain destinations, multiple destinations, or non-Pauline authorship, in various places.

3. The Acts of the Apostles, originally a second roll with Luke's Gospel, but circulating separately from it (certainly

not coming directly after it). This is categorized by extensive textual variation, found more in narrative sections than in speeches, narratives often being extended and rewritten.

4. Seven Catholic Epistles, eventually circulating together and often in a single volume with Acts and the Paulines. Obviously from different sources, and sometimes circulating with noncanonical books, they contain their own species of perplexing variation.

5. The Apocalypse, far more rarely copied than the other parts, not included in the lectionary, and itself containing many variations where the poor grammar and stylistic quirks of the seer have been removed, and intriguing variations where the subject matter perplexed readers and copyists.

Each of these books has its own set of problems. On the whole, I tend to the view that the Gospels contain the most and the most complex variants. This may be due to the importance of the sayings of Jesus in Christian tradition. It may be due to the greatest frequency of copying, a matter which I increasingly feel requires consideration.

Third, we need to enquire as to the way an editor sets about producing a critical edition. The answer is: to create a "family tree" of the text. At each place where there is variation, the editor has to work out a family tree of readings, in which the one that appears to have given rise to the rest is placed at the point of origin. Once this series of decisions has been made throughout the text, the conclusions are combined as the oldest recoverable form, the "Initial Text." This process is known as stemmatics, or the Genealogical Method. As anyone who has tried to trace their family tree will know, genealogy only takes you so far. You will reach a point where there are no records, or the records are inconclusive. That will be your oldest recoverable ancestor. But it won't be Adam.[11] Likewise, the Initial Text will be the oldest stage we can recover. It will not necessarily be the original text. Whether it is or not lies outside the realm of stemmatics, and arguably even outside the realm of textual criticism. The Initial Text will not necessarily get us back through the second century, or at any rate past the formation of the various collections I have described. There will always be a gap between the Initial Text and the starting point of the tradition. It is thus important to stress that textual criticism does not have, and never has had, the goal of recovering a text which has the supposed authority of The Author.[12]

We have then these three matters to consider: our lack of information about the forms of text that developed in the second century and earlier; the different character, developments, and copying history of the different parts of the New Testament; and the limitations upon the possible achievements of textual criticism. What then is the role of textual variation in Christian history? I suggest that it is essential to the Christian tradition. Why? Because argument is also of the essence. From the day that Paul and Peter fell out, opposing and irreconcilable points of view have been what has given life to the tradition, and the day when everyone agrees on everything will be the day when everyone also moves on to something else. Textual variation is the result of this process. It arose, not by mistake, through the carelessness, ignorance or perverseness of copyists, but because the process of passing on the text was also a means of engaging in theological and moral debate, of influencing opinion, of fostering one point of view to the exclusion of another.

How reliable is the text of the New Testament? Let me ask a different question: if the text of the New Testament were reliable, down to the last list of people in need of healing, would it even have survived? I concede that during the late Byzantine period the text was transmitted very carefully, at least in one stream of the tradition, but this phenomenon is found a millennium after the era in which we are most interested.[13] As readers of the text, we learn as much from the variation as we do from single and definitive forms of the text. We read the critical apparatus as well as the printed text, and we discuss the differences.

Which brings me to a final point: today we are used to a single printed text. Early Christians were used to the uncertainty of manuscript copies that differed from each other. They lived in fact in a textually rich world in which, if they consulted different copies, they would find different wordings. Origen, for example, sometimes comments on them. He even finds rich theological meaning in proposing that John the Baptist baptised in Bethabara and not in Bethany (Jn. 1:28). Today, our use of printed texts has impoverished our textual world, since the variations are no longer treated as belonging together in complete texts, but as short units at the bottom of the page. This is likely to be avoided in the electronic age. If we visit New Testament prototypes (http://nttranscripts.uni-muensster.de), we will find a display of the evidence that presents the same critical text as Nestle-Aland 27 with a bundle of variants underneath. But this bundle of variants can be reconstructed into the text of each manuscript, one below another, or into the text of each manuscript with its layout as you may view it on the page. The same (without the bundle of variants) is available when you view the electronic version of the Old Latin manuscripts of John's Gospel at www.iohannes.com. So in the future, we are going to see a richer textual world, one in which far more people have access to a wider range of materials than has ever been possible before for more than a handful of scholars working near big research libraries.[14] In our edition of the virtual Codex Sinaiticus (http://codexsinaiticus.org), the website contains digital images and a full transcription. It also includes some translations, that present the biblical text as it is found in that manuscript.[15]

In fact, the textual variation is not going to go away. Different forms of the text will keep appearing. What is the textual reliability of the New Testament? The answer is of only limited importance. Even if every single word were certain, the variation would remain essential to our right understanding and use of it.

5

✛

Who Changed the Text and Why? Probable, Possible, and Unlikely Explanations

William Warren

I n considering the topic of the reliability of the New Testament text, I suspect that most textual critics would agree that the text is substantially reliable in the sense that a textual critic understands the term *reliable*. But the catch here is in what is meant by saying that the text is "reliable" from the standpoint of textual criticism. What I suggest as a working definition is that in the field of New Testament textual criticism, the term *reliable* generally means that the text is attested sufficiently so that we can ascertain what is most probably the original form of the text or at least a very early form of the text such that it can serve as a suitable foundation for talking about what the text means.

Before clarifying this working definition further, a couple of points need to be made about what is sometimes meant by those outside of the field of New Testament textual criticism by the term *reliable* when applied to the New Testament text. In the larger arena of especially evangelical Christianity, the truth is that some try to claim too much when they talk about the reliability of the New Testament text.

This is due mostly to zeal for defending the text as the Word of God, a passion to claim as much as possible for God's work of inspiration, and a tremendous lack of knowledge about the actual data related to the copying and transmission of the New Testament text. For example, a few still try to defend the King James Version as the only valid English translation of the Bible. In Latin America where I worked for several years and continue to teach at times, one visiting North American preacher tried to convince students that they needed a Spanish translation that was closer to the King James Version and the *Textus Receptus*, the Greek text underlying the King James Version! That's a clear case of someone trying to claim too much about the New Testament text! Saying that our New Testament text is reliable does not mean that it was dropped down from heaven nor that it was dictated without the input of human authors. Views of inspiration are often conflated with particular stances regarding how the New Testament was transmitted and preserved, but that is not what is meant by saying that the text is reliable within the field of New Testament textual criticism.

On the other hand, some seem to be claiming too little about the reliability of the New Testament text. Is the text indeed full of uncertain wording everywhere? I mention this because many have taken Bart Ehrman's claim that "there are more differences among our manuscripts than there are words in the New Testament" to mean that we are not certain of any or hardly any of the words in the Greek New Testament.[1] Yet even Ehrman notes that most of the variants found in the manuscripts of the New Testament are "completely insignificant, immaterial, of no real importance for anything other than showing that scribes could not spell or keep focused any better than the rest of us."[2] And for all of the variants that he discusses in his well known books, such as *Misquoting Jesus* and *The Orthodox Corruption of Scripture*, Ehrman himself rarely disagrees with the text as printed in the commonly used critical editions of the Greek New Testament published by the United Bible Societies (UBS). To be more specific, he almost always ends up supporting the text as printed in those editions as being the most likely original text, with only about twenty cases where he disagrees with the text printed in our Greek New Testament editions.[3] So if Ehrman says that the text is "not reliable," based on his writings he is not saying that vast parts of the text are unstable and unknown as to the most likely original text. He is saying that some parts of the text are still being debated, and even more so, that many have been unwilling to wrestle with the work of textual critics, including Bible publishers, scholars, and preachers who often refuse to face what has been found by the field of New Testament textual criticism regarding the earliest and best readings of the New Testament text.

So what does it mean to say that the text of the New Testament is reliable and how do we substantiate such a claim? Let's look at some areas that might help on this. First, is the data sufficient so as to make such a claim? Second, was the process behind the making of the manuscripts such that we can have confidence in the data? To state this in a different way, what do we know about the scribes who could help us determine how reliable the text might be? Third, how can such a claim deal with the known variants in the text? And fourth, how do we deal with the scribal motivations that are behind some of the variants in the text?

RELIABILITY AND THE DATA

The field of New Testament textual criticism is built around a data set, a method for evaluating that data, and the analysis of the data, with the implications of the analysis following. Textual critics are generally in agreement about large areas of the field regardless of their specific views of the history of the transmission of the New Testament text and its reliability, a fact that may come as a surprise to those outside of or less familiar with the field. For example, we all agree that we have an incredible wealth of evidence for the text of the New Testament, with literally thousands of extant manuscripts and other witnesses to the text. But as an aside and challenge, while we can brag about having so many manuscripts of the New Testament, unfortunately the sad fact is that we have not yet taken the time and devoted the energy to study the vast majority of them with detailed studies and do not have full collations of most of them. So our evidence pool at present generally consists of a sampling of these manuscripts, with the Greek manuscripts best represented and the other versions and Patristic citations less so. But even so we still have a vast bounty of evidence that is increasingly at our fingertips via digital access and electronic databases.

Also, we agree that we almost certainly do not have any of the "autographs" of the New Testament books. Among the manuscripts that we have, some were not copied as well as others, and the manuscripts differ from one another in many places and ways. And we even agree that some variants arose due to theological struggles and the desire to fortify what were considered the "right" or "orthodox" ways of understanding the text.

But there are also areas of disagreement among textual critics. As for the data, we disagree sometimes over the dates of some of the manuscripts, how to arrange the data (such as the scope of a textual variant), and how these witnesses fit into the transmission history of the New Testament text, especially in the earliest period of the late first, second, and third centuries when the majority of the textual variants arose.

We also have disagreements over the best methodology for evaluating the textual evidence for specific variants. Most prefer what is called a "reasoned eclecticism" approach that seeks to weigh both the external factors related to the manuscripts themselves, including the tendencies and overall qualities of the individual manuscripts and manuscript groupings, and the internal factors such as scribal tendencies in the copy process and the proclivities of the "author/s" of the text being studied. But some textual scholars prefer an approach that relies almost totally on the external evidence for readings, with the result that they favor the text of a specific group of manuscripts almost exclusively, whether that of the Byzantine textual group or that of the Alexandrian textual group or, for a few, even that of the Western textual group. And a few scholars favor an approach that relies very heavily on the internal evidence for deciding among specific textual variants. The vast majority of textual scholars, however, follow a "reasoned eclecticism" approach, including Bart Ehrman, Dan Wallace, David Parker, Michael Holmes, and myself.

We also find that we sometimes differ when we talk about the analysis of the data that we have. At times the discussion is about how far back we can actually reach with the evidence that we have. The traditional goal of textual criticism has been to determine the text that is closest to the original of a given writing, yet over the past two decades scholars such as David Parker have raised the question of whether we can indeed talk about an original text as attainable.[4] Should we stop at the point where the external evidence stops, often rounded off to near the year 200 C.E. or the end of the second century? Or can the probability that the ascertained form of the Greek text of the New Testament is very close to the original suffice for us to talk about the resulting text as a reliable form of the New Testament text? Of course, at times there are disagreements over which readings are most likely closest to the original text, or at least the earliest attainable form of the text, as well as about the nature of the setting in which the variants arose and the reasons they arose.

When all is said and done regarding the data, however, the data is what it is. A manuscript either has a reading or it doesn't. And we either have evidence from a given time period or we don't. The fact is that we don't have the originals of the New Testament documents, but we do have quite a bit of early evidence. Up to the year 800, the evidence for the New Testament is substantial especially when compared with other ancient writings, as can be seen from this overview: from the second century we have 6 Papyri and 1 Uncial manuscript; 55 Papyri and 4 Uncials from the third; 25 Papyri, 27 Uncials, and 1 Lectionary from the fourth; 8 Papyri, 52 Uncials, and 2 Lectionaries from the fifth; 17 Papyri, 83 Uncials, and 5 Lectionaries from the sixth; 11 Papyri, 39 Uncials, and 1 Lectionary from the seventh; and 2 Papyri, 29 Uncials, and 25 Lectionaries from the eighth century, with many more extant manuscripts from the ninth century onward. To be sure, the second- and third-century manuscripts we have often contain only a small amount of text, such as the few letters extant in $\mathfrak{P}^{52}$, although a few contain substantial amounts of text, such as $\mathfrak{P}^{46}$ that contains most of the Pauline letters. One manuscript, Codex Sinaiticus from the fourth century, contains the entire New Testament, and even more than our New Testament with the *Shepherd of Hermas* and the *Epistle of Barnabas* included as well.[5] Of course, a few more substantial manuscripts from the second century would certainly be welcomed, and some autographs would be even more welcomed! But the number of manuscripts that we have is sufficient at least to allow for a responsible job to take place of recovering the earliest attainable form of the New Testament text, even if the exact results of that work may not be totally identical among those using different methods for evaluating the evidence and even, at times, among those using the same method. In other words, the amount of textual evidence allows for the logical consideration of whether we can attain a reliable form of the New Testament text or not. Without an array of evidence such as this, the question of whether a reliable form of the text is recoverable would surely invite much more skepticism than is warranted in the case of the New Testament. Of course, this does not solve the issue of whether the New Testament text is reliable or not, but it does allow for the fact that the data is sufficient to address such a question.

So, do we have enough data to be reasonably sure that we have a text that is very close to the original text? Yes and no answers are given. "No" is given by those who would say that in some places we are not certain about the text. And they are right about this. There are some places where we are not certain as to which reading is most likely the earliest attainable reading, the one closest to the original text. This is universally recognized in the field of New Testament textual studies: we have variants that we are still debating.

On the other hand, the answer yes can be given about the reliability of the text in that in the New Testament text, such as that published in the Nestle-Aland *Novum Testamentum* and the United Bible Societies' *Greek New Testament*, we have enough data to arrive at a form of the text that is very close to the original, a text with firm witnesses for most of it that go back into the late second or third centuries and for all of it into the fourth century and beyond. This data ensures that we can talk intelligently about the New Testament text, that we can evaluate the variants we find, that we can know that there is no "cover up" within the field of textual criticism that might emerge that will surprise us about the text, and that we can normally reach a broad-ranging agreement on what is the earliest attainable form of the text. For many of us, the probability of that earliest form being almost identical to the original form of the text is sufficient so as to call the text reliable without hesitation, even while we admit that the scribes made mistakes and sometimes changed the text, thereby leaving us with evidence of some variants about which we are still not certain in our choices about the earliest readings. So let's turn to the work of the scribes and the variants that they have left for us to consider.

RELIABILITY AND THE SCRIBES

The problem in talking about the scribes who copied the New Testament is that we have very limited access to the scribes, and especially so in the case of the early period from the late second century to the end of the third century, and even less so to those of the late first and early second centuries. To be more specific, while we have some manuscripts from the late second and third centuries that thereby give us access to the scribes of those manuscripts, we have only one small New Testament fragment, $\mathfrak{P}^{52}$, which gives us access to a New Testament scribe from the period of the late first and early second centuries.

Much of the access we do have comes by way of the manuscripts, which are historical artifacts in and of themselves that we've found from the past that are studied in order to understand the past even beyond the text itself. In this sense, the data for the text of the New Testament is useful for multiple enterprises, including the traditional goal of establishing the text of the New Testament, as well as other goals, such as tracing the transmission history of the text. This transmission history can include the study of the settings in which the text was transmitted and the people that were involved in its transmission. In other words, as we seek to understand the social world of early scribes and Christianity itself from the standpoint of New Testament textual criticism, some of the questions we need to ask should relate directly to what these manuscripts can tell us regarding the world from which they came: How were they made, when were they made, why were they made, where were they made, by whom were they made, who used them, how did they use them, why do they have differing texts versus other manuscripts, and other such questions. Of course, as with all artifacts, we want to know more than the artifacts can actually tell us, so we extrapolate from the information that we can ascertain, hopefully acknowledging the problematic nature of our extrapolations.

Returning to the idea of manuscripts as artifacts, archaeology has shifted from being primarily concerned with the dating of artifacts to the questions of what the artifacts tell us about the cultural processes behind them and the human lifeways that are represented by them. In many ways, a like shift has been happening in the field of New Testament textual criticism. We are now seeing interest in more than simply ascertaining the earliest form of the text to looking at the manuscripts as artifacts that can tell us also about the times from which they come. In the case of the early papyri, the study centers on the life of the church during the second and third centuries, a time that often remains shrouded in both mystery and conjecture as competing theories about how the church and the canon developed are debated by scholars who long for more evidence to support their theories, with most of us in that number I suspect. Who wouldn't like to know more about the early church of the late first and second centuries? That desire has led to new avenues of research on the manuscripts as artifacts that might inform us in part about the scribes that created these manuscripts, for which I think we should be excited and join in the discussions.

But there is a problem that arises in our knowledge of the manuscripts as artifacts. In archaeology, a major goal is to keep the context of the artifact linked to the artifact. In other words, when one is engaging in an archaeological dig and an artifact is found, say a clay lamp, every detail of the setting of an artifact should be noted, with almost no detail viewed as unimportant. This context is essential for interpreting the importance of the artifact and thereby for understanding the culture and people that created it. With manuscipts, while we rarely know their specific date of origin (although some are dated), we generally can get a fairly good sense of this. For example, $\mathfrak{P}^{75}$ is generally held to come from the early third century, with a range of plus or minus somewhere between twenty-five to fifty years. But what we rarely can ascertain with any degree of precision is the exact location where the manuscript was originally used, much less where it was made. For example, the Oxyrhynchus papyri were found in a garbage heap but, obviously, that is not where they were made or used. Nevertheless, at least we have a stable artifact in hand that can be studied to uncover as much information as possible. In this sense, the study of manuscripts remains a major part of the field of textual criticism whether one is seeking the earliest form of a text or the social history that might be seen through the manuscript.

Returning to the question of who created the New Testament manuscripts, what do we know about the scribes behind these artifacts? Based on what we see in the manuscripts, we know that they were not all copied with the same care. The expertise of the scribes ranged along a continuum between professional and documentary, with many of the New Testament scribes from the second through early fourth centuries falling into the "reformed documentary" category of expertise.[6] To clarify the difference in this range of abilities, a professional scribe would be very careful to duplicate the exemplar manuscript, whereas a documentary scribe generally worked for a merchant or family business or in the marketplace and wrote out the needed receipts and everyday literary needs of the clients with more need for input into the end product. Especially many of our earliest New Testament manuscripts were copied by scribes who were not used to copying literary works. To be sure, there were a few that came from a "professional" scribal handwriting and process, such as the scribe who wrote $\mathfrak{P}^{75}$ from the early third century. But most of the earlier New Testament manuscripts of the second and third centuries were copied with a scribal expertise below the professional level of scribes who regularly copied recognized literature. These scribes were not employed for making copies of literary texts in their normal daily scribal activities and so were not accustomed to attaining that level of copying that was the norm for works clearly literary in nature. The scribes of these early manuscripts did their work at a level generally above that of their marketplace scribal activities as represented in the vast number of documentary papyri that include receipts, transactions, notes, letters, and legal agreements such as marriage contracts, so they made good copies, but they were not on a par with the professional literary scribes attached especially to the elite stratum of society.

The majority of the scribes seem to have been Christians based on the ample and consistent use of abbreviated forms of the sacred names within Christianity, what are called *nomina sacra*, a feature that non-Christian scribes would not tend to use, and especially not in such a consistent manner. Most likely they were scribes in their day jobs based on the level of expertise demonstrated in the extant manuscripts, but whether they were copying portions of the New Testament at work or at night after working is unknown. Based on the segement of society from which they came, most of the scribes should not be characterized as "scribes by day and theologians by night." Their goal was to make a copy of a text, with extreme accuracy perhaps not always the primary concern, but on the other hand, after setting aside variants in spelling, the addition or omission of a definite article, and obvious scribal errors, the texts are quite accurate even in the midst of so many variants.

A possible scenario for some of the early copies of our New Testament might be as follows based upon this information. In this early period, say the late first and second centuries, if a new house church had people who traveled to a city where they discovered that a manuscript of the story of Jesus or some letters from Paul was present, they would be more interested in getting a copy—any copy—to take back to their church than in exactly how accurate the copy was. Not having planned to spend funds on such an endeavor, they very well would need to have one of the Christians there make the copy after work. The copy would be made well, but only up to the ability and norm of the scribe making the copy. And if other traditions related to what was in the text were known, perhaps they would be added at the request of those involved in the making of the copy. While the action of writing the text would be that of the scribe originally, the request to alter the text theoretically could come from the scribe, or from those from the city church, or those from the new church. The added text might even originate from a reader in the church setting who had added a note in the text. The fact is, we don't know exactly who all was involved in this facet of the reproduction of a manuscript, but what we do know is that the overall work of scribes was to copy the text before them, and that is what most of them did.

The results of this type of copying in the earlier stages of the New Testament text are manifest in two primary areas: the errors in the task of copying itself (and lack of concern and training to correct such errors at the moment of making the copy) and the carryover of an attitude that would allow for more changing/editing of the text than would be normal in a professional copy process. The lower standards of this type of copy process are very likely part of the explanation for the origin of many of the variants, such as some of the better known additions/omissions associated with the D-text form (formerly called the "Western" text-type). To clarify, the addition of oral traditions or well known ways of telling a story or even the replacement of uncommon words with more common words would be more natural in these types of scribal settings.

On the other hand, the great codices of the fourth century and later, such as Sinaiticus, Vaticanus, Alexandrinus, and others, ushered in a period where New Testament copies were increasingly made on a much higher level. Most of these later scribes were also Christians, but now they were professional scribes who worked in an open and institutionalized church environment in the aftermath of the shifts under Constantine and beyond. The accuracy in the copies improved remarkably, but of course the accuracy was built on exemplars that already contained variants versus other manuscripts, so these manuscripts still contain a large number of variant readings. Over time, the text was more and more standardized, with the end result being what we call the Byzantine form of the text.

So returning to the early period of especially the late first through the second centuries (and the third century to some degree), the time when most of the variant readings in the New Testament are thought to have entered into the text, can we determine why the scribes wrote these variants? To some extent we can, but our knowledge is on a scale that ranges from totally certain to totally uncertain and at all points in between. What we can determine are scribal traits in specific manuscripts when there is enough text to allow for such an analysis. These can range from seeing the care taken by the scribe in making the copy to matters of theological tendencies in given manuscripts.

For example, Barbara Aland studied the Chester Beatty New Testament papyri numbered $\mathfrak{P}^{45}$, $\mathfrak{P}^{46}$, and $\mathfrak{P}^{47}$ to see "how the scribes' view of their profession affected their products, and whether or to what extent the codices they produced met the expectations of the communities that commissioned them."[7] She found that the scribes made changes for two reasons, to clarify the reading of the exemplar, or in an attempt to copy the text rapidly such that the sense of the text is kept, although with the exact wording sometimes changed slightly.

Regarding $\mathfrak{P}^{45}$, Aland concluded that the scribe made a reliable copy, was most likely a Christian due to harmonizing some passages (non-Christians would not likely know the parallel passages), and was not carefully considering the content of what was being copied from the exemplar. On the other hand, $\mathfrak{P}^{46}$ is described as "a rough and inadequate copy of a good exemplar," while $\mathfrak{P}^{47}$ is from a scribe that

was poor on calligraphy and orthography, introduced "nonsense readings from carelessness," and tended to insert some stylistic and grammatical improvements.[8] So we can know something about the scribes
of such manuscripts and thereby determine whether or not they were
likely to make a reliable copy of the text. And from what we see in
the manuscripts that we have, the vast majority of the early scribes
did just that—they made imperfect but still reliable copies of their
exemplars. Most of the errors in the copies could easily be understood
by the church readers, so they were of no consequence in the larger
picture and did not even require correcting since the readers would
have been expected to make the corrections on the fly, so to speak,
with such errors as spelling mistakes and such. While there is more to
consider here, the bottom line is that the scribes that we can analyze
by way of the longer New Testament papyrus manuscripts from the
first three centuries seem to be ones who were making substantially
reliable copies of their exemplars.

But if this is so, then where did the more significant or "intentional"
variants that involved content changes such as shifts in the word order
and additions/omissions to the text come from and how did they enter
into the copying process? Even more so in the case of these types of
variants, we often and even normally cannot be sure about when the
variant first originated, who first made the change, why they made the
change, or the source of the change. For example, Eldon Jay Epp has
shown where the D-text in Acts as represented by Codex Bezae shows
an anti-Judaic bias at its core.[9] But this tendency likely existed at least in
part prior to the time of the scribe of Bezae itself since some of the core
elements of the D-text form are from the earliest period in the history
of the text, as noted long ago by Westcott and Hort, who held that the
"Western" text (the D-text form) originated in the early second century.[10]

While we can isolate some scribal traits for specific manuscripts,
when we shift to determining the motivations of scribes behind the
creation of specific significant variants, we move to more subjective
ground on which the levels of certainty about our conclusions are not
nearly as high. Before looking at the issue of scribal motivations, however, let's consider some of the significant variants found in the text of
the New Testament and how they relate to the issue of the reliability
of the text.

RELIABILITY AND THE VARIANT READINGS

Does the presence of significant variants such as those that change the wording of the text pose a major obstacle to claiming that the text is reliable? Facing the evidence about major variants and evaluating them to determine the earliest form of the text is not at all incompatible with the claim of having a reliable New Testament text. The question of whether a given reading was added later or altered or whatever is not a refutation of the reliability of the text in the broader sense of being able to derive a text through the process of weighing the variants and making the editorial decisions about what to print. Such work has to be done with all ancient literature, and the New Testament is not an exception. The end result, while always containing some debatable facets, can still meet the standard of presenting a text that is reliable enough to serve as a suitable foundation for talking about what the text means. While the resulting text might not be 100 percent the same as that of the original author, the probability is high that it is substantially the same and thus reliable in spite of the variants that have accrued in the transmission process. In the case of the New Testament, the unknown period between the time of the original writing events and the extant textual evidence is bridged by recourse to what is most probable even if we cannot claim total certainty. When that probability is weighed, to be sure, some will focus on the lack of total certainty, but others of us will say that the probability is so high that we have no problem in affirming that the text we have in our Greek New Testaments is reliable.

So let's look at some of the variants that have at times been put forward as casting doubt on the reliability of the New Testament text. One example is found in John 5:3-4, where the explanation about the angel of the Lord coming down and healing the first one to enter when the water was disturbed is not included in many of our earlier manuscripts. This passage is not considered to be original in the UBS *Greek New Testament*. In fact, this passage has routinely not been included in the Greek New Testament editions since the late 1800s! So what's the big issue here? We should all recognize that this passage almost certainly is a case of oral tradition from the late first century or early second century entering into the text. This tradition may indeed be exactly what the people at the pool were thinking, so it may be an accurate tradition during that time period, but nevertheless it is an addition to the text, not the earliest form that we can recover.

The same situation exists for the passage in John 7:53—8:11, the story of the woman caught in adultery. This passage also has been routinely seen as a later addition to the text for more than 125 years! In 1881, Westcott and Hort considered this passage to be a later addition that was not original to John and so printed it as a separate passage after the end of John. Likewise the ending of Mark, 16:9-20 as it is indicated in the King James Version, has long since been considered to be an addition to Mark.

The standard judgments about such variants should already be assumed for this conversation. Just to cite a few examples, the following variants are not debated much if at all anymore: the Lord's Prayer has been harmonized in Luke to bring it more into agreement with Matthew's version; in Mark 9:29, "and fasting" is an addition to the text; in Matthew 27:16-17, the name of Barabbas very well (this one is not as certain) was originally written in the text as "Jesus" but later removed so as not to dishonor the name of Jesus the Messiah; and the confession by the Ethiopian eunuch after Acts 8:36 (verse 37 in the *Textus Receptus*) is a later confessional addition. Passages such as these are not a challenge when thinking about the reliability of the New Testament text since they regularly have been deemed as secondary to the text of the New Testament for more than a century and are noted as such in modern critical editions of the Greek New Testament. Actually, it's shameful that some Bible publishers continue to print passages like these variant readings in the text when the overwhelming evidence shows that they were not in the earliest or original form of the text.

But just because these variant readings are not original to the text does not mean that they are not helpful when studying the text. These variant readings are also artifacts that can serve as early commentaries on the text when seen as the attempts of scribes, readers, and others to clarify the meaning of the text. Indeed, many times our earliest commentaries on the text are to be found in the non-original variant readings. For example, in the Mark 9:29 passage, the addition "and fasting" to the phrase "this type cannot be cast out by any means except prayer" supplies us with a window into the understanding of this passage by the early church. The variant reading indicates that the type of prayer indicated here is not superficial prayer, but intense prayer such as takes place when one is fasting. Likewise in John 5:3-4, the oral tradition added there provides an early commentary that explains why the sick were gathered by the pool. In the exegetical task, the study of variant readings such as these fills a vital role by allowing windows into the life of the early church and its understandings of these passages as well as sometimes giving us access to the oral traditions that circulated that helped clarify the passages. In the bigger picture, the presence of these non-original variant readings is the result of having enough evidence to talk about getting back to a reliable form of the text.

RELIABILITY AND SCRIBAL MOTIVATIONS

Returning to the topic of the motivations of scribes behind the creation of specific significant variants, in order to have a reliable text, we need to ascertain that there was not a major effort taking place in the "unknown" period of the late first through second centuries in which the text was extensively reworked. Work in this area has centered on analyzing the variants as guides for understanding the social history of the early church, with major studies recently by scholars such as Bart Ehrman and Wayne Kannaday leading the way.[11] In these studies the theological and apologetic struggles in the communities that produced the texts have been analyzed to discern if those struggles might have provided the motivation behind certain variant readings.

This shift to seeing variants as artifacts that can open windows into the life of the early church is in many ways helpful since it broadens the use of the information from the witnesses to the text of the New Testament. Caution has to be exercised with this approach, however, because so much about the origin of the readings is unknown, and this applies whether the study involves suggested theological motivations or other causes. Aside from specific remarks about the date of the origin of the reading by church fathers or other early writers, the date of a variant reading is extremely hard to pin down, as are the related questions of the exact setting where it might have arisen, exactly why it arose, who created it and what their motives were, and exactly how it spread to later manuscripts.

To follow the use of artifacts in archaeology, the context for the artifacts is missing in many of these discussions, with that context being the manuscripts themselves. Part of the difficulty is that many of the variants are only attested in manuscripts from later dates beyond the period under consideration. The fact is that we don't know exactly when the variant reading first appeared in most instances. We hardly ever know for certain who created it or why (sometimes credit is given by a Church Father that clarifies this some). So we can discuss possibile answers to these questions, but they are based on educated guesses and as such are matters of probability, not certainty. This is often understood within the field of New Testament textual criticism as we debate various options even while recognizing the tenuous nature of the proposed answers, but some outside of the field often don't understand that probabilities are being discussed, not certainties.

Very few textual critics would question whether or not some theologically and apologetically motivated variants were created, although the cause for a given variant arising is debated. For example, with regard to detecting theological motivations, several explanations for why a suspected theological variant arose are possible: the reading could have been created and then later used in a theological struggle; or the reading may have been created in order to support a specific viewpoint in the midst of a theological struggle; or the reading may not have been linked at all to what we might see as a related theological struggle in the early church.

The issue of how to determine when motivations such as theological or apologetic ones most likely led to the emergence of certain variant readings is still an open discussion that invites more participation as difficult questions are considered. For example, how certain can we be about ascribing motivations to the scribes who first inserted some of our variant readings? Herein is the difficulty and challenge often discussed among textual scholars. We cannot question the scribes, so how can we at least increase the level of confidence that we have in our postulations about the causes of certain textual variants?

The following proposals, while not all new, might at least help spur more discussion about how to increase our confidence level. First, the use of some passages in the writings of the church fathers to explicitly discuss a theological or apologetic concern greatly increases the likelihood that a passage might have been affected by such considerations. For example, in Matthew 27:16-17, Origen in his *Commentary on Matthew* discusses the presence (or absence) of the name "Jesus" for Barabbas in the text, so we know that this was an issue in the early church. Second, the use of certain passages or ideas in noncanonical texts from a "heretical" group's writings increases the likelihood of a theological or apologetic impact on the text. Third, when a specific manuscript has been documented as displaying a theological or apologetic tendency, then that manuscript's readings are more likely to have arisen due to such concerns. Conversely, when a manuscript does not display clear theological or apologetic tendencies, then that manuscript's readings are less likely to have arisen due to such concerns. The point is that readings should be kept in the context of the manuscripts that contain them, thereby requiring a joint study of the manuscripts and the variants, not just isolated studies of the variants. If this is to be done, we obviously need more studies of the scribal traits for the specific manuscripts in order to properly evaluate the likely cause of a given reading in a specific manuscript. Fourth, a variant should be traceable to the appropriate time period in order to be linked to a controversy from that time.

The matter of being forthright about our confidence level for assertions regarding scribal motivations and the suspected causes of textual variations especially needs to be communicated well when addressing the larger public outside of the field of New Testament textual criticism (and could be helpful even for those within the field). What we need is a system for communicating the degree of certainty about our statements on the causes of variants, especially when we posit possible scribal motivations for the creation of the readings. In a more global sense, this is what the rating system of the UBS *Greek New Testament* seeks to accomplish regarding the decisions behind their printed text. For a system related to scribal motivations and the causes of variants, I would suggest categories such as "probable," "possible," "unlikely," and "uncertain" rather than the letters used in the UBS text. The goal would be to help those outside the field understand the confidence level behind our assertions and how to weigh our results. The sense that all of our results are certain gives a skewed picture whether the results seem to favor a more positive view of the reliability of the New Testament text or a more negative view.

CONCLUDING REMARKS

So is the text of the New Testament reliable? To return to our definition of reliable, do we have a New Testament text that can serve as a suitable foundation for talking about what the text means? A form of the text common in the fourth century was a goal about 150 years ago since the extant manuscript evidence barely went back to the fourth century at that time. Today the extant manuscript evidence takes us back to about the year 200 for the New Testament text. The critical Greek New Testament editions that are used by most today at least seem to get us to this stage. Maybe we will find more manuscripts from the earlier part of the second century and push the evidence back a bit further. Of course, it would be really nice to have some first century manuscripts!

So the question remains, does our text likely represent an even earlier form or was it so changed in the period from the late first century to the late second century that we've lost too much to have confidence in what we've recovered? I would say that our text almost certainly represents a form that is almost identical to the original documents, but that is a probability statement. As mentioned earlier, even Ehrman only posits about twenty changes to the text as printed in the UBS fourth edition and the Nestle-Aland twenty-seventh edition of the Greek text of the New Testament. That sounds like a pretty solid text that is very close to the original form. Nevertheless, we live with the reality that we don't have the data to eliminate all other possibilities, so we work with probabilities. And the most probable scenario is that our text is reliable enough to allow us to have confidence in our discussions about the New Testament writings.

To be sure, we'll keep working on getting more data and working through the data that we have to see if we can shed more light on the earliest form of the text, as well as on the scribal tendencies of specific manuscripts and what the variants tell us about the social world behind the transmission of the text. There is a lot of work still to do at all levels in the field, including collating, analyzing, evaluating, and more. And we need more people involved in the field of New Testament textual criticism. So jump in, the water is great!

6

✛

Assessing the Stability of the Transmitted Texts of the New Testament and the *Shepherd of Hermas*

K. Martin Heide

How stably or unstably was the text of the New Testament transmitted? The different editions of the Greek text of the New Testament already provide us with a rough indication for estimating the stability of the text. Almost 5,000 of the 7,947 verses of the New Testament, as contained in the major text-critical editions in the last 150 years (Tischendorf, Westcott-Hort, von Soden, Vogels, Merk, Bover, Nestle-Aland), show no differences at all in the text.[1] Can the stability of the New Testament text be defined more accurately?[2]

After thirty years of intensively researching the text, Westcott and Hort provided the following evaluation of the New Testament transmission: according to their representation, at least seven-eighths of the text is accurate and requires no further text-critical research.[3] Clarity exists therefore in this portion of the transmitted text. The outstanding 12.5 percent or one-eighth remains subject to textual criticism. This 12.5 percent, however, consists mostly of minor variants with no alteration of the meaning of the text itself and, according to Westcott and Hort, has already been sufficiently clarified. This in turn leaves a marginal percentage (one-sixtieth) of the text that, according to Westcott and Hort, is unclear and should be regarded as subject to further research.

In 2005, Bart D. Ehrman published his book *Misquoting Jesus*, which appeared in a slightly revised edition in 2006 under the title *Whose Word Is It?* According to Ehrman, *Misquoting Jesus* and *Whose Word Is It?* attempt to introduce the reader in an easy-to-understand manner to the science of New Testament textual criticism. In both publications, Ehrman emphasizes that, in light of the long history of transmission, the works of the New Testament were more or less subject to the caprice of pious scribes and orthodox theologians. Whether early in the first millennium or in the Middle Ages, Christian scribes did not merely copy, but altered as well: "This conviction that scribes had changed scripture became an increasing certitude for me as I studied the text more and more. And this certitude changed the way I understood the text, in more ways than one."[4] The New Testament that we have today is different from the one the early church had, and despite the fact that it has been distorted by pious scribes, the church continues to recognise it as the genuine word of God—hence the title *Misquoting Jesus*: "We don't *have* the originals! We have only error-ridden copies, and the vast majority of these are centuries removed from the originals and different from them, evidently, in thousands of ways."[5]

Apart from these sensation-seeking remarks about the text of the New Testament, Ehrman's book *Misquoting Jesus* often meets the criteria of what one would expect from a mainstream introduction to New Testament textual criticism. The single events, quotations and backgrounds associated with the history of the text will not persuade the readers of *Misquoting Jesus* that the New Testament is a book during whose transmission successive changes have taken place. It is Ehrman's *interpretation* of these facts that is suggestive in nature.

1. Was the transmission of the New Testament text as stable as Westcott and Hort assumed it to be at the end of the nineteenth century—or as unstable as Ehrman suggests at the dawn of the twenty-first century? This paper endeavors to establish whether or not the observations (as general indicators) made by Westcott and Hort are still applicable today especially in light of the early papyri, several of which exhibit a relatively free writing style. Additionally, Ehrman's propositions will be scrutinized in light of the historical transmission of the New Testament. To begin with, the early "Alexandrian" text of the second through the fourth centuries will be compared in accordance with the available reconstructed text of the twenty-seventh Nestle-Aland edition (Nestle-Aland 27) with the subsequent Byzantine text of the ninth through the twelfth centuries.[6] The Byzantine text is in itself ideal for comparison in that it provides the same text in hundreds of manuscripts.[7] Subsequently, direct comparisons will be made between over twenty randomly chosen papyri from the second and third centuries and the texts according to Nestle-Aland 27 (the most significant early text sources being the Codices Vaticanus B and Sinaiticus ℵ) and the Byzantine text (table 6.1, below). This method allows us to compare the papyri being considered with the earliest possible reconstructed text (Nestle-Aland 27), the subsequent major majuscules that further transmitted the text of these papyri (B, ℵ), and the final product of scribal activities during the Middle Ages, namely the Byzantine text. Individual words will be the basis for comparison. That is to say, that not the individual variations are counted as an entity, but every single word that is affected by a variation. For example, if a complete sentence comprising twelve words is omitted, then this is not seen as a single variant or error, but rather as twelve error units.

Finally, the text transmission of the *Shepherd of Hermas* will be examined using the same method as described above. Campbell Bonner, the publisher of two important papyri of the *Shepherd of Hermas*, suggested such a comparison as early as 1934. Following an examination of both the linguistic peculiarities of the *Shepherd of Hermas* and the constitution of its text sources, Bonner ascertained that an eclectic edition alone does justice to the tremendous variety of this early Christian writing. Bonner suggested that, in light of the rich saturation of vulgarisms used in the language of the *Shepherd of Hermas*, even an averagely adept scribe could have come up with such ideas as, "Our pious brother has left us a work which is well fitted to build up the Christian virtues; but his language and style fall far below the elegance which now marks the doctors of the Church. Surely to improve the connection of these awkward sentences, to put the right word for the wrong one, to amend a vulgar from here and there, is only a service to the book and to the memory of him who wrote it." Bonner concluded his observations to the text of this early Christian writing with the words, "Certain it is that, whether with conscious purpose or not, diverse scribes introduced many slight changes, rarely, if ever, seriously modifying the thought and purpose of the author. How far a similar procedure, prompted by similar motives, may account for variant readings in those writings which became permanent parts of the canon of Scripture is an interesting question."[8]

Let us therefore begin with a first comparison: The story of the rich man and the beggar Lazarus (Lk. 16:19-31). The Byzantine edition of this section counts 251 words, the Nestle-Aland 27 edition 244 words. The differences appear in 15 words at 13 places of variation; individually speaking, the variants between the Byzantine text and the reconstructed Nestle-Aland 27 text are as follows:

5 words differ orthographically

7 words were added

0 words are missing

1 word was transposed

2 words were substituted

Six percent of the words from the Byzantine text differ therefore from the earlier reconstructed Nestle-Aland 27 text. This equates to a textual stability for this section of 94 percent.

The method applied in this comparison can equally be used for larger amounts of text. Four types of deviation can hereby be classified:

(1) Additions (adds)

(2) Omissions (omits)

(3) Substitutions (substitutes)

(4) Transpositions (transposes)

For the sake of simplicity, the few orthographic differences will be included under (3). Insignificant deviations such as the spelling of *nomina sacra*, the moveable endings -*ν* and -*ζ*, itacisms and accents are ignored. The relationship of the number of word changes to the sum total of words (Nestle-Aland 27) will be used to quantify the percentage of deviation. This result is then subtracted from 100 percent. The final value calculated equals the stability of the text (in other words, the amount of compared text without variation), and would, in the example above, equal 94 percent. Words in square brackets are treated as normal text.

The following tables will present some randomly taken text passages, wherein the thirteenth chapter of every major part of the New Testament (Gospels, Acts, Epistles, Revelation) is scrutinized.

Matthew 13. The deviations between the Byzantine text and Nestle-Aland 27 account to:

(1) Byzantine adds	21 words
(2) Byzantine omits	0 words
(3) Byzantine substitutes	23 words
(4) Byzantine transposes	4 words
Sum	**48 words**

The total number of words in Nestle-Aland 27 equals 1,076.

Textual stability NA27 ÷ Byz: 95.5 percent

Acts 13. Deviations between the Byzantine text and Nestle-Aland 27.

(1) Byzantine adds	28 words
(2) Byzantine omits	15 words
(3) Byzantine substitutes	27 words
(4) Byzantine transposes	5 words
Sum	**75 words**

The total number of words in Nestle-Aland 27 equals 933.

Textual stability NA27 ÷ Byz: 92 percent

Romans 13. Deviations between the Byzantine text and Nestle-Aland 27.

(1) Byzantine adds	4 words
(2) Byzantine omits	1 word
(3) Byzantine substitutes	7 words
(4) Byzantine transposes	3 words
Sum	**15 words**

The total number of words in Nestle-Aland 27 equals 270.

Textual stability NA27 ÷ Byz: 94.5 percent

Hebrews 13. Deviations between the Byzantine text and Nestle-Aland 27.

(1) Byzantine adds	2 words
(2) Byzantine omits	1 word
(3) Byzantine substitutes	6 words
(4) Byzantine transposes	0 words
Sum	**9 words**

The total number of words in Nestle-Aland 27 equals 378.

Textual stability NA27 ÷ Byz: 97.6 percent

Revelation 13. Deviations between the Byzantine text and Nestle-Aland 27.

(1) Byzantine adds	6 words
(2) Byzantine omits	6 words
(3) Byzantine substitutes	25 words
(4) Byzantine transposes	4 words
Sum	**38 words**

The total number of words in Nestle-Aland 27 equals 447.

Textual stability NA27 ÷ Byz: 91.5 percent.

One needs to note, however, that the chosen text (Revelation 13) contains an unusually high number of variants. This becomes obvious when we compare (table 6.1) chapters 12 and 13 of the book of Revelation using an earlier text. Whilst the Greek New Testament records a single minor variant with respect to Revelation 12 (Rev. 12:18), Revelation 13 comprises seven variants, some being significant in nature.

The stability of the text varies within this first survey between 91.5 percent in the Revelation and 97.6 percent in the letters. The average stability is calculated by adding all the words together and dividing by the number of variants. Out of 3,104 words, 185 variations were detected. This provides us with a text lability of 6 percent or a textual stability of 94 percent.

If one applied this type of comparison to some chapters of the New Testament (for example John 8, Mark 16, or Romans 15–16) these sections would appear far more error-ridden than others. These are, however, exceptions in the transmission and only very minimally destabilize the average textual stability of the remaining 7,850+ verses of the New Testament.

One, however, should not forget that we are dealing with a relative value of stability as a) one critical edition (Nestle-Aland 27) is compared to another critical edition (Byzantine), both editions reconstruct the prevalent text, whether the Nestle-Aland text of the second through the fourth centuries or the Byzantine text of the ninth through the fourteenth centuries; and b) the reconstructions themselves are based on coincidental findings of manuscripts. The reconstructions, however, are based on a considerable number of coincidental findings, and the Byzantine text itself is virtually the same in hundreds of manuscripts.

In the next step, a selection of earlier papyri instead of the Nestle-Aland text is compared with the Byzantine text. Shorter papyri are examined in their entirety, whereas text sections of more extensive papyri are chosen systematically to allow the same text section to be compared in different papyri.

2. As an illustration: deviations between the Byzantine text and $\mathfrak{P}^{52}$, second century, John 18:31, 33, 37-38

(1) Byzantine adds	2 words
(2) Byzantine omits	0 words
(3) Byzantine substitutes	4 words
(4) Byzantine transposes	1 word
Sum	**7 words**

The total number of words in $\mathfrak{P}^{52}$ as well as in the Nestle-Aland text equals 84.

The text under investigation has a stability of 91.7 percent.

If we disregard the orthographic variants (the itacisms of $\mathfrak{P}^{52}$, namely *hmin* (ημειν) instead of *hmein* (ημιν), then the text in the subject papyrus differs by only three words or 3.6 percent from the later Byzantine transmission. This methodology is by all means justified, as contemporary rules of orthography did not apply in antiquity. Additionally, orthographic variants only very seldomly affect the text itself. The text transmitted first by $\mathfrak{P}^{52}$ at the beginning of the second century, maintained a textual stability over a transmission period of 1,400 years (from the second century to the editio princips of the New Testament) of 96.4 percent. Not to mention that fact, that none of the variants affect the meaning of the text. $\mathfrak{P}^{52}$, however, portrays only a very small fragment of the early New Testament text. More realistic values are obtained by using more extensive papyri with greater text volumes, as well as taking random samples from different papyri.

3. In what is to follow, a preferably representative selection of the most important papyri of the second and third centuries will be studied using the same method. This will be conducted using the early majuscules of the fourth century (B, ℵ), as well as the Byzantine text. In doing so, we will proceed as follows: a) The orthographic variants (itacisms, the moveable endings -ν and -ς, haplography or dittography of consonants) will be disregarded. However, orthographic variants no longer fulfilling the above criteria, variants of small particles, morphological variants, ditto- and haplographies of words, homoioteleuta, and the like are fully considered. b) The text after the diorthosis is considered to be the final version of a papyrus, that is to say after potential corrections made by the scribe. c) Additions to the text of the respective papyri editions denoted in square brackets are counted as text. This supplemented text orientates itself in-line with the predefined text according to Nestle-Aland 27. This unfortunately proves disadvantageous in respect to the assessment of the Byzantine text (Byzantine readings could be hidden in the missing text of the papyri). Nevertheless, the evaluation of the papyri has shown up to now, that Byzantine readings are only to be expected in minor proportions. Lines that originate exclusively from a reconstructed text are disregarded and as such are not included in the comparison. Words in Nestle-Aland 27 or Byzantine that appear in square brackets are treated as normal text. d) Papyri with a low volume of text (fewer than 100 words) or highly fragmental, as for example $\mathfrak{P}^5$ or $\mathfrak{P}^{95}$, are not considered. Three of the larger papyri ($\mathfrak{P}^{45}$, $\mathfrak{P}^{46}$, and $\mathfrak{P}^{75}$) were taken into account in various books of the New Testament. e) Adjustments to word sequences are counted as follows: if the sequence 1 2 3 4 5 6 is replaced by the sequence 2 3 1 4 5 6, this results in a single transposition error; equally 2 3 4 5 1 6 and so on. The sequence 3 4 5 6 1 2 results in two transposition errors, and so forth. A gap of three words counts as three error units; if three words were substituted by three others, then this counts likewise as three error units, and so forth. f) Text that cannot always be reconstructed with surety, complex transpositions, challenging orthographic variants, errors with counting, and others, have most likely contributed to influencing the results and are therefore regarded as error tolerance.

A caveat needs to be presented, however, when making such a comparison (table 6.1): the respective values for the stability of the text do not indicate the number of deviations that took place in the course of text transmission from the second and third centuries to the fourth century (Codices B, ℵ) and through to the Middle Ages (Byzantine) that altered, in a uniformly increasing manner, the text of the New Testament. The number of variations did not increase linearly. Rather, the values for the stability of the text portray an accumulation of variants that arose during three distinct periods. At the onset of New Testament scribal activity, early scribal errors lead to variants flowing into the source text of transmission (and varied depending on the quality of the scribe from the "free" $\mathfrak{P}^{45}$ to the "strict" $\mathfrak{P}^{75}$). Then, in the course of around 500 years between the third and eighth centuries, prevalent variants were assimilated into the manuscripts. And finally, variants were introduced at the climax of the Byzantine culture during the ninth through the twelfth centuries. This accumulation of variants, however, stood in contrast to an additional development in the transmission of the text. Scribes and their correctors conducted manuscript comparisons and substituted or removed words that appeared dubious in their eyes, while adding others that seemed to have textual authority.[9] These corrections were often later regarded as the text to be copied. Under certain circumstances, very old manuscripts were used as the source material for comparison, these, however, not necessarily being the most suitable ones. The number of variants accumulates, therefore, as an integral of a non-linear function, based on manifold human interaction, errors as well as corrections, corrections of supposed errors as well as erroneous corrections of real errors, and this at different periods and of varying intensity. The number of deviations from the onset of text transmission is sometimes greater in the earlier manuscripts of the second and third centuries than in the later Byzantine manuscripts, this depending on the care of the individual scribe. The values for stability as illustrated in table 6.1 reflect these complex mechanisms of impact. The term "textual stability" needs also to be understood in this context: it merely states how much has changed during an extended period of time, not when, how, and for what reasons changes were made. To a large extent, textual criticism enables us to reconstruct the source text[10] of transmission and eliminate many of the early corruptions; theoretically speaking, and as shown in examples 1–6, the text stability could be calculated by simply comparing Nestle-Aland 27 with Byzantine. Of primary interest, however, is the comparison of actually written texts: only such texts provide the data necessary for conducting a thorough analysis of the integrity of the New Testament text.

We are therefore dealing with a *quantitative* comparison between the earliest available text of the New Testament and subsequent versions appearing later on. *Qualitative* comparisons that are often applied in various studies of textual criticism (for instance, when it is said that Codex Alexandrinus or a certain church father provides around 75 percent of Byzantine text) are then of interest, when the percentage of affiliation of a certain manuscript to a specific type of text and other manuscripts is being analyzed. Moreover, qualitative comparisons regard every variant as a single entity, not, however, every word. Furthermore, a qualitative analysis bases its reference not on the number of words of a specific section but rather on the maximum number of variants within the section being analyzed.[11]

Using John 4 as an example, a qualitative comparison of all considered manuscripts would result in a hundred places qualifying for variation (see below). If, however, an early papyrus such as $\mathfrak{P}^{75}$ agreed with Codex Vaticanus in eighty-seven of these places, or with the Byzantine text on fifty-eight of these places, then $\mathfrak{P}^{75}$ and Codex Vaticanus would be 87 percent identical, or $\mathfrak{P}^{75}$ and the Byzantine text would be 58 percent identical. Such a qualitative comparison says initially very little about which portion of a specific text remained stable over an extended period of time. This, however, is exactly the question that we should be interested in.

To begin with, let us have a look at the individual results with regard to their deviations from the major majuscules of the fourth century. table 6.1 does not offer any surprises to those who have occupied themselves with the early papyri. $\mathfrak{P}^{45}$ is the papyrus that, when measured against the Codex Sinaiticus, is at the bottom of the scale and exhibits a textual stability of 88.8 percent only (89.3 percent when measured against the Codex Vaticanus). Kenyon's remark concerning $\mathfrak{P}^{45}$ is self-explanatory: "It is true that it is very imperfect, but it covers such a substantial portion of the Gospels that it is legitimate to draw general conclusions from it, and these show us in the early part of the third century a text of the Gospels and Acts identical in all essentials with that which we have hitherto known on the evidence of later authorities."[12] This has also been confirmed by more recent analysis. The scribe of $\mathfrak{P}^{45}$ "added or omitted trivialities, most probably consciously, or at least semiconsciously [. . .] the scribe occasionally omitted conjunctions, but occasionally he included them as well [. . .] the scribe also added words that he had forgotten to the next suitable passage, this leading naturally to transpositions" and generally "producing many harmonizations toward a narrower context."[13] However, all these variants did not arise with the intention of altering the text. "The nature and method of copying in $\mathfrak{P}^{45}$ is both intelligent and liberal: intelligent, because the sense of the exemplar is quickly grasped and in essence precisely reproduced; and liberal, because involved

Papyrus / Text	W_{NA}	W_{Byz}	B	St. B	ℵ	St. ℵ	NA	St. NA	Byz	St. Byz	Delta
$\mathfrak{P}^{45}$, III, Jn. 10:7-25.29-11:5	598	606	64	89.3%	67	88.8%	58	90.3%	77	87.1%	3.2%
$\mathfrak{P}^{101}$, III Mt. 3:10-12; 3:16-4:3	111	114	7	93.7%	8	92.8%	7	93.7%	11	90.1%	3.6%
$\mathfrak{P}^{37}$, III-IV, Mt. 26:19-52	587	601	40	93.2%	44	92.5%	36	93.9%	61	89.6%	4.3%
$\mathfrak{P}^{90}$, II, Jn. 18:36-19:7	242	241	18	92.5%	18	92.5%	14	94.2%	26	89.2%	5.0%
$\mathfrak{P}^{108}$, III, Jn. 17:23-24; 18:1-5	120	120	13	89.2%	4	96.7%	7	94.2%	4	96.7%	-2.5%
$\mathfrak{P}^{72}$, III, 2 Pet. 1:1-21	384	384	18	95.3%	41	89.3%	22	94.3%	27	93.0%	1.3%
$\mathfrak{P}^{45}$, III, Mt. 20:24-32; 21:13-19; 25:41-26:17; 26:18-39	912	929	60	93.4%	56	93.9%	47	94.9%	76	91.7%	3.2%
$\mathfrak{P}^{77+103}$, II-III, Mt. 13:55-56; 14:3-5; 23:30-34. 35-39	186	188	13	93.0%	12	93.5%	9	95.2%	13	93.0%	2.2%
$\mathfrak{P}^{66}$, II-III, Jn. 12:1-50	892	889	45	95.0%	44	95.1%	40	95.5%	75	91.6%	3.9%
$\mathfrak{P}^{106}$, III, Jn. 1:29-35. 40-46	221	225	10	95.5%	11	95.0%	10	95.5%	17	92.3%	3.2%
$\mathfrak{P}^{53}$, III, Mt. 26:29-35	186	189	8	95.7%	10	94.6%	8	95.7%	12	93.5%	2.2%
$\mathfrak{P}^{46}$, II-III, Rom. 9:1-32	507	514	25	95.1%	25	95.1%	23	95.5%	38	92.5%	3.0%
$\mathfrak{P}^{15}$, III, 1 Cor. 7:18-8,4	419	419	19	95.5%	17	95.9%	13	96.9%	46	89.0%	7.9%
$\mathfrak{P}^{75}$, II-III, Jn. 12:3-50	830	827	26	96.9%	35	95.8%	22	97.3%	63	92.4%	4.9%
$\mathfrak{P}^{100}$, III, Jak 3:13-4:4; 4:9-5:1	292	297	10	96.6%	22	92.3%	9	97.1%	19	93.6%	3.7%
$\mathfrak{P}^{115}$, II, Rev. 12:1-5.8-10.12-16	299	302	–	–	9	97.0%	8	97.3%	9	97.0%	0.3%
$\mathfrak{P}^{46}$, II-III, Heb. 4:1-16	291	292	8	97.2%	8	97.2%	6	97.9%	9	96.9%	1.0%
$\mathfrak{P}^{64+67}$, II-III, Mt. 3:9.15; 5:20-22. 25-28; 26:7-8.10.14-15. 22-23. 31-33	194	196	5	97.4%	3	98.4%	4	98.0%	11	94.3%	3.7%
$\mathfrak{P}^{49}$, III, Eph. 4:16-29.31-5:13	359	358	6	98.3%	11	96.9%	7	98.0%	15	95.8%	2.2%
$\mathfrak{P}^{75}$, II-III, Lk. 12	1033	1058	25	97.6%	50	95.2%	21	98.0%	68	93.4%	4.6%
$\mathfrak{P}^{13}$, III, Heb. 4:1-16	291	292	7	97.6%	8	97.2%	5	98.3%	9	96.9%	1.4%
$\mathfrak{P}^{98}$, II, Rev. 1:13-2:1	191	193	–	–	15	92.2%	3	98.4%	9	95.3%	3.1%
$\mathfrak{P}^{39}$, III, Jn. 8:14-22	160	164	0	100%	7	95.6%	2	98.7%	9	94.4%	4.3%
$\mathfrak{P}^{20}$, III, Jas. 2:19-3:2. 3-9	259	264	5	98.7%	9	96.5%	3	98.8%	18	93.0%	5.8%
$\mathfrak{P}^{1}$, III, Mt. 1:1-9.14-20	276	279	5	98.2%	5	98.2%	3	98.9%	16	94.2%	4.7%
$\mathfrak{P}^{27}$, III, Rom. 8:12-22.24-27; 8:33-9:3.5-9	423	427	10	97.6%	7	98.3%	1	99.7%	14	96.7%	3.0%
Sum total / average	10263	10368	447	95.6%	546	94.7%	388	96.2%	752	92.6%	3.6%

Table 6.1

Textual variants in the New Testament text. The first column indicates the respective papyrus, followed by the century it is usually assigned to (II=2nd, III=3rd century) and the text of concern. Shorter papyri are examined in their entirety and appear in bold type, whereas more extensive ones such as $\mathfrak{P}^{66}$ are partially examined. The next two columns indicate the sum total of words contained in these passages in the Nestle-Aland 27 and the Byzantine texts respectively. The beginning and end of the respective passage conform to the Comfort/Barret 2001 edition of the respective papyri. Column 4 indicates the number of deviations existing between the text of the subject papyrus and Codex B (if B has been subject to scribal corrections at this place, then B* is used), column 6 indicates the number of deviations existing between the text of the subject papyrus and Codex ℵ (if ℵ has been subject to scribal corrections at this place, then Codex ℵ* is used), the stability on the text being indicated in columns 5 and 7 respectively. Columns 8 and 10 indicate the corresponding values for Nestle-Aland 27 and Byzantine, the stability on the text being indicated in columns 9 and 11 respectively. The equation for the stability is: Stability = 100 percent * [1 – X/WNA], whereby the value of X is to be taken from columns 4 (B), 6 (ℵ) 8 (NA) and 10 (Byz) respectively. For example, the stability of $\mathfrak{P}^{101}$ measured against B: Stab. $\mathfrak{P}^{101}$ = 100% * [1 – 7/111] = 93.7 percent. For practical reasons, the reference for the volume of words in a passage remains the text according to Nestle-Aland 27, incurring an error of about ± 0.1 percent. The final column indicates the delta between columns 9 (stability measured against NA) and 11 (stability measured against Byzantine).

expressions and repetitious words are simplified or dropped."[14] "The scribe has a marked tendency to omit. . . . Harmonization is a frequent cause of error. . . . Stylistic improvements are sometimes attempted."[15] The errors and corruptions of this papyrus did not arise because of certain editorial inclinations impacting upon the text. Rather, sloppy negligence was the responsible factor. If we examine the considered text in John 10 (row 1), we ascertain that a large omission (a secondary sentence in John 10:35) further contributes to a poor result;[16] in Matthew 20 (row 7), the text of the same papyrus has a considerably higher stability. $\mathfrak{P}^{45}$ is counted as "free" text.[17] This is similarly the case with $\mathfrak{P}^{37}$ (although minimally conforming to the D-text, $\mathfrak{P}^{37}$ does not exhibit any of the typical D-paraphrases or interpretative additions and as such is more comparable to $\mathfrak{P}^{45}$) and $\mathfrak{P}^{66}$. $\mathfrak{P}^{46}$ should be assigned to the same category: "The excellent quality of the text represented by our oldest manuscript, $\mathfrak{P}^{46}$, stands out again [. . .] We must be careful to distinguish between the very poor work of the scribe who penned it and the basic text which he so poorly rendered. $\mathfrak{P}^{46}$ abounds with scribal blunders, omissions, and also additions [. . .] Once they have been discarded, there remains a text of outstanding (although not absolute) purity."[18] Besides numerous orthographical and grammatical errors as well as omissions and harmonizations to the immediate context, some of the variants of $\mathfrak{P}^{46}$ seem to have been motivated by theological considerations (Gal. 1:6; 2:20; 3:17-19; 4:6-7). These variants, however, most of them omissions, can be fit easily into the pattern that the scribe of $\mathfrak{P}^{46}$ establishes elsewhere.[19]

The other end of the scale is dominated by papyri fulfilling the criteria of "strict" text whereby especially $\mathfrak{P}^1$, $\mathfrak{P}^{27}$, and $\mathfrak{P}^{75}$ are worthy of mention, as well as $\mathfrak{P}^{39}$ and $\mathfrak{P}^{64+67}$. The value though of $\mathfrak{P}^{75}$ in John 12 suffers due to two homoioteleuta (Jn. 12:8, 34); without these, the corresponding text would exhibit an equally high stability as in Luke 12.[20] $\mathfrak{P}^{75}$ seems to have been copied with care, "but not with the unusual care that has been sometimes ascribed to him."[21]

Let us now take a look at the overall result. The considered 10,263 words make out approximately 7.5 percent of the entire New Testament word pool. The stability of the New Testament text under consideration, from the early papyri to the Byzantine text, achieves an average of 92.6 percent. Errors need to be taken into account when evaluating the number of variants; an overall error of ±1 percent is assumed. Despite applying the assumed tolerance of ±100 words per 10,000 words (that is to say, four extremely unfavorable summed up collation errors per manuscript), a value of over 90 percent is still achieved.

What is striking about the analysis above is the difference between the Nestle-Aland 27 and Byzantine textual stabilities (Stability NA27 versus Byz). Based on the papyri, the Byzantine text in comparison to the reconstructed Nestle-Aland 27 text is, on average, 3.6 percent less stable. This difference rises minimally when calculating the text stability against Codex Vaticanus (see graph 6.1, below). It can, however, also be concluded that papyri which have a "strict" text can at the same time be considered as relatively close to the Byzantine text. It cannot be said that those early papyri with a "free" text are closer to the Byzantine text simply because some of their readings seem to be Byzantine in character. And even though these papyri show evidence of early corrective measures on a small scale that were later assimilated into the Byzantine text, they still exhibit far more unique renderings. These early variants are to some extent a by-product of their liberal writing style and not an indication of the existence of a Byzantine text at an early point in time. Only $\mathfrak{P}^{108}$ is apparently closer to the Byzantine text than to the early text. This result may well be influenced by the limited volume of text of $\mathfrak{P}^{108}$ (Jn. 17:23-24; 18:1-15). The manuscripts ℵ, A, and W also contain minor variants that can be found in the Byzantine text. Likewise, $\mathfrak{P}^{115}$ (Rev. 12:1-5, 8-10, 12-16) is conspicuous: apart from minor variation, its text remained stable over a period stretching from antiquity into the second millennium. This, however, does not surprise us. It is well known that the Byzantine text of the book of Revelation (with a few exceptions such as Rev. 13) does not exhibit the corrections, additions, and harmonizations to the extent observable in the remaining books of the New Testament.

If we focus our attention exclusively on the antique text of the second through the fourth centuries and disregard the Byzantine transmission, then we achieve average textual stabilities of 94.7 percent (against Codex ℵ) and 95.6 percent (against Codex B) respectively. If the unique renderings of the majuscules B and ℵ are eliminated (which is one of the important tasks of the critical edition according to Nestle-Aland 27), then a value as high as 96.2 percent (against Nestle-Aland 27) is achieved (see graph 6.1 below).

In comparing the text, whose early papyri already contained corruptions and which reached editorial finality in the Byzantine text of the Middle Ages, we are able to ascertain the greatest possible lability of the New Testament text during a preferably large period of time. The value, however, proves to be on average 7.4 percent, which is lower than expected. Epp,[22] Ehrman,[23] Parker,[24] and others endeavored to demonstrate that, among all the mistaken synonyms and substitutions in the area of particles and conjunctions, among the additions, transpositions and gaps, some interesting and dogmatically motivated variants exist, variants that are not to be attributed to pure coincidence or negligence. One, however, cannot deduce from the aforementioned that the New Testament is distorted, theologically discolored by early and latter scribes, thereby making the reconstruction of the earliest attainable form of the text very difficult if not impossible.

An often repeated observation in a wide range of discourses pertaining to New Testament textual criticism must not be forgotten: most of the early papyri are of an informal, somewhat private nature.[25] By taking this factor into account, the stability of the New Testament text

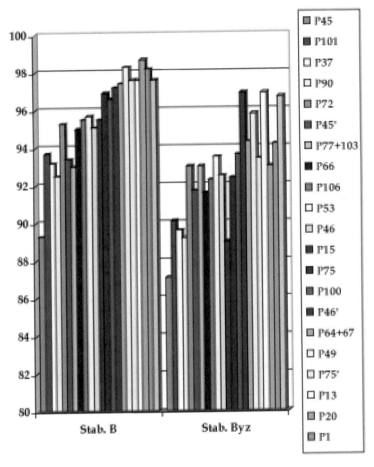

Graph 6.1
A graphical illustration of the stability of the text according to the early papyri, measured against Codex Vaticanus and the Byzantine text. For the purposes of clarity, $\mathfrak{P}^{108}$ (an extreme value for Byzantine) and $\mathfrak{P}^{39}$ (an extreme value for B) have been excluded from this illustration.

that was calculated using these largely informal early papyri should be greater by a few percent than the values in table 6.1. It is well known that this is confirmed by $\mathfrak{P}^{75}$, which, in contrast to most papyri, exhibits a relatively precise copying technique;[26] minimal intrusions into the text imply a very high regard for the text that had to be copied.[27] Despite the informal character of the early papyri (these having a much larger abundance of variants than the subsequent homogeneous copies of the Byzantine period), we are able to ascertain "that one is always dealing with variants of a specific text that behave within expected boundaries [. . .] Fundamentally new information is not produced. Rather, variation inherent to scribes is observed." The text being offered "is the text of the first century. This text was copied while errors were introduced by scribal activity. We are able to reconstruct this text, naturally apart from certain details varying in number. "The papyri are 'copies of a specific text in a specific form of text.'"[28]

Nevertheless, one may object that the text stability according to table 6.1 applies merely to a certain portion of text of a single papyrus, which is compared to another manuscript (Byzantine). Theoretically speaking, if one were to compare 2,500 papyri instead of the twenty-five papyri used in the calculation above, then our spectrum of variation would be a hundred times greater. This would result in a lower stability per section of text. Concerning the text stability in table 6.1, however, the average value would hardly be affected by this increase in manuscript comparison. Single manuscripts could well alter the upper and lower text stability values; however the average value would become more and more stable with an increasing number of manuscripts. This can be clearly seen on the graph: around half of the very early papyri (papyri against Codex B) vary above the average of 95.6 percent, the majority above a value of 92 percent. A similar trend can be seen with the comparison of the Byzantine text: seventeen out of twenty-four of the papyri reach a value higher than 92 percent.

Furthermore, through comparison, singular readings and orthographic errors, writing errors such as homoioteleuta, ditto- and haplographies could be recognised and isolated; many subordinate variants less important for the generation of the text such as harmonizations (to the immediate or remote context) could be eliminated. In other words, if we had 2,500 early papyri containing the same portion of text at our disposal, then this would enable us to reconstruct the source text of transmission with much greater reliability compared to the text reconstructed from a single papyrus. This procedure for text-critical analysis had been fittingly presented by Bentley around 300 years ago. Bentley, however, was mistaken to believe that the New Testament text could with ease be completely reconstructed utilizing the manuscripts available at the time. For in those days, only a few hundred manuscripts were known, to say nothing of Codex Sinaiticus and the papyri.

Additionally, the text of the older translations and church fathers was to a large extent unexplored. Even today, no one would dare to claim that the "original Greek" could be reconstructed perfectly. Bentley's remarks, however, to a text-critical methodology are, in principle, accurate. They were adapted to a large extent by Lachmann and the other text researchers of the nineteenth century and continue to enjoy validity into the twenty-first century; if we only had one manuscript of New Testament, then, according to Bentley, we would admittedly have no variants, but a text with hundreds of undiscovered and irreparable errors.

This sobering statement may be illustrated by using the newly discovered Gospel of Judas that was recently unveiled to the public.[29] According to the editors, they have reproduced the text as accurately as possible and present us with an authentic text of antiquity that portrays Judas and Jesus in a completely different light. Furthermore, and with a high degree of certainty, the Gospel of Judas can be traced back to the second century, as even Irenaeus seems to make mention of it (*adv. haer.* I, 31,1).

Bentley, however, already warned 300 years ago of the danger of presenting a transmitted text as good on the basis of a single extant manuscript alone. His warning should equally be applied *mutatis mutandis* to the Gospel of Judas, especially when considering the so-called Gospel of Thomas, a document having partial similarity to that of the Gospel of Judas and which blatantly underwent continuous elaboration within the same period of time: "If there had been but one manuscript of the Greek Testament, at the restoration of learning about two centuries ago, then we had had no various readings at all. And would the text be in a better condition then, than now that we have 30,000? So far from that; that in the best single copy extant we should have had hundreds of faults, and some omissions irreparable. Besides that the suspicions of fraud and foul play would have been increas'd immensely."[30] Accordingly, whether the edited Sahidic manuscript of the Gospel of Judas, the Codex Tchacos, is able to provide us with the text of the Gospel of Judas from the second century with a tolerable textual stability remains very doubtful.

Bentley remarks further with respect to the text-critical work on the New Testament: "It is good therefore, you'll allow, to have more anchors than one; and another manuscript to join with the first would give more authority, as well as security. Now choose that second where you will; there shall be a thousand variations from the first, and yet half or more of the faults shall still remain in them both. A third therefore, and so a fourth, and so on, are desirable; that by a joint and mutual help all the faults may be mended: some copies preserving the true reading in one place, and some in another. And yet the more copies you call to assistance, the more do the various readings multiply upon you, every copy having its peculiar slips, though in a principal passage or two, it does singular service. And this is fact, not only in the New Testament, but in all ancient books whatever [. . .] where the copies of any author are numerous, though the *various readings* always increase in proportion; there the text by an accurate collation of them made by skillful and judicious hands is ever the more correct, and comes nearer to the true words of the author."[31]

If we therefore possessed a hundred or even 2,500 early papyri instead of only $\mathfrak{P}^{45}$ in John 10, then we would be able to reproduce a text exhibiting a greater textual stability in relation to the "Ausgang-stext der Überlieferung" [the earliest attainable text starting the trans-mission]. Particularly good papyri such as $\mathfrak{P}^{75}$ "shorten" naturally such a reconstruction. Besides, we would also discover in these papyri here and there dogmatically motivated alterations.

Many of the rejected variants that are identified as such in the course of a text-critical reconstruction are interesting objects of study: how and why did they arise, why were they (or were they not) trans-mitted, why are some of these readings extremely tenacious,[32] why do some of them only appear in certain text types (D-text, Byzantine text) and should they not after all be used in certain passages, and so forth?

4. Greater insight into the textual stability of the New Testament can be gained by analyzing the textual stability of a comparative text. The text used in this analysis is the *Shepherd of Hermas*, which underwent an appropriate investigation to provide the necessary results. The *Shepherd of Hermas* was composed in Rome around 150 c.e. and was regarded in the early church as one of the most popular books. Along with the other writings of the New Testament, the *Shepherd of Hermas* played an important role in church gatherings and Christian homes. The wide dissemination of the book within the Alexandrinian church—the *Shepherd of Hermas* was used to instruct catechumens—is very well attested by numerous findings.[33] The *Shepherd of Hermas* was also mentioned in the works of the early church fathers. Despite its great popularity, though, certain church fathers such as Tertullian rejected it and, according to the words of the *Canon Muratori*, it should most certainly be read in private; therefore, public readings to the people at church were forbidden, as the *Shepherd of Hermas* was neither reckoned among the prophets nor among the apostles.[34] Eusebius had already relegated the *Shepherd of Hermas* to the noncanonical writings (*Historia ecclesiae* III 25:4), and toward the end of the fourth century it merely enjoyed attention in the east, according to Hieronymus (*De viris illustribus 10*: "apud Latinos paene ignotus est"). Two essential witnesses of the "*visiones*," the Codex Sinaiticus and the papyrus Bodmer 38, originate from this period however.

So far, a total of twenty-three papyri manuscripts (or, to be more exact, fragments) of the PH have been published, including more recently the papyri manuscripts P.Oxy 4705—4707 dating back to the second and third centuries.[35] The manuscripts of the *Shepherd of Hermas* (including the later pergament manuscripts), however, do not provide evidence that a direct relationship or dependency exists among them.[36] Until the sixth century, the *Shepherd of Hermas* is even more widely attested than many books of the New Testament;[37] as many as eleven manuscripts were written before the fourth century. Because of the often fragmentary text pool, only a few manuscripts are suitable to be used in researching textual stability. Nonetheless, we are able to oversee the Greek transmission from the end of the second until the fifteenth century. One of the oldest manuscripts of the *Shepherd of Hermas* is the P.Michigan 129, dated to the second half of the third century. Further *Shepherd of Hermas* manuscripts considered are the P. Bodmer 38, two Oxyrhynchus papyri, the P.Berlin inv. 5513, and the Codex Sinaiticus. As a representative of the Byzantine text, the Codex Athous (fifteenth century) will be utilized. Furthermore, the excerpts of the *Shepherd of Hermas* in another minuscule, the Codex Lavra K96 as published by M. Bandini in 2000, enable the P.Michigan to be collated against both the Codex Athous as well as the Codex Lavra. The volume of text was evaluated using the critical edition according to

Leutzsch (1998). Apart from the Codex Lavra K 96, all remaining manuscripts were collated, their variants being accessible within the text critical apparatus of this edition.

With five text sources taken into consideration, the text of the *Shepherd of Hermas* as transmitted by the relatively well preserved P. Michigan 129 (*Sim.* 2:8–9:5.1) provides us with 977 variants.[38] This text is comprised of approximately 7,000 words. A comparison with the New Testament illustrates the following: when taking into account twenty-five significant text sources, John 4, comprised of 950 words, has approximately 100 variants;[39] John 14, which has as an equivalent volume of text, has, when considering eighteen text sources, more

	H	collated	Dev	Stab.	Athous	Stab. A	Lavra	Stab. L
Codex ℵ, IV, vis I	981				132	86.5%		
P. Bodmer 38, IV-V, vis I	981	ℵ	86	91.2%	155	84.2%		
P. Oxy 1172, IV, sim II 4-10	359				57	84.1%		
P. Berlin inv. 5513 III, sim II 7-10	174	Oxy 1172	4	97.7%	22	87.3%		
P. Mich 129, III, sim III-IV	418				62	85.2%		
P. Mich 129, III, sim VI	1270				230	81.9%	214	83.1%
P. Oxy 1599, IV, sim VIII 6:4-8:3	422	Mich 129	100	76.0%	103	75.3%		
Sum total / average	4605	1577	190	87.9%	761	83.5%	214	83.1%

Table 6.2

Variants in transmission of the *Shepherd of Hermas*. The first column indicates the respective Codex, followed by the date of its compilation and the relevant text. Shorter papyri are examined in their entirety and appear in **bold** type, whereas more extensive ones such as P. Mich 129 are partially examined. The second column (H) indicates the sum total of words contained in these passages according to the Leutzsch edition 1998. The third column (collated) indicates the Codex against which it was collated, so as to evaluate the deviation among the early manuscripts in column 4 (Dev). Column 6 (Athous) indicates the degree of deviation (number of error units) of the Codex Athous from the early text. The smaller *lacunae* of the manuscripts were not considered, that is to say that they were regarded as unaltered text and were included as such in the calculation. The corresponding stability of the text is seen in columns 5 (early manuscripts against each other), 7 (early manuscripts against Codex Athous) and 9 (P. Mich 129 against Codex Lavra). The equation for the stability is: Stab. = 100 percent*[1 − X/H], whereby the value of X is to be taken from columns 4 (Dev), 6 (Athous), and 8 (Lavra) respectively.

than 200 variants.[40] To achieve a similar value with the *Shepherd of Hermas*, 950 words provide us with 133 variants (977/7,000*950). This rough calculation provides us with a preliminary assessment for the transmitted text of the *Shepherd of Hermas*: the number of variants existing with merely five text sources is only present in the New Testament when taking into consideration double or even triple the number of manuscripts. We now go on to investigate a larger related volume of text of the *Shepherd of Hermas* (see tables 6.2 and 6.3) using the same criteria that applied in table 6.1. In doing so, two larger portions of text from the *Shepherd of Hermas*'s early manuscript, P. Michigan 129, were considered.

Due to the fragmentary nature of most of its papyri, large passages of text of the edition Leutzsch 1998 are based on merely a few Greek manuscripts. To gain an impression of the volume of variation in the early period, therefore, two important early manuscripts need to be collated. Due to the partially fragmented nature of the papyri, however, the sum total of text needs to be specified using the Leutzsch 1998 edition of the text (this resulting in a probable error no greater than ±0.2 percent).

As can de deduced from table 6.2 (above), the stability of the *Shepherd of Hermas* text between the third and fifteenth centuries attains on average a value of 83 percent. When disregarding some homoioteleuta (table 6.3, opposite), a text stability of up to 86 percent can be achieved. The average text lability of 14 percent is therefore almost twice as large as that of the New Testament. Average values of 86 percent do not even reach the lowest value of the New Testament text, as represented by $\mathfrak{P}^{45}$ (graph 6.2, below). Greater text stability cannot even be attained during the early period; the transmission of the *Shepherd of Hermas*, with its associated average text lability of 10 percent, lies greatly below that of the New Testament text (papyri measured against Codex B). In addition, both comparisons (the comparison of the New Testament papyri and that of the *Shepherd of Hermas* papyri) have one manuscript in common—namely, the Codex Sinaiticus. Here the textual stability of a certain portion of the papyrus Bodmer 38, when collated against ℵ, reaches a textual stability of 91 percent, a value attained by some of those New Testament papyri collated against ℵ, which are regarded as having a "free" text.

	H	collated	Dev	Stab.	Athous	Stab. A	Lavra	Stab. L
Codex ℵ, IV, vis I	981				125	87.3%		
P. Bodmer 38, IV-V, vis I	981	ℵ	86	91.2%	148	84.9%		
P. Oxy 1172, IV, sim II 4-10	359				57	84.1%		
P. Berlin inv. 5513 III, sim II 7-10	174	Oxy 1172	4	97.7%	22	87.3%		
P. Mich 129, III, sim III-IV	418				62	85.2%		
P. Mich 129, III, sim VI	1270				149	88.3%	167	86.8%
P. Oxy 1599, IV, sim VIII 6:4-8:3	422	Mich 129	60	85.8%	76	82.0%		
Sum total / average	4605	1577	150	90.5%	639	86.1%	167	86.8%

Table 6.3

Variants in transmission of the *Shepherd of Hermas* (cf. table 6.2), omitting the large homoioteleuta of Codex Athous (*Vis.* 1.2.2; *Sim.* 6.1.4; 2.3; 3.6), Codex Lavra K 96 (*Sim.* 6.3.4; 4.5; 5.7), P. Mich 129 (*Sim.* 8.7.4) and P.Oxy 1599 (*Sim.* 8.7.1, 3).

Noteworthy is the good result of P. Berlin inv. 1533, which needs to be labelled as "too good." Not only does the small volume of text diminish this "good" result but, additionally, the fact has to be taken into account that this papyrus had to be reconstructed by almost 40 percent.[41]

According to some church fathers, the *Shepherd of Hermas* had a quasi-canonical position.[42] Despite its high popularity at the time, it was not copied as precisely as the New Testament writings. Despite enjoying intermittent recognition as official church literature (from the second through the fourth centuries and this restricted to certain regions), greater emphasis was placed on its role in private usage. An obvious consequence was that the text of the *Shepherd of Hermas* received less attention than the writings of the New Testament. Although the *Shepherd of Hermas* in the Codex Sinaiticus was linked to some degree to the canonical writings (which surely increased its esteem), it cannot, thus, be concluded that the *Shepherd of Hermas* had scriptural authority equal to other writings of the New Testament. A further point worth mentioning is that the earliest manuscripts of the *Shepherd of Hermas* from the second century (P. Michigan 130; P.Oxy 4706) were written on scrolls and not bound in the form of the codex,

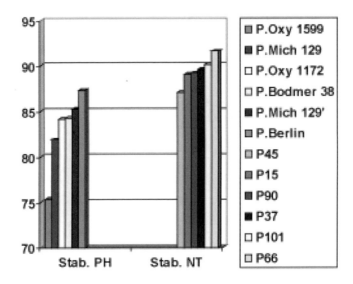

Graph 6.2

Stability of the *Shepherd of Hermas* papyri according to table 6.2 (calculated against Codex Athous) and the New Testament papyri whose text had the worst values when compared against the Byzantine text.

as is the case with the earliest known New Testament manuscripts. Theological discourses and excerpts were also written on scrolls; the Codex style, however, was the prevalent technique of writing among canonically relevant manuscripts.[43]

The original copying method of the *Shepherd of Hermas* is sometimes compared to the copying method of the early New Testament papyri.[44] *Vis.* 2.4.3-4 conveys to us on the sidelines a method of reproducing Christian literature that was applied early on: Hermas manifests himself to the church as an elderly lady and wants to propagate her teachings in the form of a book. This is carried out by "producing two copies of the small book, one of which should be sent to Clemens and the other one to Grapte. [. . .] Grapte should use the book to exhort the widows and orphans. You yourself, however, should read them in this town with the elders who oversee the church." Initially, the *Shepherd of Hermas* was copied for private reasons. Hermas himself, as Lusini suspects, most likely amended his "original" several times, which can further be substantiated by the large number of variants found in the

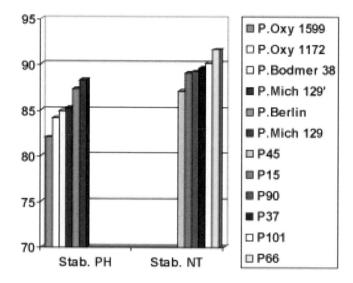

Graph 6.3

Stability of the *Shepherd of Hermas* papyri according to table 6.3 (calculated against Codex Athous and disregarding the homoioteleuta) and the New Testament papyri whose text had the worst values when compared against the Byzantine text.

early manuscripts: "It is more plausible to suppose that Hermas, transcribing many copies of his Apocalype, sometimes changed his mind and produced the the competitive readings in question."[45] Similarly, Bonner and Osiek remark, "It is doubtful whether there ever was an authoritative text after the writer's autograph copy had perished."[46] "If the text was composed over a long period of time and on the basis of oral use, it is even doubtful whether the author had one authoritative text. The enormous variety of readings within a relatively small range of manuscripts witnesses to the diverse uses to which the text was put."[47] In the course of propagating this literary work, dwindling discipline among the scribes provided an additional source for variants to creep in. The text in question was being copied capriciously, simply because there were no rules governing the aspects of transmission. The wide circulation of the early church writings throughout the entire Mediterranean and the intensive usage they enjoyed did, however, not leave them untouched; this far more so regarding the *Shepherd of Hermas*: "The tradition is rather contaminated, an indication that the work knew for some time an intense and transverse circulation in the different communities of the (late?) ancient Mediterranean, from Gaul to Egypt to Ethiopia."[48]

In contrast, the reproduction of the New Testament writings was subject to greater scrutiny. The text itself (whose early corruptions in the papyri were often not passed on and whose Byzantine "face lifting" only took place in a very restricted manner) testifies to certain factors that accompanied its transmission: similarly to Judaism, the copying of biblical manuscripts in the early church was most likely only permitted when using reference copies that were to be found at the churches or in the possession of church leaders.[49]

The insight we gain from the suggested methods of early Christian copyists portrayed in *Vis.* 2 of the *Shepherd of Hermas*, however, seems not to provide us with an accurate picture of the scribes of the New Testament papyri and their copying methods. The lability of the *Shepherd of Hermas* text both in the fourth and fifth centuries (compare the Codex Sinaiticus with the Papyrus Bodmer 38), as well as in the thirteenth (Codex Lavra K 96) and fifteenth (Codex Athous) centuries, is almost twice as large compared to the average lability of the New Testament text. Even additional early fragments of the *Shepherd of Hermas* that have not been used in this assessment provide a large number of unsystematic variants.[50] The transmitted text based upon the oldest text sources (P. Michigan 130, 2. Jh), "written scarcely more than two generations after the commonly accepted date of Hermas,"[51] exhibits already in a small passage containing sixty-six words (mand II,6—III,1), twelve deviations from Codex ℵ and nineteen deviations from Codex Athous, thus revealing in the course of its transmission a certain disposition to gradual "improvement." These "improvements" (as can been seen in other *Shepherd of Hermas* manuscripts) can generally be attributed to relatively capricious word transpositions without changes to meaning. They can already be observed with P. Michigan 129 (third century), this being substantiated by comparisons of this codex with other early Greek fragments.[52] The subsequent P.Michigan 129 was written by a scribe with average to good accuracy, who oversaw only a few orthographic errors. He reproduced the relatively simple language of the *Shepherd of Hermas* with all its vulgarisms (thanks to the autograph) correctly, despite the fact that some errors crept in on his part.

In contrast to the earlier fragments, the Codex Sinaiticus provided a further "improved" or amended text: "the itacisms and such-like minor defects are far grosser than one commonly meets with; moreover, the numerous corrections—partly by a contemporary hand [. . .], but largely also by a hand of about the sixth century [. . .] show that the text was felt at a quite early date to call for systematic improvement."[53] Another important papyrus, the already mentioned papyrus Bodmer 38 (fourth to fifth centuries) is accepted as a witness that agrees generally with Codex Sinaiticus but deviates nevertheless many times from the aforementioned codex.[54] In contrast to the texts of the early period, many passages of the fifteenth-century Codex Athous text underwent doctoring to better adapt its Greek to the Byzantine style. Conjunctions have been inserted, the word order changed, individual words replaced by synonyms, and even theological concerns have led to alteration.[55] This applies equally to what remains of the *Shepherd of Hermas* in Codex Lavra K98 (*Sim.* 6–7 and *Sim.* 9:31.4–33.3). Even though this thirteenth-century textual witness contains some of the older readings as recorded in the P. Michigan, its greater affinity is definitely toward the Codex Athous,[56] which not only can be observed in their common errors, but also in frequent word transpositions and substitutions. The Byzantine transmission did *not* bring forth a definite text of the *Shepherd of Hermas*. Not to mention the orthographic variants, merely 30 out of 135 readings of the Codex Lavra K96 in *Sim.* 6 are in agreement with the Codex Athous. This agreement in less than 25 percent of the readings is far from what we know to be the case, as can be seen with the Byzantine manuscripts of New Testament. The remaining variants encompass mainly peculiar readings consisting of morphological variants, transpositions and substitutions, additions or omissions of particles, articles, prepositions and personal pronouns that can only very rarely be ascribed to known variants. Numerous of these errors could easily have been avoided.

Noteworthy, however, is that the early acceptance and later rejection of the *Shepherd of Hermas* did not lead to dogmatically motivated changes of the text. Whittaker,[57] as well as Ehrman,[58] mention *Vis.* 1.1:7 as the only example; here *thean* (θεάν) (Codex ℵ, P. Bodmer 38) was replaced by *thygatera* (θυγατέρα) (Codex Athous). Other frequent substitutions such as *kyrios* (κύριος) instead of *theos* (θεός) can hardly be interpreted as dogmatically motivated. Ehrman generally assumes that "there appears to be no noticeable difference in the kinds of alteration one finds made by scribes in New Testament writings, on the one hand, and writings of the Apostolic fathers, on the other."[59] These alterations, however, (and those of dogmatic nature) neither dominate the tradition of the *Shepherd of Hermas* nor change the general meaning of its text.

Despite its ugly appearance, hardly recognisable accents,[60] and frequent inconsistency in thought and other scribal blunders, the Codex Athous provides a text, "from which the Sinaiticus varies in small details but apparently not in substance,"[61] and has solely managed to preserve the correct text at certain places.[62] Similar can be said of the Codex Lavra K96.[63] A noncanonical text such as the *Shepherd of Hermas* could have experienced the same fate as other apocryphal texts: "The copying of the text [. . .] serves to answer topical questions [. . .] these texts serve to edify people whose current situation is in a state of flux; as a consequence, the texts themselves are changed also." It is a characteristic of the apocryphal literature to be continually in variance.[64]

Other noncanonical texts of the early period (for example the Epistle of Barnabas as transmitted in the Codex Sinaiticus) achieve at best a text stability similar to that of the *Shepherd of Hermas*, particularly as not a single type of text resembles the earliest text of the Epistle of Barnabas.[65] Even the Codex Sinaiticus transmits a mere recension of Barnabas. No later than the seventh century did this recension experience change—change, however, of insignificant nature.[66] Some of these apocryphal and often pseudepigraphal texts that were transmitted in a relatively large quantity of manuscripts exhibit, however, unlike the New Testament, a far greater abundance of variants. A good illustration of this is the Protevangelium of James, a text originating around 150 c.e. and found in many textual witnesses. Theological interests and piety destabilized the text of these manuscripts far beyond the stability of the text of the canonical gospels.[67] According to Cullmann, this observation, which applies to many apocryphal gospels, can be applied all the more to the Protevangelium of James.[68] The variants of this text "are reduced to variations of a classical kind, as there exist everywhere among different witnesses of the same text."[69] A collation of the first three chapters, comparing manuscripts between the third and the ninth through the sixteenth centuries,[70] whereby the previ-

ously mentioned methodology was applied (cf. tables 6.1–3), resulted
in 87 deviations from a total of 414 words producing a text stability
of less than 80 percent. Furthermore, the minuscules used by Tischendorf do by no means have the homogeneity of the New Testament
minuscules. A collation therefore of single manuscripts with the Codex
Bodmer 5 would most likely lead to even worse results. Additionally,
the Codex Bodmer 5 papyrus is the result of an earlier, unintelligent
abridgement.[71] As one approaches the end of the Protevangelium of
James, the differences between the earlier and Middle Age transmissions manifest themselves so prominently that the text can only be
edited according to its respective recensions.

5. On comparing the average transmission quality of the *Shepherd of Hermas*
with the corresponding values of the New Testament, we find that both
the early transmission of the New Testament as well as the more timely
advanced Byzantine transmission achieve significantly better values. In
other words: the transmission stability of the *Shepherd of Hermas* reaches
at best values that compare to values achieved by New Testament manuscripts that have been produced by negligent and careless scribes (graphs
6.2 and 6.3). For the New Testament transmission, relatively poor values
result, for example, from a comparison between $\mathfrak{P}^{45}$ and the Byzantine
text, or between $\mathfrak{P}^{75}$ and Codex D (for Codex D see further remarks below).

   Unlike the manuscripts of the *Shepherd of Hermas*, the New Testament manuscripts reveal a clearly identifiable development thrust: the
formation of the Byzantine text. The stability gradient between the
early and Byzantine text was fixed to some extent: it was primarily created in the fourth century, further refined between the fifth and ninth
centuries, and reinforced beyond the ninth century. Seen from this
perspective, the Byzantine transmission is truly a jackpot in history:
despite the creeping in of certain new readings into the text during
the fourth to the ninth centuries, the text was transmitted with large
stability into the medieval period (and in some cases the old text too,
for example, minuscule 1739). Table 6.1 indicates this in that the Byzantine transmission does not orientate itself toward the "free" text of
the early papyri but toward the manuscripts with "strict" text.

   Therefore, and in light of both the restrictions confronting
early scribal activity, as well as the controlled Byzantine phase of

transmission, the entire transmission of the New Testament has produced a very stable text. We are truly indebted to the proto-orthodox and orthodox scribes of the New Testament for the text we have today. The transmission of the *Shepherd of Hermas*, which occurred parallel to that of the New Testament, illustrates very clearly the consequence of sloppy transmission, especially in the early period: "The text of Hermas is probably far from good: the evidence of the papyri shows that neither ℵ nor A is completely trustworthy,"[72] even though the meaning of the text as a whole hardly changed, as both Bonner's ("diverse scribes introduced many slight changes, rarely, if ever, seriously modifying the thought and purpose of the author"[73]) and Milne and Skeat's ("varies in small details but apparently not in substance"[74]) statements substantiate. Hilhorst similarly remarks: "These differences are for the most part insignificant: morphological variations, little changes in word order, additions or suppressions of particles, articles, prepositions, personal pronouns."[75]

After a comparison of the textual transmission of the *Shepherd of Hermas* with other postapostolic writings, Ehrman concludes that these writings were altered by the scribes in the course of their transmission "probably about the same degree as were the writings of scripture. When these books *were* copied, however, they were subject to the same kinds of textual corruption that one finds attested among the manuscripts of the New Testament. They were accidentally altered on occasion by careless, tired, or inept scribes to probably about the same degree as were the writings of Scripture. And they were intentionally changed by scribes in light of their own historical, theological, and social contexts. [. . .] In short, the factors that affected the transmission of the texts of the New Testament played a similar role in the transmission of the early proto-orthodox writings that came to be excluded from the canon of sacred Scripture."[76] Such generalizations, however, lack substance and do not cope with the analysis carried out above, which portrays the true quality of the New Testament transmission in light of the most widely distributed postapostolic writing, the *Shepherd of Hermas*. The history of the text of the New Testament is not characterized by error and alteration, but far more by a high degree of stability. Despite an abundance of variants, the text of the New Testament is good and reliable.[77]

6. In *The Orthodox Corruption of Scripture*, Ehrman's approach to examining the errors of New Testament transmission is purely qualitative in nature. He refuses to examine these errors quantitatively: "it is pointless [. . .] to calculate the numbers of words of the New Testament affected by such variations [. . .] the importance of theologically oriented variations, on the other hand, far outweighs their actual numerical count."[78] Ehrman's method of emphasizing variants that he believes belong to the category of "orthodox corruptions" is to some degree understandable. However, one cannot capsize the idea of quantitative analysis as casually as Ehrman does. It is also very questionable whether the significance of dogmatically motivated variants "far outweighs their actual numerical count." On closer examination, many of Ehrman's so-called orthodox corruptions, such as Mark 1:1-2; Luke 2:33; John 1:18, 7:8; 1 Timothy 3:16, turn out to be trivial contextual adaptions—adaptions, for instance, geared toward the needs of the audience at church. This was ultimately the motivation for copying manuscripts—not for the defence of heretical opinions and views.[79] It is truly unfortunate that Ehrman is, on one hand, unwilling to accept the scientific method of quantitative analysis out of fear that his ideas of "orthodox corruptions" could be torpedoed, yet, on the other hand, is willing to apply this technique to the transmission of the New Testament text as long as the results portray the transmission in a bad light: "We have only error-ridden copies, and the vast majority of these are centuries removed from the originals and different from them, evidently, in thousands of ways."[80] Neither is the first point convincing (the dogmatic alterations are by no means as significant as Ehrman suggests; some of them, such as Matthew 20:30 and 26:39, are merely scribal errors) nor the last one (the transmission of the New Testament is not characterized by error-ridden copies containing thousands of deviations from the original).

Besides, most of the dogmatically motivated variants known of come from manuscripts that descended from a less precise ancillary line or from manuscripts whose scribes did not impose upon themselves the necessary discipline required for work of such magnitude and significance.[81] For instance, the copying habits of the scribe of the D-text can be described as follows: every manuscript of the D-text adopted as a whole the prevalent "Western" text, modified, however—

each individually, though in line with "Western" editorial techniques (that exceeded greatly the style of the composer at the time)—beyond the existing *Vorlage*.[82] Scribal meticulousness comparable to that of the transmission line $\mathfrak{P}^{75}$–B cannot be identified between the third and fifth centuries among those manuscripts that belong in a broad sense to the D-text ($\mathfrak{P}^{38}$, $\mathfrak{P}^{48}$, 0171, $\mathfrak{P}^{69}$). Even the minuscules (614, 2412) that lag behind the actual D-text confirm this.[83] If we harbor low expectations with respect to the quality of the text of the early papyri belonging in a broad sense to the D-text, then this is far more the case with its prominent end product, the Codex Bezae Cantabrigiensis.

And exactly for these reasons do the peculiar D-readings in most cases belong to those readings that have been discarded. Even the first chapter of Mark contains a relatively large number of variants. With 706 words (Nestle-Aland 27), Codex D contains 106 error units and achieves a text stability of merely 84.9 percent, whereby the Byzantine text as compared to Nestle-Aland 27 achieves a text stability of 89.5 percent (not considering the *euthys–eutheōs* (εὐθύζ–εὐθέωζ) substitutions). The one and only dogmatically motivated alteration in the Byzantine text is located in Mark 1:2. One ascribed the quotation in this verse not only to Isaiah, but to the "prophets" as well, overseeing, however, the fact that Mark quoted Exodus 23:20 as well; Malachi 3:1, on the other hand, contributes only minimally to the entire quotation. The D-text, however, goes beyond this type of alteration and frequently uses terminology to reinforce expressions, such as paraphrasing terminology found in Mark 1:26-31 and 34. If we use Acts 2 (824 words according to Nestle-Aland 27) as an additional example, then the Byzantine text, containing 63 error units, achieves a textual stability of 92.3 percent. Codex D, on the other hand, containing 122 error units, achieves a textual stability of 85.2 percent, or a textual lability twice as high. Hence, the textual stability of Codex D achieves equally low values as the transmission of the *Shepherd of Hermas*.

The quality of the alterations contained within the Codex Bezae is certainly of a different nature: whereas the variants of the *Shepherd of Hermas* very often meander uncontrollably in numerous directions, contain frequent transpositions, substitutions, and few indications of dogmatically motivated changes, the variants of Codex Bezae, on the other hand (especially as observed in the book of Acts), are well known for their frequent usage of augmented paraphrases and harmonized abridgement, as well as anti-Jewish,[84] pro-Roman,[85] and socially motivated tendencies.[86] The text of the *Shepherd of Hermas* shows us what a transmission of the New Testament could have looked like if less care had been applied in copying. Negligible, dogmatically motivated influence crept in and many transpositions arose.[87] In contrast, the D-text shows us what the transmission of the New Testament would look like if strong paraphrasing, accompanied by occasional dogmatic inclinations, were at work. The scribes of the early papyri found in Egypt (table 6.1) did not always transmit the text word by word. They did, nevertheless, hand down the books of the New Testament with a high stability, quite unlike the transmission of the D-text or the *Shepherd of Hermas*. A further stability gradient, commencing from the early text, developed between the fourth and fifth centuries. This occurred as a result of the appearance of related Byzantine readings, which in turn led to the formation of the early Byzantine text itself. Due to a meticulous transmission, however, the scribes of the early and subsequent Byzantine text were able to rapidly fixate the stability gradient and thereby transmit the text almost unchanged into the medieval period.

Trivial dogmatic alterations appear naturally in the best manuscripts as well, for example in $\mathfrak{P}^{75}$. The changes in these instances (e.g., Jn. 10:7), however, are sometimes unique: the scribe tried to place more emphasis on the style of the author rather than introducing his own preconceived notions of the text.[88] Similarly, certain peculiar readings of the Codex Vaticanus appear to be more "markian" than Mark's text itself.[89] As recently pointed out by Barbara Aland, the scribe of the early and relatively unreliable $\mathfrak{P}^{66}$ consciously produced an aspect of referencing, as can be observed with some of his singular readings, whether during the course of his own familiarization with the text or in refering the reader of his text to parallel verses (within the text of John). He was obviously confident though that his readers would understand the meaning of these references."[90]

Westcott and Hort estimated that around 0.1 percent of the variants of the New Testament impact on the meaning of the text.[91] One speaks today of between 150,000 and 250,000,[92] or occasionally 400,000 variants of the New Testament. This number represents the sum total of variants found in all analyzed manuscripts. Even in light of the numerous findings in ancient times and assuming that some 0.2 percent of the New Testament variants were categorized as exhibiting "substantial variation," then what we see, first and foremost, is that this relatively low number of (at least in some cases) dogmatically motivated variants is contained in hundreds and thousands of manuscripts (including the old translations) and not merely in *one* specific manuscript. Most of these, however, can be discarded as secondary as soon as text critical methods are applied. Why should passages such as Mark 1:1—2:41, 16:9-20; Luke 2:27, 33, 41, 43, 48; John 1:18, 7:8; Romans 8:28; 1 Corinthians 6:26; 1 Timothy 3:16, or even obsolete discussions concerning the Comma Johanneum (1 Jn. 5:9), jeopardize the text critical reconstruction of the source text of transmission? The low quantity (and in most cases low quality) of these alterations shows us, however, that the New Testament was excellently transmitted (with scrupulous avoidance of conscious interference). Besides, a general tendency to falsify early manuscripts for dogmatic reasons cannot be observed; sporadic appearance as such occurs here and there and can—but must not—be interpreted as intentional "cosmetic improvement."[93]

After K. W. Clark remarked (as others before and after him as well) that there are certainly some dogmatically motivated variants in the New Testament, he concluded his observation with the words "When all such points of textual variation are considered together it is clear that they comprise a substantial body of critical issues which only textual criticism can resolve."[94] Having said that though, the words "substantial body" are to be understood in a relative sense (Clark presented only a handful of such variants from the Pauline letters), and the challenge remains to deal with such variants appropriately (the correlation between the variants and the text of the New Testament), whether they are seen as (proto) orthodox or having other motivations behind them. Accordingly, the variants are then either included or excluded from the text.

Where confidence once existed with respect to the accuracy of New Testament transmission, an unfortunate development toward distrust appears to be gaining momentum. According to E. J. Epp, the New Testament contains "myriad variation units, with their innumerable competing readings and conceptions, as well as the theological motivations that are evident in so many."[95] If an average of 7 percent corresponds to deviation in the text, whereof only a fraction of these deviations alter the essence thereof (a fraction of these, however, being theologically motivated and these mostly in favor and not against the meaning of the text), then do these percentages—"myriad variation units, with their innumerable competing readings and conceptions"— force us to abandon the reconstruction of the earliest attainable text of the New Testament? It can certainly be said that the reconstruction of the "original Greek" on a formal level (extending to the smallest orthographic and morphological units) remains a phantom, as clear definitions continue to elude us (the following may apply: "the term 'original text' has exploded into a complex and highly unmanageable multivalent entity").[96] Whereby controversial variants (independent of the discussions surrounding them) that could possibly be seen as belonging to the "original Greek" would only be able to alter the overall picture of the New Testament with great difficulty. We focus primarily on the deviations in the manuscripts and forget amidst the variants the commonality between the transmissions.[97] It was and is the great goal of textual criticism to know how the New Testament was read in its original form. "Even though in many crucial questions this desire will perhaps never be gratified [. . .], yet it is worthwhile to continue with all available means."[98]

The quotation above from Clark concludes with this noteworthy imperative: "Therefore, it is the great responsibility of textual criticism to refine the New Testament text toward an ever increasing purity. It must lay the foundation on which alone doctrinal interpretation of the New Testament may be soundly based."[99]

7

Textual Criticism and Textual Confidence: How Reliable Is Scripture?

Craig A. Evans

B oiled down, there are two basic questions that relate to the issue of the reliability of Scripture. First, we must ask how faithful the manuscript tradition is. That is, do the manuscripts we possess provide us with a very close approximation of the original writings? We need not press for exact correspondence, in some sort of mathematical sense. We simply want to know if, for example, our copies of Romans in Greek are close enough to what Paul actually dictated to Tertius (cf. Rom. 16:22), so that we might have confidence that we truly know what Paul originally said. Secondly, we must ask how accurate the originals themselves are, that is, how accurate were the biblical writers, when they assert facts (that is, so-and-so said this, or so-and-so did that) and teach (that is, "No one is justified by works of law"; or "all have sinned").

A superficial review of the data of Scripture could lead one to declare that the scribes who transmitted biblical literature and the authors who wrote it in fact fail both tests. That is, the surviving manuscripts are filled with errors, and so we should suppose that we really do not know what Paul or Jesus originally said, or that Paul and Jesus were not themselves always accurate. Let's consider a few examples that some critics could and sometimes do cite as significant manuscript errors, that is, errors in the copying of Scripture, and significant factual errors, that is, errors on the part of the biblical characters (such as Jesus) or writers (such as Paul).

SIGNIFICANT ERRORS IN MANUSCRIPT TRANSMISSION

Despite their care and respect for Christianity's sacred literature, scribes did make many errors in making new copies of Scripture. Most of these errors are very minor, but some of them are quite significant. I will look at three very obvious examples and three others that are far from certain.

Perhaps the best-known glitch in the transmission of the Greek New Testament concerns the ending of the Gospel of Mark, which narrates the appearances of the risen Jesus to Mary and the eleven disciples. When Erasmus published his first edition of the Greek New Testament in 1516 and when the English translation authorized by King James of England appeared in 1611, no one doubted the originality of the last twelve verses of Mark, known as the "Long Ending," that is, Mark 16:9-20. But when major and much older manuscripts of the Greek New Testament were discovered in the nineteenth and twentieth centuries, the picture changed. The last twelve verses of Mark are not present in the great codices (or books) Sinaiticus and Vaticanus, copies of the Greek Old and New Testaments dating to the first half of the fourth century. Other Greek manuscripts and translations also omit these verses. Still other manuscripts included the verses, but with marks indicating uncertainty. Some manuscripts include a different, shorter ending (and, of course, some manuscripts include both the Long Ending and the Short Ending). Examination of the vocabulary and grammar of Mark 16:9-20 has confirmed in the minds of many grammarians, textual critics, and commentators that these verses were not in fact part of Mark's original text. Authentic Mark ends, it seems, with frightened women who tell no one what they had seen, "for they were afraid" (v. 8).[1]

If it is agreed that Mark 16:9-20 is not the original ending of Mark's story, what have we lost? Very little, and in a certain sense, perhaps nothing. After all, the Gospels of Matthew, Luke, and John narrate several appearances of the risen Jesus to Mary and the disciples. Paul also provides an early catalogue of resurrection appearances (1 Cor. 15:5-8). Moreover, some scholars suspect that Mark's original ending is imbedded in the resurrection narrative found in the Gospel of Matthew. So, we may be left with the mystery of the missing ending (Did Mark end at 16:8? If not, what happened to the ending?), but, so far as the other Gospels are concerned, there is no doubt with respect to why the tomb of Jesus was found empty and what transpired after.

We have another case where a passage comprising twelve verses turns out not to be part of the original edition of a Gospel. This time it is the Gospel of John. Once again, when the older Greek manuscripts came to light—long after the publication of the King James—a well-known passage was missing.

The famous passage of the woman caught in the act of adultery, John 7:53—8:11, is not found in two old papyrus manuscripts dating to the beginning of the third century, nor in the two fourth-century codices already mentioned (Sinaiticus and Vaticanus), nor in many other manuscripts, versions, and quotations by fathers of the church. Moreover, some manuscripts place these twelve verses somewhere else in John 7, other manuscripts include only parts of the passage, some include it but with marks indicating doubt, and a few manuscripts place the passage at the end of the Gospel of Luke! Analysis of the vocabulary and the literary context of John 7–8 confirms the manuscript evidence: the passage was not penned by the author of the Gospel of John.[2]

If John 7:53—8:11 was not an original part of the Gospel of John, have we lost something important? No, I really don't think so. The depiction of Jesus in this passage is entirely consistent with what we see in other Gospel stories, whose textual authenticity is not in doubt. For example, one thinks of the sinful woman defended by Jesus in Luke 7:36-50. In fact, John 7:53—8:11 is so consistent with the way Jesus regarded sinners and the way he responded to those who judged harshly, that many scholars suspect the story is historically authentic, even if textually uncertain.[3] Accordingly, what we have lost is the original context and setting of the story, but not an insight into the thinking and action of Jesus otherwise unknown to us.

The Gospel of Luke presents us with another interesting example. In this case, we have an embellishment of a story. The Synoptic Gospels narrate the story of Jesus' anguished prayer in a place on the Mount of Olives called Gethsemane (Mt. 26:36-46; Mk. 14:32-42; Lk. 22:39-46). But in some manuscripts, the story in Luke provides two very interesting details. We are told that while Jesus was praying an angel from heaven appeared, strengthening him (v. 43), and that Jesus prayed so fervently that sweat fell from his face like drops of blood (v. 44). These two verses are not found in our oldest authorities. These include a papyrus manuscript that dates to the third century, the fourth century books already mentioned, and several other manuscripts. However, these interesting details were popular and incorporated into the story at least as early as the fifth century and became pretty standard.[4]

It is probable that these verses were added to the story to enhance the drama and agony of the prayer in Gethsemane. Moreover, early Christians were interested in angels and heavenly actions. This could be what lies behind the mention of the angel who periodically agitated the water in the pool of Beth-zatha (Jn. 5:1-9). Verses 3b-4 (". . . waiting for the moving of the water, for an angel went down at a certain season into the pool, and troubled the water . . .") are not found in our oldest manuscripts. Verse 4, along with the last part of v. 3, has been added to the story to explain the significance of the crippled man's reference to the healing power of the pool's "troubled water" (v. 7).[5]

There are other significant passages where some suspect a scribal addition or error, but the manuscript evidence is either inconclusive or nonexistent. An example of inconclusive manuscript evidence is seen in the case of Rom. 5:1, where according to some manuscripts Paul says: "Therefore, since we are justified by faith, *we have* peace with God through our Lord Jesus Christ" (emphasis added). But according to other manuscripts Paul says: "Therefore, since we are justified by faith, *let us have* peace with God through our Lord Jesus Christ" (emphasis added). These two readings differ significantly and it all boils down to one letter in one word: Either Paul meant to say "we have" (Greek: *echomen*) or "let us have" (*echōmen*). Did he mean to use the letter omicron (that is, the short *o* in *echomen*) or the letter omega (that is, the long *o* in *echômen*)? If he intended to use the omicron, he meant to say "we have," that is, "we have peace with God." But if he intended to use the omega, he meant to say "let us have," that is, "let us have peace with God."

Most textual critics and commentators think Paul meant to say "we have peace with God."[6] This makes the most sense in the light of his argument in Romans 4–5. Because believers are justified by faith (in the same way Abraham was justified by faith) they have peace with God. However, the Greek manuscripts themselves actually favor the "let us have peace with God" reading. In this particular case it seems that the better attested reading is in all probability not the original reading, or at least the reading the apostle (who was dictating to a scribe named Tertius; cf. Rom. 16:22) intended. So even though the letter omega has stronger textual support, we suspect the letter omicron was the original, intended letter. If this isn't confusing enough, it has even been suggested that Tertius the scribe misheard Paul, and wrote the wrong form of the verb. If this is what happened, then we have an example where a scribal error found its way into the original manuscript itself!

We also have passages of Scripture where interpreters think a couple of verses have been added to the text, but we are not in possession of clear manuscript evidence (at least not yet) that supports this suspicion. One of these passages is found in 1 Corinthians 14, where Paul is instructing the Corinthian Christians in proper worship. He urges the Corinthians to do all things decently and in order (v. 40). After all, "God is not a God of confusion but of peace" (v. 33a). Then quite abruptly, the text reads: "As in all the churches of the saints, the women should keep silence in the churches. For they are not permitted to speak . . ." (vv. 33b-36). At v. 37 the apostle returns to the theme expressed in vv. 26-33a, when he challenges his readers: "If any one thinks that he is a prophet, or spiritual, he should acknowledge that what I am writing to you is a command of the Lord."

Many interpreters suspect that vv. 33b-36 constitute a scribal interpolation, perhaps inspired by the similar passage in 1 Timothy 2:11-15 ("Let a woman learn in silence . . . I am not permitting a woman to teach or to have authority over men . . ."). Interpreters think this because these verses interrupt the flow of thought in

1 Corinthians 14:26-40 and stand in tension with Paul's instruction earlier in the letter, where he says women who pray or prophesy in church should cover their heads (1 Cor. 11:5). How are women to pray and prophesy and at the same time keep silent? Accordingly, interpreters suspect vv. 33b-36 are not original to the letter. This suspicion is strengthened when it is observed that some old manuscripts (e.g., Sinaiticus) place marks around these verses, probably indicating doubt, and other manuscripts place the verses after v. 40, the last verse in the chapter, perhaps indicating doubts about whether the passage really belongs in 1 Corinthians 14.[7]

Finally, we may consider the very strange narrative of the dead saints, who with Jesus are raised up. According to Mark, when Jesus died the curtain of the temple was torn and the centurion confessed that Jesus was truly the Son of God (Mk. 15:38-39). The narrative in Matthew has additional details. Not only was the temple curtain torn, "the earth shook, and the rocks were split; the tombs also were opened, and many bodies of the saints who had fallen asleep were raised, and coming out of the tombs after his resurrection they went into the holy city and appeared to many" (Mt. 27:51b-53). The detail of the earth shaking and the rocks splitting is probably Matthew's addition to the narrative. But what about the rest of what we read in vv. 52-53? Were dead saints (or holy ones) also raised up that first Easter?

Although we have no manuscript evidence of which I am aware that suggests that these verses are not part of Matthew's original narrative, I suspect that they, too, were added to the text by an early Christian scribe, perhaps inspired by the Greek version of Zechariah 14:4-5 ("the mount of Olives shall be split . . . in the days of the earthquake . . . the Lord my God will come and all the holy ones with him"). I say this because of the temporal awkwardness introduced by the curious incident of the resurrected saints. We are told that when earth shook and the rocks split, the tombs were opened and the sleeping saints were raised (v. 52). But that was Friday afternoon, the day that Jesus died. These awakened saints do not actually leave their tombs and enter Jerusalem (the holy city) until "after (Jesus') resurrection" (v. 53).[8]

This is puzzling. The sleeping saints were raised up Friday, the day Jesus died (and so preceded Jesus in his resurrection), but loitered in their tombs until Sunday (so as not to precede Jesus?). One must also wonder how anyone would know that these raised persons were in fact deceased saints. Would they not simply be taken for residents of Jerusalem or visiting pilgrims for the Passover? And, moreover, whatever became of them? Did they return to their tombs?[9] The Matthean evangelist tends to tie up loose ends and to simplify chronological difficulties (as seen, for example, in comparison with Mark's accounts of the entry into Jerusalem, the cursing of the fig tree, the return to the city, the demonstration in the temple precincts, and the discovery of the withered fig tree). The addition of the story of the raised saints is chronologically clumsy and in my opinion does not reflect the literary skill of the Matthean evangelist. It may well be a scribal gloss that attempts to enhance the story of the resurrection. Should we someday recover a second century Greek manuscript that preserves the latter part of Matthew 27, I shall not be surprised if vv. 52-53 are not present.

The examples that have been reviewed are among the most significant textual errors and uncertainties that exist in the manuscripts of the Greek New Testament. Others could be cited (for example, the reworked 1 Jn. 5:7-8),[10] but the ones treated above suffice to make the point: errors, deliberate and accidental, crept into the manuscripts over the course of time. Most of them have been recognized and the text has been corrected, bringing it much closer to the form of the original writings. Further manuscript discoveries may well lead to further correction. But no discovery yet has called into question significant New Testament teaching. Anyone who claims that the Greek manuscript tradition is so riddled with errors that we really don't know what the New Testament writers actually wrote is sadly misinformed.

SIGNIFICANT FACTUAL ERRORS IN THE NEW TESTAMENT WRITINGS

Readers may well agree with me up to this point, acknowledging that we really can know from the manuscripts that we indeed have a text that is very, very close to the original wording of the New Testament writings. But are all of the claims and statements of the New Testament accurate? What about alleged mistakes on the part of the writers or on the part of Jesus whom the evangelists quote? Are there not at least a few demonstrable errors of this nature? Let us consider a few candidates.

Jesus' reference to the actions of David and his men "when Abiathar was high priest" (Mk. 2:23-28) has been recently cited as an example of a factual error, either on the part of the evangelist Mark or on the part of Jesus himself. According to the story in 1 Sam. 21: 1-6, Ahimelech, father of Abiathar, was high priest when David and his men made their appeal for assistance. Only after the later death of Ahimelech did Abiathar succeed his father as high priest. Perhaps sensing the difficulty, Matthew and Luke abridge Jesus' saying, omitting reference to the high priest (Mt. 12:3-4, Lk. 6:3-4). Indeed, some manuscripts of Mark also omit the phrase. So, was Jesus (or Mark) mistaken? Is the reference to "Abiathar the high priest" (Mk. 2:26) a factual error?[11]

The solution to the problem lies in the recognition that there seem to have been two traditions with regard to the priestly figures Ahimelech and Abiathar. The better-known tradition narrates Abiathar as the son of Ahimelech. Accordingly, the latter is the priest who gave the bread to David and his men. This is the tradition we find in 1 Samuel 21–22. But there is also a lesser-known tradition, in which Ahimelech (or Abimelech in some manuscripts) is said to be the son of Abiathar, who survives and serves David alongside Zadok (2 Sam. 8:17, 1 Chron. 18:16, 24:3-31; contrast 1 Kings 4:4, where it is Abiathar who serves alongside Zadok). The saying attributed to Jesus apparently reflects the lesser-known tradition.[12]

This example in the Gospel of Mark is not unusual. Parallel versions of Old Testament stories are attested not only in Old Testament Scripture itself, but in some of the writings produced in the two centuries leading up to the time of Jesus. Indeed, thanks to the Dead Sea Scrolls, we now know that there were as many as four versions of Hebrew Scripture circulating among the Jewish people prior to the great rebellion against Rome (c.e. 66–70). There are also several scrolls that paraphrase this or that part of Scripture. When Jesus referred to Abiathar as high priest, he cited one of the versions of this part of ancient Israel's history. The evangelists Matthew and Luke, both familiar with the better-known version, chose to delete this detail. After all, who the high priest was at the time does not impact the point of the story. With or without the name of the high priest, the point Jesus makes is quite clear and right on target.

Some critics allege that Jesus committed an error of botany when he referred to the mustard seed as "the smallest of all the seeds on earth" (Mk. 4:31). It is pointed out that there are other seeds that are in fact smaller than the tiny mustard seed.[13] But to raise this objection is to fail to appreciate the proverbial quality of the saying, as seen in various sayings of the Rabbis (for example, *m. Nid.* 5:2 "even as little as a grain of mustard seed"; *y. Pea* 7.4 "I had a mustard plant . . . as (high) as a fig tree"; *b. Ber.* 31a "they are so strict that if they see a drop of blood no bigger than a mustard seed they wait seven days").[14] The mustard seed is often cited, for its tiny size contrasts dramatically with the great size of the mustard plant, which becomes a shrub and if allowed, becomes a small tree, large enough for birds to build nests. Had Jesus appealed to a seed that in scientific terms was truly the smallest seed or spore on earth, his hearers would have had no idea what he was talking about. His appeal to the tiny mustard seed was understood and readily acknowledged as the smallest seed with which the people of his time and place were familiar. Again Jesus has communicated clearly, invoking images and realities which were known to his contemporaries.

Sometimes discrepancies are observed when trying to harmonize parallel Gospel stories. According to Mark 11 Jesus entered Jerusalem and then after viewing things in the temple precincts he left the city. The next day he returned and demonstrated in the precincts. But according to Matthew 21 Jesus entered the city and demonstrated in the temple precincts the same day. In telling the story this way the Matthean evangelist has smoothed out Mark's disjointed narrative. We see this again in the story of the cursed fig tree. According to Mark 11:12-21, the fruitless tree is cursed and not until the next morning is it discovered withered. But in Matthew 21:19-20 Jesus curses the tree and it is withered "at once." To be sure, these are genuine chronological discrepancies, but in themselves they do not cast doubt on the event.

Comparison with the fourth Gospel reveals an even more dramatic chronological discrepancy. According to Mark (cf. Mk. 11:15-19), followed by Matthew and Luke (cf. Mt. 21:12-13; Lk. 19:45-48), Jesus demonstrates in the temple precincts at the *end* of his ministry, only days before he is arrested. But according to John (cf. Jn. 2:13-21), Jesus demonstrates in the temple in what seems to be the *beginning* of his ministry. Moreover, the Synoptic Gospels give us the impression that the Last Supper was the Passover meal (Mt. 26:17-29; Mk. 14:12-25; Lk. 22:7-23), but John's Gospel makes it clear that the Last Supper was eaten the day *before* the Passover (Jn. 13:21-30, 18:28, 19:14, 31, 42). According to John, after handing Jesus over to Pilate, the ruling priests hurry home to prepare for the evening Passover meal (Jn. 18:28).

Some critics have cited discrepancies such as these as evidence of factual errors in the Gospel narratives. These are discrepancies to be sure, but discrepancies do not mean that the events in question did not happen, any more than discrepancies in almost all of recorded history does not mean that we are not in position to know what happened. The Gospel writers agree that Jesus demonstrated in the temple precincts, that he celebrated a final meal with his closest followers, and that he did many other things. What is not always known is exactly when these events took place.[15] But not knowing exactly when and in what order does not mean we can have no confidence in the reliability of Scripture.

We have another interesting example from Paul, in his own words. The apostle and founder of the church at Corinth is exasperated with the divisions and party loyalties that plague the community. Paul is particularly annoyed that the church is divided along the lines of loyalties to specific apostolic figures, including himself. With reference to this issue Paul says in 1 Corinthians 1:14-16:

> 14 I am thankful that I baptized none of you except Crispus and Gaius; 15 lest any one should say that you were baptized in my name. 16 (I did baptize also the household of Stephanas. Beyond that, I do not know whether I baptized any one else.)

Paul is relieved that he had not baptized a large number of the Corinthian converts. Given what is going on in the church, those baptized by Paul would probably have formed a faction of Paulinists. So, Paul begins by saying that he is grateful that he only baptized Crispus and Gaius (v. 14). By the time he finishes his sentence (v. 15), he remembers that he also baptized the household of Stephanas (v. 16a). (Perhaps one of his colleagues reminded him?) Thus, Paul has corrected what he said in v. 14. As Paul gives the matter more thought, he realizes that he is not sure. Had he baptized others? His memory has failed him. So he says, "Beyond that, I do not know whether I baptized any one else" (v. 16b).

The truthfulness of the point that Paul is making—that believers belong to Christ and not to one celebrated Christian leader or another—is quite clear, however many people the apostle baptized. The fallibility of Paul's memory does not nullify the truthfulness and validity of what he has said.

WHAT ARE THE REAL ISSUES?

Christians are keenly interested in the integrity and accuracy of sacred Scripture; and rightly so. If the New Testament writings do not describe historical events accurately, or if the writers do not really know what they are talking about, or if the scribes who made the copies of these writings did such a poor job that what the original writings said is hopelessly garbled, then Christians have a serious problem. Ultimately Christian faith is much more than platitudes and happy thoughts. It centers on a set of very special events, summed up by what God achieved in Christ. These events are historical events. They have theological meaning to be sure, but they are historical events nonetheless.

Did Jesus do and say the things that the evangelists say he did? Do we have good reason for having confidence in their writings? In my view there is every reason to respond to these questions in the affirmative. There is credible, early testimony to the effect that the material in the four New Testament Gospels reaches back to the original followers of Jesus and that this material circulated and took shape during the lifetimes of eyewitnesses. There is no good reason to think that the contents of the New Testament Gospels lack a solid historical basis.

Do we have apostolic, first-hand eyewitness tradition? Again, the answer is yes. Not everything in the New Testament is first-hand, but an important core is, a core that reaches back to Jesus, what he taught and what he did.[16] Later Gospels and Gospel-like writings supplemented and altered this early tradition, but these later writings reflect ideas that emerged in the second century and beyond, not the ideas articulated by Jesus and passed on by his disciples.

And finally, has this eyewitness, apostolic tradition been accurately preserved? Again, I think the answer is yes. With respect to the words and deeds of Jesus, we have four Gospels and at least two independent literary streams within these writings. The multiplicity of witnesses safeguards against the danger of idiosyncratic tradition emerging and gaining traction. The antiquity of the tradition of the four New Testament Gospels supports this contention. Idiosyncratic tradition would have been recognized for what it is by those who had walked with Jesus and had seen his deeds and heard his words.

Given the evidence, we have every reason to have confidence in the text of Scripture. This does not mean that we possess 100 percent certainty that we have the exact wording in every case, but we have good reason to believe that what we have preserved in the several hundred manuscripts of the first millennium is the text that the writers of Scripture penned.

8

Authors or Preservers? Scribal Culture and the Theology of Scriptures

Sylvie T. Raquel

In *Misquoting Jesus,* Bart Ehrman claimed that the current New Testament has been the object of so many recensional activities that it cannot be trusted as a sacred text. He gauges the "invalidity" of the text on textual evidences, a line of study that led him to recant his former fundamentalist approach to the writing. Ehrman explained how, following a "born again experience,"[1] he engaged in and committed to the world of biblical literature through the lens of the inerrancy culture, although he never explained how the text personally touched and transformed him. He continued that path until another enlightenment moment (a reverse born again experience, so to speak) prompted by his own research on Markan textual variants: the alteration of the text proved to him the unauthentication of the message. I also have studied New Testament textual criticism and, by contrast with Ehrman, have found confirmation about the validity of the text; it enhanced my knowledge of the God I encountered years ago. How could two individuals such as Ehrman and I, both trained as New Testament textual critics, come to such different conclusions? I believe

174 THE RELIABILITY OF THE NEW TESTAMENT

that his philosophical presuppositions have led him down a different path than mine. At the risk of oversimplifying, Ehrman focuses on the 10 percent empty glass while I focus of the 90 percent full glass. These presuppositions have caused him to misjudge the scope of scribal contributions.

Ehrman has built his case on the following reasoning: if God existed and wanted to convey a written message to his people, he would produce a God-given, God-inscribed, immutable text. Ehrman confuses the means with the end. Taking the Scriptures as the end of knowing God personally borders on bibliolatry. The God of the Bible did not convey his message solely in a written form but fully disclosed himself in the person and ministry of Jesus Christ. God first revealed himself personally and always used human mediums, as imperfect as they were, to propagate his message. Ehrman assumes that early Christian scribes espoused his own conception of sacred writing. He argues that their careless alterations or theological fabrication occurred either because they did not honor the text as sacred or because they plainly invented its content. Thereby he imposes on the New Testament a modern point of view on the theology of Scriptures that early Christian scribes did not share and thus criticizes them inappropriately. He does not take into consideration that they understood the original medium of revelation to be personal, dynamic, and living. How did early scribes really understand the nature of the biblical text? Did their handling of the manuscripts reflect their theology of Scriptures? As a result, how should one think of Scriptures? I propose to investigate these questions and continue the conversation Dale Martin initiated[2] by exploring scribal attitude toward a historical theology of Scriptures.

THE CASE FOR CAUTIOUS SCRIBES

Even if Christianity rapidly moved from a Palestinian-Judaic to a Greco-Roman milieu, it is unfair to think that early Christian scribes always acted toward their writings in a typical Greco-Roman manner and only reflected the ideology and values of the Greco-Roman world. Certainly early Christian scribes were the product of their cultural (mostly Gentile) milieu, but they also inherited their understanding of Scripture from a Jewish perspective. After all, grounded in Judaism,

Christianity immediately claimed the Jewish Scriptures as its own set of sacred texts and, unlike other religions of the time, relied heavily on those texts to gain knowledge of God and discern his will. The fact that Christianity embraced, reproduced, and disseminated its own early writings so quickly, although imperfectly, proves that it mirrored Judaism in becoming a religion of the book. Surely early Christian literature "aimed to be serviceable to Christian communities, mainly in communication, instruction, documentation, edification, evangelism, and organization,"[3] but its practical value rested on the content of its message which promoted its continuity with Jewish monotheistic views, ethics, and values. Paul's letters to the Corinthians, for example, became essential not only because they helped bring order to a chaotic situation, but because they also provided indispensable insights on ecclesiology. Practicality may have been the original force behind the work of early Christian scribes, but it was not dissociated from orthodoxy. Practicality and orthodoxy converged and coalesced in a symbiotic relationship.

The practicality of the text expressed itself first in the context of early Christian worship. The gatherings reinforced the community's appreciation for its early writings as Christians came together to hear valuable teachings from the founders of the faith. The collective readings replaced personal instruction from the apostles. The first copying of early Christian literature happened in this worship context when churches circulated among themselves the apostolic tradition. Early churches modeled their worship order and style on the synagogue services, which included the reading aloud of sacred texts. Early Christian scribes, whether Gentile or Jewish, were influenced by this reverence to religious books, which motivated them to treat their own writings differently. As Gamble suggested, "we ordinarily bring a consumer attitude to texts and reading. . . . But liturgical reading depends upon another attitude, for the same texts are read over and over again, yet lose none of their value in the process, but rather gain in esteem."[4] Additionally, because copies were rare and expensive, most members, including the copyists, regarded the book or scroll as a special object that deserved care and reverence.[5]

The Oxyrhynchus manuscripts illuminate our understanding of how the books that became canonical received special treatments.

Larry Hurtado lists the following reasons: (1) The use of *nomina sacra* shows the existence of scribal conventions that the community would understand; as he noticed, such conventions by nonprofessional scribes are the more notable; (2) The presence of reading aids—breathing marks, punctuation, spacing—confirms that the manuscripts were meant for public usage; (3) The preference for the codex over the scroll form for noncanonical literature provided an early distinction and classification of Christian writings.[6] The repeated public reading may have led to stylistic improvements, but the most important factor is that the community itself served as a controlled setting that verified the quality of the manuscripts, a sort of *ad hoc* check-up point. The congregation could pinpoint any major deviations to a text because the repeated collective readings had allowed members to memorize most of its content.

In the Greco-Roman world, the transmission of literature resulted from networks of scribes and readers by means of personal acquaintances.[7] As Christian circles came to rely on written documents and grew in Gentile circles, Christian copyists followed the same practice to secure, transcribe, and disseminate copies of biblical documents.[8] Individuals who aspired to acquire written exemplars of the first Christian documents likely belonged to the upper economic classes.[9] They probably owned slave *librarii*[10] who had to perform expertly because the cost of book production was so high that they could not afford to squander precious materials.[11] An unsatisfactory copy meant a waste of money that called for disciplinary action or unemployment.

THE CASE FOR TRAINED AND UNTRAINED SCRIBES

If early Christian scribes perceived sacredness in their writings, why did they demonstrate carelessness or freedom in changing the text? Many scholars have contrasted the fluidity of Christian texts' transmission with the optimal care that Jewish scribes used to handle their Scriptures. However, one cannot in all fairness compare a finished product with a work in progress. Indeed, by the end of the first century, the process of Old Testament canonization had come to completion whereas Christianity was a nascent movement that struggled to affirm its identity. Nevertheless, Christianity being grounded in Judaism, Jewish scribal activities influenced somewhat the work, purpose, and vision of Christian scribes who followed their example in dealing with holy books. Did Jewish scribes always follow strict copying regulations or did they also take liberty to modify the text? In the pre-exilic period, the evidence of scribal activities is scarce because the centrality of corporate worship limited the need for copies of the Law. In the exilic period, alongside the oral tradition, the Jews began to emphasize written records with the archiving of the Law and prophetic utterances. In the post-exilic period, "scribal activity [was] commonly associated with priests and Levites."[12] Following the example of Ezra they functioned as teacher, leader, and priest. According to Old Testament specialists these scribes were the "authors, commentators and transmitters of the Biblical texts."[13] Contrary to Saldarini's view, by "author" I understand redactor and preserver, not creator. As the Qumran community seems to indicate, scribes of priestly background or subordinate to the priests remained as faithful as possible to the text because they were the guardians of the sacred writings.[14] Yet, even the Qumran manuscripts reflect the existence of textual complexions or shades, meaning that the text transmission was not always word-perfect.

Josephus distinguished three types of scribes in first-century Palestinian Judaism: the Temple scribes and the scribes of middle and lower classes.[15] The scribes of priestly or lowest status most likely participated in the original spread of the written record of Jesus' words and deeds. For sure, "the shift from understanding scripture as sacred story to sacred text was long and gradual"[16] and involved a period of textual dynamism. The Temple scribes were probably the copyists who "had an effect on the preservation of prophecy, wisdom writing and the Pentateuch,"[17] therefore were trained to keep accurate records of religious and spiritual works. Thus, scribes of lowest status produced more textual variants, not because they were not committed to a correct work, but because they did not operate in a culture of exactitude. Textual flux did not necessarily mean complete freedom and wild transmission but a semicontrolled context.

These approaches to the copying of spiritual texts persisted in the Gentile community. Christian scribes reflected the socially diverse nature of society, and therefore its corresponding level of literacy. The

10 to 15 percent level of literacy in the Roman Empire comprised all levels from signatureliteracy to semiliteracy to sophisticated erudition.[18] Gamble recognized that "The vast majority of Christians were illiterate, not because they were unique, but precisely because they were in this respect typical members of ancient society [which] operated mainly through oral communication."[19] When Kim Haines-Eitzen agreed with Ehrman that scribes who copied early Christian literature probably "did not have a specific training or extensive experience in copying literary texts,"[20] she did not share stunning information. To find a low concentration of high-level literacy among Christian scribes is a legitimate expectation. Moreover, no proofs of differences between common Greco-Roman copyists and Christian copyists have surfaced. Even if Christian literacy was mainly a grass-roots movement, highly educated Christian scribes also participated in the transmission of the New Testament writings. The problem is that Ehrman classifies the former as incapable copyists[21] and the latter as motivated by ulterior motives in modifying the text. Did Christians really entrust their sacred texts to the hands of incapable or untrustworthy copyists?

THE CASE FOR MODIFICATIONS OF MANUSCRIPTS

Several reasons why poor copying can be found in early New Testament manuscripts have not been sufficiently explored. Untrained and uneducated Christian scribes were responsible mostly for unintentional variants that are easy to discern even for their own sources. In his study of the most extant New Testament papyri, Royse showed that copyists, even as careless as the one of $\mathfrak{P}^{72}$, corrected their own copies, which indicates that they could pinpoint their textual alterations, whether intentional or unintentional.[22] Some of the modifications sprang from a lack of knowledge of the proper language and its nuances. Christian scribes reproduced as well as they could a text which they valued but could not transpose properly. For example, although Greek was the *lingua franca* of the Roman Empire, the same exact language was not spoken in each province. People groups kept their primary languages, cultural identities, writings, social constructs, philosophical approaches, and modes of communication. They adapted the texts to their own native languages, thus creating Greek patois. Scribes who grew up with such vernacular were not purposely careless but simply relied on their regional use of the Greek language.

Some intentional textual changes also depended on the immediate linguistic context. For example, the scribe of $\mathfrak{P}^{47}$ prefers a singular verb with a neuter plural subject.[23] Was it a personal preference or did the grammatical changes fit the idiomatic expressions of his dialect? His transcription may have necessitated this adjustment to make the text more readable or pleasant to the immediate readership. Educational circumstances can also explain some of the existing textual variants. Raffaella Cribiore indicated that students copied maxims for their training.[24] An exemplar may have been used for writing exercises in Christian schooling. If Christian schoolmasters followed the pattern of their contemporary counterparts, they probably used religious texts in lieu of philosophical or poetic works. One can imagine how some students handled their own copies! Moreover, in advanced education, this type of exercise allowed some initiative and originality with longer passages, leading to possible modifications of the tradition.[25]

Literate copyists had the potential to modify ideologically an original copy.[26] Ehrman posited that they performed more of a creative than a conservative task. Yet, Fee indicated that trained copyists aspired to precision and aimed at textual accuracy.[27] As Hurtado postulated, "the copying of early Christian texts in the second century involved emergent scribal conventions that quickly obtained impressive influence, and, at least in some cases and settings, that there was a concern for careful copying."[28] The early church fathers followed that expectation: Irenaeus (c.115–c. 202) expected the most scrupulous accuracy for the copy of texts[29] and Origen (c.185–c. 254) operated in a controlled working environment—a scriptorium—in which supervision and correction took place. Still, "scribes . . . [did] not always act in completely predictable ways."[30] Christian scribes were influenced by Alexandrian and Jewish practices in their concern with preserving the text,[31] but even in their most instrumental roles, they continued to "impose their style, language, and ideas on the text . . . to suit the conventions of the written genre and his interpretations of the oral tradition."[32]

The emergence of schools, libraries, and the growth of a reading public in Hellenism created favorable conditions for the propagation of a culture of literacy.[33] In the second century, Christians embraced this avenue of communication to promote orthodoxy and ecclesiastical unity as a response to nascent heresies and deviant instructions.[34] Early Christian scribes followed the pattern of their time. At the example of Latin as well as Greek historians, they relied on their memories and used information from personal experiences and oral testimony over written materials.[35] However, they cited their sources in a more conservative way than many classical historians.[36] By the second and third centuries, Christians encouraged literacy because the written text had become central for the spread and survival of the faith:[37] some withdrew their children from the Greco-Roman schools for ideological purposes,[38] and others built congregational and individual libraries.[39] At this stage of inscripturation, getting *ipsissima vox* rather than *ipsissima verba* was of overriding importance. Nevertheless, some communities such as one discovered at the Oxyrhynchus site showed evidences of literary activity and scholarly editing.[40]

Scriptorium frameworks developed but they did not necessarily lead to recensional activities as the case of Origen indicates. Origen's interest in "textual criticism" developed when he came in contact with various regional text forms during his travels.[41] According to Eusebius, he used three types of assistants, most likely trained at Ambrose's home with a tutor or a *paedagogus*:[42] tachographs (*tachygraphoi*) or shorthand writers (*bibliographoi*) or writers of books, copyists or scribes, and kalligraphs (*kalligraphai*)—ladies, if you please—or penpersons trained for beautiful writing.[43] It seems plausible that the tachographs wrote first under Origen's dictations, then the copyists multiplied the documents, perhaps putting the writing into good grammatical form, and eventually the kalligraphs provided embellished manuscripts for specific buyers. His shorthand writers required an adequate level of literacy since they recorded the teachings and commentaries their master delivered orally. Assuming that the copyists transcribed the tachographs' notes into a customary written form, they had to display the same level of literacy and scribal competency. Therefore, more than 100 years before the first church council, Origen was careful to cite accurately with the probable use of a control text and instilled in his scribes awareness of some standard of reproduction.

THE CASE FOR INSPIRATION

The fluidity of the Christian tradition and the fact that the oral tradition was still active in the first two or three centuries has disturbed
more than one with regard to inspiration and canonization. Ehrman's
hypothesis for this issue is that trained scribes formulated an "inspiration conspiracy." However, there is a difference between devising
a theory and recognizing something that already exists. I am afraid
Ehrman imposes on the Bible his own perception of authorship. As
Dutch scholar Karel Van Der Toorn writes, "The notion of the author
as an autonomous agent of creation genius is a historical construct. It
is not a fixed truth but was born in early modern times."[44] Applied to
the act of revelation, this notion views God as the sole actor and the
human party as the passive instrument in the act of revelation. Van
Der Toorn explains, "Our concept of the author as an individual is
what underpins our concern with authenticity, originality, and intellectual property. The ancient Near East had little place for such notions.
Authenticity is subordinate to authority and relevant only inasmuch
as it underpins textual authority; originality is subordinate to the cul-
tivation of tradition; and intellectual property is subordinate to the
common stock of cultural forms and values."[45] Early Christian scribes
performed in their cultural milieu and wrote according to the cultural
norms of their time. They did not create the text *ex nihilo* but built
on an original, mostly oral tradition accompanied by a few written
notes, which resulted from the participation of an entire fellowship.
The community, not the individual, imputed authority to a writing.
Even independent scribes were subject to the scrutiny and approval of
the larger group. One may ask the nature of their writings, did early
Christians count the final product as inspired or did they consider the
entire process to be under the guidance of the Holy Spirit?

The early Christians built their theology of Scripture on Judaism.
Although the Jews connected written statements with the knowledge
and will of their God, they did not dismiss the primacy of orality in
the process of revelation and revere a nontextual mode of communication with God.[46] For example, they used the Urim and Thummim
and the words of the prophets to seek His will and favor. Jeremiah 36

provides an interesting insight on the recording process of the prophets' utterances: after King Hezekiah burned Baruch's first copy, Jeremiah dictated once more the message to his scribe who "added few words."[47] These last words are significant because they constitute a blatant admission to authorial and scribal voluntary modifications that did not even need the scrutiny of text critics. Obviously, later Jewish scribes did not find this passage embarrassing or compromising their theology of Scriptures since they kept a record of the event. This passage indicates that, for Jeremiah: (1) the source and content of the message had value, not the writing itself; (2) God's message was not stagnant; and (3) a human medium was never perfect and his work sometimes necessitated corrections. Interestingly, Ezra conferred authority to "the word of Jeremiah" (Ezra 1:1) indicating the authentication of the human medium.

Following the tradition of the prophets, early Christians relied on the oral dissemination of their story. "So long as there [was] no industrial production of written texts, the spoken word [remained] the main channel of communication."[48] In the same spirit, "Paul claimed no more authority for his letters than for his oral teaching: when he taught as Christ's apostle to the Gentiles, the medium made no difference to the authority behind the words."[49] However, in a society that was becoming increasingly document-minded, Christianity, as a nascent movement, rapidly found the need to validate its ethos and *raison de vivre* and to strengthen the fluid and shifting form of the word of mouth with a written record. The written word validated the life and ministry of Jesus Christ and documented and archived the Christians' historical and spiritual origin. The recognition of special contemporary writings as Scriptures came rapidly with Christianity's growth among Gentiles. First, the letters of Paul were treasured and considered essential to guide in faith and practice. Then, the Gospels became a spiritual testament, an "aide-memoire . . . to be used secondarily as an extension or even a substitute for memory,"[50] especially after the death of the apostles.

First, the written documents still needed the validation of oral tradition, although Christians increasingly used Scriptures for worship, intellectual growth, and apologetic purposes. Both oral and written modes coexisted in the production and in the use of texts[51] and were mutually validating. Jean Duplacy agrees: "Especially for the main

books, the handwritten translation has always been more or less duplicated by an oral tradition: originally, for the Gospels and possibly for
Acts, the oral traditions and memories didn't have to fade overnight."[52]
For example, Papias, bishop of Hierapolis, declared that he would
rather listen to the oral account of eyewitnesses or those who had direct
access to them than learn it from books.[53] Yet, Christians captured rapidly the potential of a written means of delivery and circulated letters
and codices among house-churches.[54] The written message became
available to the "masses," which may have led to unsystematic copying
processes by undisciplined scribes. Yet, as Holmes writes, the evidence
leads toward mega-conservation and mini-alteration of the original
writings.[55] In other words, although the texts were subjected to modifications, the level of stability remains remarkable. No other ancient
text presents that level of stability.[56] Furthermore, if the New Testament had remained untouched from the beginning and the number
of canonical books clearly stated,[57] Ehrman would be the first to call
it a fraud.

How did God's people measure the "correctness" of certain
writings, discern their inspiration, and recognize their status as Holy
Scriptures? Early Christians recognized biblical authority on the basis
of inspiration, antiquity, apostolicity, orthodoxy, catholicity, and traditional use.[58] I disagree with S. T. Coleridge that merely "the spirit
of the Bible" and not the "detailed words or sentences" should be
considered "infallible and absolute."[59] This contradicts Jesus' view of
the Scriptures and of His own spoken words.[60] I prefer what Richard
Bauckham[61] calls the coincidence view which prevailed in early Christianity. This means that the content of apostolic tradition coincided
with the content of the Scriptures; the apostolic tradition was found
in the apostolic writings as well as in the oral tradition handed down
from the apostles. The criterion of inspiration is complex. Daniel
Hoffman explains inspiration as the "work of the Holy Spirit in guiding human authors to compose and record God's selected message in
the words of the original documents."[62] Rodney L. Petersen's definition acknowledges the reader's engagement in this endeavor; the work
of the Holy Spirit is also essential to decipher the message of the Bible
because he "[stimulates] the faithful in understanding and in the per-
formance of acts of virtue or charity."[63] The text itself is useless unless

the reader properly interprets it and personally applies its principles.[64] Therefore, the meaning of the text is as important as the technicality of the language.[65]

Paul Feinberg also connected inerrancy to hermeneutics. He considered the terms "indefectibility," "infallibility," and "indeceivability" inadequate to qualify inerrancy.[66] For him, "Inerrancy means that when all facts are known, the Scriptures in their original autographs and properly interpreted will be shown to be wholly true in everything that they affirm, whether that has to do with doctrine or morality or with the social, physical, or life sciences."[67] It involves the work of God (Scriptures as completely true), the Holy Spirit (necessary enlightenment), and human beings (interpretation not infallible). Kevin Vanhoozer also declined to approach Scripture only with the historical-actualist or the verbal-conceptualist view. "Scripture is neither simply the recital of the acts of God nor merely a book of propositions. Scripture is rather composed of divine-human speech acts that, through what they say, accomplish several authoritative, cognitive, spiritual, and social functions."[68] Scripture does not contain a stagnant message but "a way to venture" in knowing God.[69] After all, all that the first Christians had was the Jewish Scriptures and the *kerygma*. The work of their scribes attests to the fact that they viewed their holy texts as a dynamic and vibrant world. Inerrancy was not a primary doctrinal concern for the propagation of the faith. Ehrman's limited and negative understanding of inerrancy ("the Bible is without error") does not capture the early Christians' view of Scriptures. By contrast, Dan Wallace's open and positive terminology ("inerrancy is that the Bible is true in what it touches")[70] moves toward the early Christians' take on the nature of their canonical literature.

CONCLUSION

In this brief excursus in scribal handling of the sacred texts, I have tried to show that Ehrman's generalization on who changed the New Testament neglected factors that controlled and preserved the text and that examine early Christian understanding of Scriptures. Jesus' followers delivered and promulgated his message first orally, but Christianity became rapidly a textual movement. The biblical writers and copyists' task was to transpose into writing the riches of God's message, a daunting task. The process of transcribing oral tradition into a written form presented problems. As Jaroslav Pelikan writes, "What is lost when the spoken word is reduced to writing must be balanced against what is preserved in that same process and by means of it."[71] Contrary to modern views of inscripturation, biblical scribes were active in the recording process and focused on the gist of the message rather than the precise wording of the tradition. Nevertheless, early Christian scribes quickly developed a scriptural attitude toward their texts while guarding themselves against the Pharisees' "scripturolatry." Prompted by a reverence for religious writings that they inherited from their Jewish precursors and the exactitude of the Alexandrian bookmakers, they showed some conservative copying practices although exactness was not the dominating trend. Scribes "were more interested in making the message of the sacred text clear than in transmitting errorless [manuscripts]."[72] So, when Ehrman deplores their lack of accuracy, he criticizes them anachronistically. Their understanding of the nature of Scriptures did not involve a word-perfect transmission of the text.

By defective reasoning, misuse of evidence, and a misconception of inerrancy, Ehrman fails to build a case for the unreliability of the New Testament text as a sacred and inspired text. The existing textual variants give different shadings to the text but do not transform the essence of the message. Scripture is not the only way the God of the Bible reveals himself. He makes himself known in nature, epiphanies, worship, service, and relationships. Yet, the most permanent, accurate, and complete way of knowing God happens "through his gracious self-disclosure in scripture breaking in on [the] minds and hearts in the power of the Spirit. This requires not only the Spirit's work to remove our willful incapacity to believe and recognize the truth . . . but . . . also requires Spirit-empowered willingness to adopt a quite different worldview."[73] This worldview usually baffles our understanding and rationality.[74] Ehrman *par principe* rejects it and places his trust in the evidential perspective of textual criticism.

NOTES

Introduction

1. For a brief, general discussion of the chief considerations and criteria that New Testament text critics take into account in doing their work, see Bruce M. Metzger and Bart D. Ehrman, *The Text of the New Testament: Its Transmission, Corruption, and Restoration*, 4th ed. (New York: Oxford University Press, 2005), 300–43, esp. 302–5.

2. "Reasoned eclecticism" is the approach to textual criticism in which some factors outside the New Testament manuscripts, such as "the age, weight, and diversity of witnesses to a variant," are considered and "play a significant role in textual decisions." Gordon D. Fee, "Rigorous or Reasoned Eclecticism—Which?" in Eldon Jay Epp and Gordon D. Fee, eds., *Studies in the Theory and Method of New Testament Textual Criticism*, (Grand Rapids: Eerdmans, 1993), 124. Reasoned eclecticism is a middle road between the historical-documentary method and rigorous or thoroughgoing eclecticism. The historical-documentary method relies upon *external* data and "attempts to reconstruct the history of the New Testament text by tracing the lines of transmission back through our extant manuscripts to the very earliest attainable stages" and then seeks to choose "the reading that represents the earliest attainable level of the textual tradition." Rigorous or thoroughgoing eclecticism relies upon *internal* criteria such as "the context of the passage, the author's style and vocabulary, or the author's theology, while taking into account such factors as scribal habits." Reasoned eclecticism combines elements of these two methods because both approaches have much to commend but neither is fully adequate on its own to deal with what critics realistically find in the manuscripts. Eldon Jay Epp, "Decision Points in New Testament Textual Criticism," in Epp and Fee, eds., *Studies in the Theory and Method of New Testament Textual Criticism*, 31–36.

3. For more on the history of New Testament textual criticism and New Testament text critical method, see Metzger and Ehrman, *The Text of the New Testament*, 205–49, as well as the following in *The Text of the New Testament in Contemporary Research: Essays on the Status Quaestionis*, ed. Bart D. Ehrman and Michael W. Holmes (Grand Rapids: Eerdmans, 1995): Daniel Wallace, "The Majority Text Theory: History, Methods, and Critique," 297–320; J. Keith Elliott, "Thoroughgoing Eclecticism in New Testament Criticism," 321–35; and "Reasoned Eclecticism in New Testament Textual Criticism," 336–60. For a defense of thoroughgoing eclecticism, see J. K. Elliott, "The Case for Thoroughgoing Eclecticism," in *Rethinking New Testament Textual Criticism*, ed. David Alan Black (Grand Rapids: Baker Academic, 2002), 101–24.

4. Bart D. Ehrman, *The Orthodox Corruption of Scripture: The Effect of Early Christological Controversies on the Text of the New Testament* (New York: Oxford University Press, 1993).

5. Ehrman no longer claims to be a Christian of any stripe; he presently is agnostic regarding the existence of God. He does not address these issues, however, in Bart D. Ehrman, *Misquoting Jesus: The Story behind Who Changed the Bible and Why* (New York: HarperOne, 2007).

6. Most modern translations remove Acts 8:37 and have a quite different text for 1 John 5:7 than is found in the King James Version.

7. The "apparatus" lies at the bottom of the page in modern editions of the Greek New Testament, contains some (not all) of the more significant variants, and tells the knowledgeable reader which manuscripts contain alternate readings.

8. Virtually all modern translations begin with the Nestle-Aland Greek text. They may make alterations in places, but the Nestle-Aland Greek text will be the starting point.

9. Strictly speaking, "probability" means a likelihood of greater than 50 percent. "Plausibility" refers to the likeliest explanation—i.e., which of the available explanations (wordings) has the best chance of being correct. This is not something that can be quantified, but it can be recognized—as can its absence.

10. Georg Luck, "Textual Criticism Today," *American Journal of Philology* 102 (1981): 166.

11. D. C. Parker, *The Living Text of the Gospels* (Cambridge: Cambridge University Press, 1997), 92.

12. Ibid., 209.

13. Ibid., 207–12. Parker's use of language is confusing at times, making his argument difficult to follow. On a single page (209), he says the manuscripts transmit the tradition, then says they are the tradition, and then declares that they carry a tradition.

14. Ibid., 209–13.

15. Eldon Jay Epp, "Issues in New Testament Textual Criticism: Moving from the Nineteenth Century to the Twenty-First Century," in Black, ed., *Rethinking New Testament Textual Criticism*, 17–76, esp. 55–61.

16. Daniel B. Wallace, "Challenges in New Testament Textual Criticism for the Twenty-First Century," *Journal of the Evangelical Theological Society* 52, no. 1 (2009): 79–100, esp. 80–85; Moisés Silva, "Response," in Black, ed., *Rethinking New Testament Textual Criticism*, 141–49. I take Wallace and Silva to mean that text critics possess the necessary data to retrieve the original reading, but that, due to the number of extant New Testament manuscripts, we may be unable to know that we have done so, even if we should do so.. Consider the statement of Eldon Jay Epp in "Decision Points in New Testament Textual Criticism" (31): "The point is that we have so many manuscripts of the New Testament and that these manuscripts contain so many variant readings that surely the original reading in every case is somewhere present in our vast store of material."

17. Bertrand Russell, *The Problems of Philosophy* (London: Oxford University Press, 1954), 17.

18. The fact that it is probably the case that nobody living today knows what the original said in each and every respect does not mean that nobody could know or even that nobody will know someday.

19. Metzger and Ehrman, *Text of the New Testament*, 181. Cf. *Oxford Dictionary of National Biography* 8, ed. H. C. G. Matthew and Brian Harrison (Oxford: Oxford University Press, 2004), 805.

20. Metzger and Ehrman, *Text of the New Testament*, 181.

21. Ehrman, *Misquoting Jesus*, 211.

22. "If A, then B.
A.
Therefore, B."

23. "If A, then B.
Not-B.
Therefore, not-A."

24. For an antecedent to "entail" its consequent, the antecedent must be a sufficient condition for the consequent *necessarily* to follow. For instance, if I am a widower, then (necessarily) I have been previously married. It could not possibly be otherwise. Though it is possible that God might choose to preserve the New Testament manuscripts (indeed, it makes sense to many people), it is not impossible that God would choose not to.

25. No doubt Burgon believed that he had such warrant. I disagree.

26. A variant is not deemed viable if it is found in a single late manuscript or group of manuscripts that by themselves have little or no likelihood of going back to the original text.

Chapter 1

1. Bart D. Ehrman, *Misquoting Jesus: The Story behind Who Changed the Bible and Why*; 1st paperback ed. (New York: HarperOne, 2007), 253. All quotations are from the paperback edition.

2. Those who are "reasoned eclectics" (the dominant school of thought in New Testament textual criticism, of which both Bart and I are members) would agree with each other on the vast majority of textual problems.

3. Robert W. Funk, Roy W. Hoover, and the Jesus Seminar, *The Five Gospels: The Search for the Authentic Words of Jesus* (New York: Macmillan, 1993), 6 (italics added).

4. Those whose writings are very influential in the marketplace of ideas but who are not biblical scholars make even more unguarded statements. For example, Earl Doherty in *Challenging the Verdict* (Ottawa: Age of Reason, 2001), 39.

5. Bart D. Ehrman, "*Novum Testamentum Graecum Editio Critica Maior*: An Evaluation," *TC: A Journal of Biblical Textual Criticism*, 1998, a revision of a paper presented at the Textual Criticism section of the 1997 Society of Biblical Literature conference

in San Francisco. http://rosetta.reltech.org/TC/vol03/Ehrman1998.html, accessed July 12, 2009.

6. Bart Ehrman, *The New Testament: A Historical Introduction to the Early Christian Writings*, 3rd ed. (New York: Oxford University Press, 2003), 481.

7. Ehrman, *Misquoting Jesus*, 10.

8. Ibid., 98.

9. Bart Ehrman, *Lost Christianities: The Battles for Scripture and the Faiths We Never Knew* (New York: Oxford University Press, 2003), 219.

10. For example, the recently cataloged codex 2882, a tenth- to eleventh-century minuscule of Luke, has twenty-nine singular readings not found in any other manuscripts. Yet the manuscript is, for the most part, an ordinary Byzantine manuscript, and none of the singular readings is even remotely compelling.

11. Of course, if a lone manuscript also had corrections, those readings would count as variants.

12. Although Ehrman does both, he seems to emphasize the former far more than the latter. See Craig L. Blomberg, "Review of *Misquoting Jesus: The Story behind Who Changed the Bible and Why*," *Denver Journal* 9 (2006), http://www.denverseminary.edu/article/misquoting-jesus-the-story-behind-who-changed-the-bible-and-why/, accessed July 12, 2009.

13. Bruce M. Metzger and Bart D. Ehrman, *The Text of the New Testament: Its Transmission, Corruption, and Restoration*, 4th ed. (New York: Oxford University Press, 2005), 126.

14. Specifically, 43 percent, but this does not necessarily mean that every portion of each of these verses is in these manuscripts. Thanks are due to Brett Williams for doing the painstaking work of tabulating the number of verses that are found in the second-century manuscripts.

15. Ehrman does not say this in any of his books, as far as I am aware, but he does discount the number of early manuscripts by noting their fragmentary character. Cf. *Lost Christianities*, 219.

16. *Charlotte Observer*, December 17, 2005. Italics added.

17. See C. L. Porter, "Papyrus Bodmer XV (p. 75) and the Text of Codex Vaticanus," *JBL* 81 (1962): 363–76; *idem*, "An Evaluation of the Textual Variation between Pap75 and Codex Vaticanus in the Text of John," in *Studies in the History and Text of the New Testament in Honor of Kenneth Willis Clark*, Studies and Documents 29, ed. Boyd L. Daniels and M. Jack Suggs (Salt Lake City: University of Utah Press, 1967), 71–80; Gordon D. Fee, "𝔓75, 𝔓66, and Origen: The Myth of Early Textual Recension in Alexandria," in *Studies in the Theory and Method of New Testament Textual Criticism*, ed. Eldon J. Epp and Gordon D. Fee, Studies and Documents 45 (Grand Rapids: Eerdmans, 1993), 247–73.

18. Ehrman, *Lost Christianities*, 219.

19. Cf., e.g., Metzger and Ehrman, *Text of the New Testament*, 277–78, 312. Hort believed that when A and B agreed, their reading went back to a very ancient common ancestor. That it was not a near ancestor was demonstrated by the thousands of disagreements between these two manuscripts, suggesting that there were several

intermediary ancestors between the common ancestor and these two uncial documents. B. F. Westcott and F. J. A. Hort, *Introduction [and] Appendix*, vol. 2 of *The New Testament in the Original Greek* (Cambridge: Macmillan, 1882), 212–50. Cf. also Metzger and Ehrman, *Text of the New Testament*, 312: "With the discovery . . . of 𝔓⁶⁶ and 𝔓⁷⁵, both dating from about the end of the second or the beginning of the third century, proof became now available that Hort's Neutral text goes back to an archetype that must be put early in the second century."

20. Ehrman, *Misquoting Jesus*, 124.

21. Ibid., 131.

22. So Ehrman, *Misquoting Jesus*, 131.

23. Brooke Foss Westcott, *Some Lessons of the Revised Version of the New Testament*, 2nd ed. (London: Hodder & Stoughton, 1897), 8–9 (italics added). Credit is due to Keith Small for pointing out this reference to me.

24. Even in the earliest form of the text, we see spelling variations by the same author. Perhaps the most notable example is to be found in John 9:14-21. In the space of eight verses, the evangelist manages to spell the third person singular aorist active indicative of ἀνίγω three different ways: ἀνέῳξεν in v. 14; ἠνέῳξεν in v. 17; ἤνοιξεν in v. 21.

25. See Moisés Silva, "Response," in *Rethinking New Testament Textual Criticism*, ed. David Alan Black (Grand Rapids: Baker, 2002), 149.

26. Ehrman, *Misquoting Jesus*, 207–8.

27. "The Gospel according to Bart: A Review Article of *Misquoting Jesus* by Bart Ehrman," *Journal of the Evangelical Theological Society*, 49 (2006): 327–49.

28. Ehrman, *Misquoting Jesus*, 95, 110, 204, 209, 223 n. 19, 224 n. 16.

29. Bart D. Ehrman, *Studies in the Textual Criticism of the New Testament* 33, New Testament Tools and Studies, ed. Bruce M. Metzger and Bart D. Ehrman (Leiden: Brill, 2006), 333.

30. Ehrman, *Misquoting Jesus*, 204.

31. Ehrman argues that it would have been an anti-Adoptionist variant and that the versional evidence confirms this.

32. Athanasius is the first father to mention any problem with the Son's omniscience when discussing this passage. See discussion in Adam Messer, "Patristic Theology and Recension in Matthew 24.36: An Evaluation of Ehrman's Text-Critical Methodology," *Revisiting the Corruption of the New Testament: Manuscript, Patristic, and Apocryphal Evidence*, vol. 1, *The Text and Canon of the New Testament*, ed. Daniel B. Wallace (Grand Rapids: Kregel, forthcoming), 34 (prepublication draft).

33. So Messer, "Patristic Theology," 26, 30, 31–33. Specifically, Messer challenged Ehrman's claim that Origen knew of the shorter reading (ibid., 31).

34. See discussion in ibid., 26.

35. Irenaeus, *Against Heresies* 3.11.8.

36. It is not until Basil (mid- to late-fourth century) that we see a patristic writer affirm the omission *and* argue that "alone" in Mt. 24:36 does not exclude the Son. See Messer, "Patristic Theology," 43. Basil could have easily changed the text or argued that

"alone" was not found in all the manuscripts, if that were the case. But the fact that he attempts to adjust to the passage with the "alone" as a lone speed bump shows that, like other fathers, he "tended to clarify [his] theology rather than change [his] texts" (ibid., 60).

37. Bart D. Ehrman, *The Orthodox Corruption of Scripture: The Effect of Early Christological Controversies on the Text of the New Testament* (New York: Oxford University Press, 1993), 282 n. 16.

38. Ibid.

39. Matthew P. Morgan, "Egregious Regius: Sabellianism or Scribal Blunder in John 1:1c?" (unpublished paper read at the Southwestern Regional Meeting of the Evangelical Theological Society, March 29, 2008, at Southwestern Baptist Theological Seminary, Houston Campus), 31.

40. Messer, "Patristic Theology," 68.

41. Silva "Response," 149.

42. Gordon D. Fee, "Review of *The Orthodox Corruption of Scripture*," in *Critical Review of Books in Religion* 8 (1995): 204.

43. See, e.g., Ehrman, *Misquoting Jesus*, 62.

44. Bart D. Ehrman, "Jesus and the Adulteress," *New Testament Studies* 34 (1988), 22–44.

45. C. S. Lewis, *Miracles: A Preliminary Study*, 1st Touchstone ed. (Touchstone, 1996) 95.

46. Ehrman, "Jesus and the Adulteress," 22–44.

47. That is, the supplement to Codex W. This refers to an eighth-century replacement quire for John 1.1–5.11 in that codex. It was added most likely because the original quire had disappeared from the manuscript.

48. Bart D. Ehrman, *The Orthodox Corruption of Scripture: The Effect of Early Christological Controversies on the Text of the New Testament* (New York: Oxford University Press, 1993), 179 n.187.

49. Bart D. Ehrman, "Jesus and the Adulteress," *New Testament Studies* 34 (1988), 22–44.

50. C. S. Lewis, *Miracles: A Preliminary Study*, 1st Touchstone ed. (Touchstone, 1996) 95.

51. Ehrman, "Jesus and the Adulteress," 22–44.

52. That is, the supplement to Codex W. This refers to an eighth-century replacement quire for John 1.1–5.11 in that codex. It was added most likely because the original quire had disappeared from the manuscript.

53. Bart D. Ehrman, *The Orthodox Corruption of Scripture: The Effect of Early Christological Controversies on the Text of the New Testament* (New York: Oxford University Press, 1993), 179 n.187.

Chapter 2

1. For an illuminating analysis (both quantitative and qualitative) of the number and extent of manuscripts of the New Testament during the first millennium of its

existence, see Eldon Jay Epp, "Are Early New Testament Manuscripts Truly Abundant?" in *Israel's God and Rebecca's Children: Christology and Community in Early Judaism and Christianity*, ed. David B. Capes et al. (Waco: Baylor University Press, 2007), 77–117 and 395–99. Epp lists only three or four second-century manuscripts: $\mathfrak{P}^{52}$, $\mathfrak{P}^{90}$, $\mathfrak{P}^{104}$, and perhaps $\mathfrak{P}^{98}$ (pp. 83, 98); a slightly more generous estimate of the number of second-century texts is offered by J. Keith Elliott, "The Nature of the Evidence Available for Reconstructing the Text of the New Testament in the Second Century," in *The New Testament Text in Early Christianity/Le texte du Nouveau Testament au début du christianisme*, ed. Christian-B. Amphoux and J. Keith Elliott (Lausanne: Éditions du Zèbre, 2003), 1011.

2. Cf. David Parker: "At present, the central question is the degree to which we can recover forms of the text older than the end of the second century. . . . Before that lies a period for which we have no manuscript attestation, and in which we know the greatest amount of change and variation to have arisen" ("Textual Criticism and Theology," *Expository Times* 118.12 [2007]: 586).

3. I am using the phrase "in whatever form a particular document began to be copied and circulate" in lieu of "original text" because of the multivalent and problematic character of that term in recent discussion. See Eldon Jay Epp, "The Multivalence of the Term 'Original Text' in New Testament Textual Criticism," *Harvard Theological Review* 92 (1999): 245–81 (repr. in Epp, *Perspectives on New Testament Textual Criticism: Collected Essays, 1962–2004* [Leiden: Brill, 2005], 551–93), and Michael W. Holmes, "Westcott & Hort at 125 (& Zuntz at 60): Their Legacies and Our Challenges" (paper presented at the annual meeting of the Society of Biblical Literature, Washington, D.C., November 2006), 27–29.

4. David Trobisch, *The First Edition of the New Testament* (New York: Oxford University Press, 2000).

5. Trobisch, *First Edition*, 6.

6. Evidence of this alleged editorial activity includes (a) utilization of the codex format, (b) consistent use of *nomina sacra*, (c) standardization and uniform arrangement of contents, (d) standardized titles, (e) editorial cross-references between books, and (f) the addition of John 21 (a final editorial appendix).

7. Trobisch, *First Edition*, 102–3; 24, 34. In his survey of New Testament manuscripts from the first seven centuries (pp. 24–34), he finds only five exceptions, four of which ($\mathfrak{P}^{46}$, D/05, D/06, and W/032) "may be understood as a deliberate redactional rearrangement of the same material" as found in the rest, while the fifth exception ($\mathfrak{P}^{72}$) is "an irregular and singular exemplar, one that left no traces in the later manuscript tradition" (34).

8. Trobisch, *First Edition*, 62–65.

9. Consult F. H. A. Scrivener, *A Plain Introduction to the Criticism of the New Testament* (4th ed.; 2 vols.; London, 1894; repr., Eugene, Ore.: Wipf and Stock, 1997) 1:72–74.

10. Cf. Bruce M. Metzger, *The Canon of the New Testament: Its Origin, Development, and Significance* (Oxford: Clarendon, 1987), 295–300.

11. Cf. Michael W. Holmes, "The Biblical Canon," in *The Oxford Handbook of Early Christian Studies*, ed. Susan Ashbrook Harvey and David Hunter (Oxford: Oxford University Press, 2008) 406–26.

12. Kurt Aland and Barbara Aland, *The Text of the New Testament: An Introduction to the Critical Editions and to the Theory and Practice of Modern Textual Criticism*, 2nd, rev. and enl. ed. (Grand Rapids: Eerdmans, 1989).

13. Aland and Aland, *Text*, 291, 292.

14. Ibid., 294.

15. Ibid., 296.

16. Bruce M. Metzger, *A Textual Commentary on the Greek New Testament*, 2nd ed. (Stuttgart: Deutsche Bibelgesellschaft, 1994 [1st ed.: London and New York: United Bible Societies, 1971; corr. ed., 1975]), 393–5 (a decision with which both Kurt Aland and Metzger disagreed).

17. Metzger, *Textual Commentary*, 395–96.

18. See Jeffrey Kloha, "1 Corinthians 6:5: A Proposal," *Novum Testamentum* 46 (2004): 132–42.

19. G. Zuntz, *The Text of the Epistles: A Disquisition upon the* Corpus Paulinum (Schweich Lectures, 1946; London: Oxford University Press for the British Academy, 1953), 15.

20. Metzger, *Textual Commentary*, 352.

21. Zuntz, *Text of the Epistles*, 31–32; Gordon D. Fee, *The First Epistle to The Corinthians* in the *New International Commentary of the New Testament* (Grand Rapids: Eerdmans, 1987), 364, 367.

22. Jerome, *Against Pelegius*, 2.15.

23. Manuscripts 1505 and 2495, according to Reuben J. Swanson, *New Testament Greek Manuscript: Variant Readings Arranged in Horizontal Lines Against Codex Vaticanus: Romans* (Wheaton, Ill.: Tyndale House, 2001), 39.

24. Aland and Aland, *Text*, 292 (emphasis added).

25. William L. Petersen, "What Text Can New Testament Textual Criticism Ultimately Reach?" in *New Testament Textual Criticism, Exegesis, and Early Church History: A Discussion of Methods*, ed. Barbara Aland and Joël Delobel (Kampen: Kok Pharos, 1994), 136–51; William L. Petersen, "The Genesis of the Gospels," in *New Testament Textual Criticism and Exegesis: Festschrift J. Delobel*, ed. A. Denaux (Leuven: Leuven University Press and Peeters, 2002), 33–65; William L. Petersen, "Textual Traditions Examined: What the Text of the Apostolic Fathers tells us about the Text of the New Testament in the Second Century," in *The Reception of the New Testament in the Apostolic Fathers*, ed. Andrew Gregory and Christopher Tuckett (Oxford: Oxford University Press, 2005), 29–46; William L. Petersen, "Patristic Biblical Quotations and Method: Four Changes to Lightfoot's Edition of Second Clement," *Vigiliae Christianae* 60 (2006): 389–419. Cf. also François Bovon, "The Synoptic Gospels and the Non-canonical Acts of the Apostles," in *Studies in Early Christianity* (Grand Rapids: Baker Academic, 2005), 209–25 (cf. esp. 210, 221; repr. from *Harvard Theological Review* 81 [1988]: 19–36); Helmut Koester, "The Text of the Synoptic Gospels in the Second Century," in *Gospel Traditions in the Second Century: Origins, Recensions, Text, and Transmission*, ed. William L. Petersen (Notre Dame and London: University of Notre Dame Press, 1989), 19–37; Helmut Koester, *Ancient Christian Gospels: Their History and Development* (London: SCM, 1990).

26. Petersen, "Textual Traditions Examined," 34 (author's italics); cf. 45–46.

27. William L. Petersen, "The Genesis of the Gospels," 62; cf. 53–54: "We know next to nothing of the text of the gospels in the first century, for we have no manuscript evidence and few (if any) Patristic writings." Cf. also William L. Petersen, *Tatian's Diatessaron: Its Creation, Dissemination, Significance, and History in Scholarship* (Leiden: Brill, 1994), 9–34.

28. Petersen, "The Genesis of the Gospels," 54; cf. also Petersen, "Traditional Traditions Examined," 38–39. In an earlier work he phrased the matter more clearly when he spoke of the "variety" and "instability" of second century "traditions" rather than texts (*Tatian's Diatessaron*, 33).

29. Petersen, "Genesis," 35–36.

30. Petersen, "What Text," 142–43.

31. On Justin's use of multiple sources, cf. Oskar Skarsaune, "Justin and His Bible," in *Justin Martyr and His Worlds*, ed. Sara Parvis and Paul Foster (Minneapolis: Fortress Press, 2007), 64–68; differently T. K. Heckel, *Vom Evangelium des Markus zum viergestaltigen Evangelium* [*From the Gospel of Mark to the Fourfold Gospel*], WUNT 120 (Tübingen: Mohr Siebeck, 1990), 326–27. On Justin's use of a harmonized sayings collection, cf. Arthur J. Bellinzoni, *The Sayings of Jesus in the Writings of Justin Martyr*, Supplements to *Novum Testamentum* 17 (Leiden: Brill, 1967), 49–100; Leslie L. Kline, "Harmonized Sayings of Jesus in the Pseudo-Clementine Homilies and Justin Martyr," ZNW 66 (1975): 223–41; Koester, *Ancient Christian Gospels*, 360–402; William L. Petersen, "Textual Evidence of Tatian's Dependence upon Justin's ΑΠΟΜΝΗΜΟΝΕΥΜΑΤΑ," *Novum Testamentum* 36 (1990): 512–34; Petersen, *Tatian's Diatessaron*, 27–9; Craig D. Allert, *Revelation, Truth, Canon and Interpretation: Studies in Justin Martyr's* Dialogue with Trypho (Leiden: Brill, 2002), 195–202; G. N. Stanton, "Jesus Traditions and Gospels in Justin Martyr and Irenaeus," in *The Biblical Canons*, ed. J.-M. Auwers and H. J. de Jonge (Leuven: Leuven University Press, 2003), 353–70, esp. 364–65 (repr., *Jesus and Gospel* [Cambridge: Cambridge University Press, 2004], 92–109); differently (but unpersuasively) G. Strecker, "Eine Evangelienharmonie bei Justin und Pdeudoklemens?" *Novum Testamentum* 24 (1978): 297–316. There is no indication that this harmonized sayings source was a complete gospel or meant to replace earlier gospels: cf. Graham N. Stanton, "The Fourfold Gospel, *Novum Testamentum* 43 (1997): 329–35 (repr., *Jesus and Gospel*, 75–81), contra Koester, "Text of the Synoptic Gospels," 28–33.

32. For a more detailed discussion of these texts, see Joseph Verheyden, "Assessing Gospel Quotations in Justin Martyr," in *New Testament Textual Criticism and Exegesis: Festschrift J. Delobel*, ed. A. Denaux (Leuven: Leuven University Press and Peeters, 2002), 363–70.

33. Petersen, "What Text," 145.

34. Cf. William R. Schoedel, *Ignatius of Antioch*, Hermeneia (Philadelphia: Fortress Press, 1985), 226–27 ("probably not . . . a loose version of the Lukan text"; "perhaps most likely that Luke and Ignatius rely on common tradition"); Andrew Gregory, *The Reception of Luke and Acts in the Period before Irenaeus*, WUNT 2.169 (Tübingen: Mohr Siebeck, 2003), 70–75.

35. Sabrina Inowlocki, *Eusebius and the Jewish Authors: His Citation Technique in an Apologetic Context*, Ancient Judaism and Early Christianity 64 (Leiden: Brill, 2006) 40. Cf. also Frances M. Young, *Biblical Exegesis and the Formation of Christian Culture*

(Cambridge: Cambridge University Press, 1997); Christopher D. Stanley, *Paul and the Language of Scripture: Citation Technique in the Pauline Epistles and Contemporary Literature*, Society for New Testament Studies Monograph Series 74 (Cambridge: Cambridge University Press, 1992).

36. Cf. Skarsaune, "Justin and His Bible," 53–76; also Oskar Skarsaune, *The Proof From Prophecy: A Study in Justin Martyr's Proof-Text Tradition: Text-Type, Provenance, Theological Profile*, Supplement to *Novum Testamentum* 56 (Leiden: Brill, 1987).

37. Ibid., 67.

38. It is not that Petersen is unaware of these matters (for example, "The character of Justin's gospel text is difficult to determine, for he may be citing from multiple sources" ["Genesis," 45]), but rather that they play no evident role in his discussion and assessment of specific texts.

39. Petersen, "Genesis," 62.

40. D. C. Parker, *The Living Text of the Gospels* (Cambridge: Cambridge University Press, 1997); David Parker, "Textual Criticism and Theology," *Expository Times* 118 no. 12 (2007): 583–89.

41. Parker, "Textual Criticism and Theology," 585.

42. Ibid., 587–88.

43. Michael W. Holmes, "Polycarp's *Letter to the Philippians* and the Writings that Later Formed the New Testament," in *The Reception of the New Testament in the Apostolic Fathers*, ed. Andrew Gregory and Christopher Tuckett (Oxford: Oxford University Press, 2005), 187–227 (cf. in particular 188–89).

44. Regarding the Apostolic Fathers, consult: Andrew Gregory and Christopher Tuckett, eds., *The Reception of the New Testament in the Apostolic Fathers* (Oxford: Oxford University Press, 2005); Andrew Gregory and Christopher Tuckett, eds., *Trajectories through the New Testament and the Apostolic Fathers* (Oxford: Oxford University Press, 2005). Regarding apocryphal writings: James Keith Elliott, "The Influence of the Apocrypha on Manuscripts of the New Testament," *Apocrypha* 8 (1997): 265–71; Stanley E. Porter, "Apocryphal Gospels and the Text of the New Testament Before A. D. 200," in *The New Testament Text in Early Christianity/Le texte du Nouveau Testament au début du christianisme*, ed. Christian-B. Amphoux and J. Keith Elliott (Lausanne: Éditions du Zèbre, 2003), 235–59. Regarding the Egerton Gospel: Stuart R. Pickering, "The Egerton Gospel and New Testament Textual Transmission," in *The New Testament Text in Early Christianity*, 215–34; Porter, "Apocryphal Gospels." Re Marcion and Tatian: Ulrich Schmid, "How Can We Access Second Century Gospel Texts? The Cases of Marcion and Tatian," in *The New Testament Text in Early Christianity*, 139–50. Also on Tatian: Tjitze Baarda, "The Diatessaron of Tatian: Source for an Early Text at Rome or Source of Textual Corruption?" in *The New Testament Text in Early Christianity*, 93–138.

45. For a similar outcome, arrived at on different grounds, cf. Barbara Aland, "Die Rezeption des Neutestamentlichen Textes in den ersten Jahrhunderten," in *The New Testament in Early Christianity: La réception des écrits néotestamentaires dans le christianisme primitive*, ed. Jean-Marie Sevrin (Leuven: Leuven University Press, 1989), 1–38.

46. Petersen, "Genesis," 53–54 ("We know next to nothing of the text of the gospels in the first century, for we have no manuscript evidence and few [if any]

Patristic writings. Therefore, our only route of inquiry is to take what we have discovered thus far, from our study of the second century, project these trends and tendencies back into the first century, and see what they suggest"); similarly Frederik Wisse, "The Nature and Purpose of Redactional Changes in Early Christian Texts: The Canonical Gospels," in *Gospel Traditions in the Second Century: Origins, Recensions, Text, and Transmission*, ed. William L. Petersen (Notre Dame and London: University of Notre Dame Press, 1989), 44–47.

47. Cf. Wisse, "Nature and Purpose," 42.

48. Kim Haines-Eitzen, *Guardians of Letters: Literacy, Power, and the Transmitters of Early Christian Literature* (New York: Oxford University Press, 2000), 106; cf. Larry W. Hurtado, "The New Testament Text in the Second Century: Text, Collections and Canon," in *Transmission and Reception: New Testament Text-Critical and Exegetical Studies*, ed. J. Childers and D. C. Parker (Piscataway, N.J.: Gorgias, 2006), 14–19.

49. For these and other adjectives (e.g., "uncontrolled," "unedited," "free") cf. J. H. Petzer, "The History of the New Testament—Its Reconstruction, Significance and Use in New Testament Textual Criticism," in *New Testament Textual Criticism, Exegesis, and Early Church History: a Discussion of Methods*, ed. Barbara Aland and Joël Delobel (Kampen: Kok Pharos, 1994), 30–31; Aland and Aland, *Text*, 59–64; Ernest C. Colwell, *Studies in Methodology in Textual Criticism of the New Testament*, NTTS 9 (Leiden: Brill, 1969), 166–67 n. 3.

50. Even without titles, "To the ancient reader the Gospels of Matthew and Luke did not look like interpolated versions of the Gospel of Mark. The obviously different beginnings and endings of these Gospels were sufficient indication that they were distinct texts" (Wisse, "Nature and Purpose," 42).

51. Regarding Marcion, see John Barton, "Marcion Revisited," in *The Canon Debate*, ed. L. M. McDonald and J. A. Sanders (Peabody, Mass.: Hendrickson, 2002), 341–54. On Marcion's handling of Luke, see Koester, *Ancient Christian Gospels*, 35–37. With regard to Marcion's text of the Pauline epistles, recent work has demonstrated that Marcion, rather than creating a text, passed along the wording of texts already in existence: cf. Ulrich Schmid, *Marcion und Sein Apostolos: Rekonstruktion und Historische Einordnung der Marcionitischen Paulusbriefausgabe* [Marcion and His Apostle: Reconstruction and Historical Classification of the Marcionite Edition of the Pauline Letters], ANTF 25 (Berlin and New York: De Gruyter, 1995); John J. Clabeaux, *A Lost Edition of the Letters of Paul: A Reassessment of the Text of the Pauline Corpus Attested by Marcion*, Catholic Biblical Quarterly Monograph 21 (Washington, D.C.: CBAA, 1989); Gilles Quispel, "Marcion and the Text of the New Testament," *Vigiliae Christianae* 52 (1998): 349–60.

52. The two major sections, 1–24 and 25–114, were written and at first circulated separately. Later the two sections were combined and Parables 9 and 10 were added to unify the two parts into a single document. Cf. Carolyn Osiek, *Shepherd of Hermas*, Hermeneia (Minneapolis: Fortress Press, 1999), 10–16.

53. The Gospel of Mark would be included on this list by some, largely on the basis of the alleged testimony of Clement of Alexandria about the so-called Secret Mark (e.g., Koester, "Text of the Synoptic Gospels," 34–37; Koester, *Ancient Christian Gospels*, 293–303). I remain unpersuaded, however, that the letter attributed to Clement is anything other than a hoax or forgery. Moreover, even if one were inclined to accept it as authentic, it is not at all clear that "Secret Mark" is part of the prehistory

of canonical Mark (so Koester) rather than its post-history (so Scott G. Brown, "On the Composition History of the Longer ["Secret"] Gospel of Mark," *Journal of Biblical Literature* 122 [2003]: 89–110). For an overview and bibliography of the debate about "Secret Mark" consult Adela Yarbro Collins, *Mark: A Commentary*, Hermeneia (Minneapolis: Fortress Press, 2007), 484–93. For yet another view of Mark, cf. Christian-B. Amphoux, "Une édition «plurielle» de Marc," in *The New Testament Text in Early Christianity/Le texte du Nouveau Testament au début du christianisme*, ed. Christian-B. Amphoux and J. Keith Elliott (Lausanne: Éditions du Zèbre, 2003), 69–80.

54. Zuntz, *Text of the Epistles*, 217–20.

55. Origen, *Comm. Matt.* 15.14 (Greek text as reconstructed by Klostermann on the basis of the Latin translation; cf. GCS 40 = *Origenes Werke* 10).

56. See James R. Royse, *Scribal Habits in Early New Testament Papyri* (Leiden and Boston: Brill, 2008).

57. E.g., the scribe of 𝔓⁴⁵: cf. Royse, *Scribal Habits*, 103–97; J. Keith Elliott, "Singular Readings in the Gospel Text of 𝔓⁴⁵," in *The Earliest Gospels: The Origins and Transmission of the Earliest Christian Gospels—The Contribution of the Chester Beatty Gospel Codex P⁴⁵*, ed. Charles Horton (London: T & T Clark, 2004), 122–31; Barbara Aland, "The Significance of the Chester Beatty Biblical Papyri in Early Church History," in Horton, *The Earliest Gospels*, 108–21.

58. Colwell, *Studies in Methodology*, 117 (cf. 167–68); cf. Royse, *Scribal Habits*, 704 ("The overall impression is that the scribe copies with care, but not with the unusual care that has sometimes been ascribed to him").

59. *Diorthōsis* was an activity routinely performed by readers who wished to have a reliable copy of a manuscript, especially if reading a newly copied one (in which the presence of copying errors in need of correction was taken for granted). The evidence of the papyri indicates that in performing this routine activity some readers (including some copyists, but certainly not all) often "felt themselves free to make corrections in the text, improving it by their own standards of correctness, whether grammatically, stylistically, or more substantively" (Aland and Aland, *Text*, 69). For a discussion of the meaning and scope of *diorthosis* in antiquity see Michael W. Holmes, "Codex Bezae as a Recension of the Gospels," in *Codex Bezae: Studies from the Lunell Colloquium, June 1994*, ed. D. C. Parker and C.-B. Amphoux (Leiden: Brill, 1996), 143–45, 149–50.

60. Indeed, if the corrections were especially thorough, it is entirely possible for a given manuscript (*D*), copied from (*C*), itself in turn a copy of (*A*) corrected according to (*B*), to look more like (*B*) than (*A*), even though it is the putative grandchild of the latter.

61. Holmes, "Codex Bezae," 147–50; Michael W. Holmes, "The Text of 𝔓⁴⁶: Evidence of the Earliest 'Commentary' on Romans?" in *New Testament Manuscripts: Their Text and Their World*, ed. Tobias Nicklas (Leiden: Brill, 2006), 189–206.

62. Klaus Wachtel, *Der Byzantinische Text der Katholischen Briefe: Eine Untersuchung zur Entstehung der Koine des Neuen Testaments* [The Byzantine Text of the Catholic Epistles: A Study of the Formation of the Koine of the New Testament], ANTF 24 (Berlin and New York: De Gruyter, 1995), 159–202; Zuntz, *Text of the Epistles*, 271–72; J. N. Birdsall, "The New Testament Text," in *The Cambridge History of the Bible*, vol. 1, *From the Beginnings to Jerome*, ed. P. R. Ackroyd and C. F. Evans (Cambridge: Cambridge University Press, 1970), 328; cf. Colwell, *Studies*, 49–53.

63. Zuntz, *Text of the Epistles*, 267–80.

64. J. Neville Birdsall, "Rational Eclecticism and the Oldest Manuscripts: A Comparative Study of the Bodmer and Chester Beatty Papyri of the Gospel of Luke," *Collected Papers in Greek and Georgian Textual Criticism* (Piscataway, N.J.: Gorgias, 2006), 99; Gordon D. Fee, "𝔓⁶⁶, 𝔓⁷⁵ and Origen: The Myth of Early Textual Recension in Alexandria," in *New Dimensions in New Testament Study*, ed. by M. C. Tenney and R. N. Longenecker (Grand Rapids: Zondervan, 1974), 19–45; Carlo M. Martini, S.I., *Il problema della recensionalità del codice B alla luce del papiro Bodmer XIV* [The Problem of the Recensional Character of Codex B in light of Papyrus Bodmer XIV] (Rome: Pontifical Biblical Institute, 1966).

65. Wisse, "Nature and Purpose," 44–45.

66. Hurtado, "The New Testament Text in the Second Century," 12–13.

67. Continuing to use, as at the beginning of the essay, "in the late first century" as shorthand for "the time when the various documents that now comprise the New Testament began to be copied and circulate" (whenever and in whatever form that was for a particular document).

68. For Mark 16 consult James A. Kelhoffer, *Miracle and Mission: The Authentication of Missionaries and Their Message in the Longer Ending of Mark*, WUNT 2.112 (Tübingen: Mohr Siebeck, 2000); for the endings of Romans consult Robert Jewett, *Romans: A Commentary*, Hermeneia (Minneapolis: Fortress Press, 2007), 4–9, 985–1014. Though some form of the *pericope adultera* (John 7:53—8:11) may have been known to second century figures such as Papias (cf. Michael W. Holmes, *The Apostolic Fathers: Greek Texts and English Translations*, 3rd ed. [Grand Rapids: Baker Academic, 2007], 724–27), it does not make an appearance in the manuscript tradition until ca. 400, in Codex Bezae.

69. For examples from the Gospels, cf. Wisse, "Nature and Purpose," 47–51.

70. During the forum, the point was repeatedly made that "we just don't know whether we can approximate the original or not." True enough; it is, however, equally true that we don't know that we can't recover it. In any case, the claim is a bit of a red herring, inasmuch as history deals with probabilities, not certainty of knowledge.

71. Epp, "Are Early New Testament Manuscripts Truly Abundant," 105.

Chapter 3

1. I have explored the ideas presented in this essay more expansively in my book *Pedagogy of the Bible: An Analysis and Proposal* (Louisville: Westminster John Know, 2008).

2. For a fuller demonstration of these points, see *Pedagogy of the Bible*, esp. chapter 1.

3. I grew up in Texas in Churches of Christ, which share a broader history with the Disciples of Christ (Christian Church) and independent Christian Churches in what has been called "the Restoration Movement" or "the Stone-Campbell Movement." For histories of the movement, see David Edwin Harrell, *A Social History of the Disciples of Christ*, 2 vols. (Nashville: Disciples of Christ Historical Society, 1966–73); Nathan O. Hatch, *The Democratization of American Christianity* (New Haven: Yale University Press, 1989); Richard T. Hughes, *Reviving the Ancient Faith: the Story of Churches of Christ in America* (Grand Rapids: Eerdmans, 1996); Henry E. Webb, *In Search of Christian Unity: a History of the Restoration Movement*, rev. ed. (Abilene, Tex.: Abilene Christian University Press, 2003).

4. Bart D. Ehrman, *Misquoting Jesus: The Story Behind Who Changed the Bible and Why* (San Francisco: HarperSanFrancisco, 2005), 7.

5. Even pronouncements by Roman Catholic hierarchy and councils that the Latin Vulgate is the *editio typica* for official use in Catholic churches do not identify only the Vulgate as scripture. See "Vulgate," in *New Catholic Encyclopedia*, 2nd ed. (Washington D.C.: Catholic University of America; Farmington Hills, Mich.: Thomson Gale, 2003), 14.591–600.

6. Some Christians have designated the physical, socially delineable institution(s) as "the visible church" and the full, unseen body of Christ as "the invisible church." But Christian theologians, at least many of them, prefer not to speak of the local congregation as the "visible church" and the entire body of Christ as the "invisible church," because, for one thing, as David Kelsey has put it, "the church universal is as concretely actual as is any local congregation" (David H. Kelsey, *To Understand God Truly: What's Theological About a Theological School.* [Louisville:Westminster/John Knox, 1992], 149).

7. Again, Kelsey: "The greater church, with which particular congregations are in some way 'one,' that is, the church 'catholic' or 'ecumenical,' while always necessarily localizable, always present as particular congregations—though not necessarily *only* present as local congregations (whether or not it is present in other ways can remain an open question)—is never localized, never exhaustively present as nor simply identical with a local congregation" (*To Understand God Truly*, 150–51).

8. The point is well made by Mark Jordan when speaking about Thomas Aquinas's beliefs about translation of scripture: "Thomas's confidence in the possibility of translation is a theological confidence. It extends just to the essentials of faith. . . . It must be possible to articulate truths essential to faith in every language" (Mark D. Jordan, *Rewritten Theology: Aquinas After His Readers* [Malden, Mass.; Oxford; Carlton, Victoria, Australia: Blackwell, 2006], 26, 27).

9. The usually cited impulse for "narrative theology" and its understanding of scripture as narrative is Hans Frei, *The Eclipse of Biblical Narrative: A Study in Eighteenth and Nineteenth Century Hermeneutics* (New Haven: Yale University Press, 1974); but now there are hundreds of books and many more articles on the theme. David Kelsey (*To Understand God Truly*, 170–71) explicitly makes the points I have highlighted here: that the other genres of scripture are often taken by Christians as imbedded within the major, larger narratives Christian scripture is thought to contain.

10. For a fuller treatment of these ideas, see my *Sex and the Single Savior: Gender and Sexuality in Biblical Interpretation* (Louisville: Westminster John Knox, 2006), 170–81.

11. I stress that I am here speaking of Ehrman's rhetoric as contained in *Misquoting Jesus*. Ehrman is quite aware of the necessity and vagaries of interpretation, as he makes clear toward the conclusion of his book (see p. 216, for example). But he never gives his reader any clue that perhaps since interpretation is always necessary and variable, *therefore* the inaccessibility of the "original words" of the text is not as challenging for Christian faith in scripture as he elsewhere in the book implies. He never hints that other, more adequate understandings of the nature of scripture are even available— much less the dominant theological tradition in the history of Christianity.

12. Rowan A. Greer, *Anglican Approaches to Scripture: From the Reformation to the Present* (New York: Crossroad, 2006). This quotation of John Locke is found on p. 78.

13. See Augustine, *On Christian Doctrine* 1.35.40; Martin, *Sex and the Single Savior*, 12, 49, 168; and *Pedagogy of the Bible*, 83–84.

14. Bart D. Ehrman, *The Orthodox Corruption of Scripture: The Effects of Early Christological Controversies on the Text of the New Testament* (New York: Oxford University Press, 1993).

Chapter 4

1. W. D. Davies and D. C. Allison, *A Critical and Exegetical Commentary on the Gospel According to Saint Matthew*, vol. 2 (Edinburgh: T. and T. Clark, 1991), 567 n. 23.

2. Readings that are of no particular interpretative significance may be valuable for stemmatological analysis, and so perhaps more significant text-critically than readings that have a profound influence on the meaning of the text.

3. The age of a reading is not the same as the age of the oldest manuscript in which it is found. Of course, unless it can be cogently argued that a reading was brought into being in that manuscript, it will always be older than that manuscript, at least by the difference in age between that manuscript and the one from which it was copied. Moreover, variant readings in the New Testament seem to have been preserved for a long time, so that sometimes readings had hitherto been believed to be Byzantine in origin turn up in papyrus manuscripts many centuries older.

4. This gives rise to some interesting situations, since although the Hebrew is the original tongue and the Greek a derivative of it, the Septuagint was made a thousand years before the manuscript which best represents the Massoretic text, and on occasion provides an older and more intelligible form of text.

5. This is true of Roman Catholicism, which until rather recently adhered to a particular early printed form of the Latin Vulgate text. It is now only a few Protestant groups that cling stubbornly to the form of text as it happened first to be printed.

6. The Peshitta is the Syrian equivalent of the Latin Vulgate, a form of text given authority in the fifth century by Rabbula, Bishop of Edessa, much as the Latin was authorised by Pope Damasus. And also as with the Latin, it is a particular form of the Syriac which is accepted in its printed form.

7. See C. Hempel, "The Literary Development of the S-Tradition. A New Paradigm," *Révue de Qumran* 22 (2006): 389–401.

8. In fact, today we possess more multiple forms than any other generation, for in the past couple of centuries we have been able to recover increasingly ancient forms of text, first in the discovery of older witnesses in libraries, more recently through the recovery of papyrus texts from desert sites.

9. In D.C. Parker, *The Living Text of the Gospels* (Cambridge: Cambridge University Press, 1997), 102.

10. This is similar to the way in which we tend to associate details from other Gospels with the version in a particular Gospel.

11. For a more detailed explanation (and the same analogy of tracing one's family tree), see D. C. Parker, *An Introduction to the New Testament Manuscripts and Their Texts*, (Cambridge: Cambridge University Press, 2008).

12. Apart from the genealogical reasons for this already given, it is sometimes asked whether the concept of the all-significant author is not a modern imposition upon antiquity.

13. I am thinking of the so-called Kr text, exemplified in carefully-copied manuscripts such as 19 or 35, which provides the basis for the orthography of modern editions.

14. The digital tools available from Birmingham and Münster, even in their current stage of development, should be the port of call for anyone interested in the New Testament text.

15. See D. C. Parker, *Codex Sinaiticus: The Story of the World's Oldest Bible* (London: The British Library; and Peabody, Mass.: Hendrickson, 2010).

Chapter 5

1. Bart Ehrman, *Misquoting Jesus: The Story Behind Who Changed the Bible and Why* (New York: HarperSanFrancisco, 2005), 10.

2. Ibid., 207.

3. See Barbara Aland, Kurt Aland, Johannes Karavidopoulos, Carlo Martini, and Bruce Metzger, eds., *Novum Testamentum Graece* 27th rev. ed. (Stuttgart: Deutsche Bibelgesellschaft, 2001), and The Greek New Testament 4th rev. ed., (Stuttgart: United Bible Societies, 1994).

4. See David Parker, *The Living Text of the Gospels* (Cambridge: Cambridge University Press, 1997), 3–7.

5. The fifth century Codex Alexandrinus also contains books not presently in the New Testament, namely *1&2 Clement*, which follow Revelation in the manuscript.

6. For a good characterization of the reformed documentary hand, see among others Harry Y. Gamble, *Books and Readers in Early Christianity: A History of Early Christian Texts* (New Haven: Yale University Press, 1995), 70–74.

7. Barbara Aland, *The Significance of the Chester Beatty Biblical Papyri in Early Church History in The Earliest Gospels: The Origins and Transmission of the Earliest Christian Gospels— The Contribution of the Chester Beatty Gospel Codex P45*, Charles Horton, ed. (New York: T. & T. Clark, 2004), 108.

8. Ibid., 116.

9. See Eldon Jay Epp, *The Theological Tendency of Codex Bezae Cantabrigiensis in Acts* (Eugene, Ore.: Wipf & Stock, 2001), with an excellent summary of his findings on pages 165–71.

10. B. F. Westcott and F. J. A. Hort, *Introduction to the New Testament in the Original Greek with Notes on Selected Readings* (New York: Harper and Brothers, 1882/Reprint by Hendrickson Publishers, 1988), 145.

11. See Bart Ehrman, *The Orthodox Corruption of Scripture: The Effect of Early Christological Controversies on the Text of the New Testament* (New York: Oxford University Press, 1993); Ehrman, *Misquoting Jesus*; and Wayne Kannaday, *Apologetic Discourse and the Scribal Tradition: Evidence of the Influence of Apologetic Interests on the Texts of the Canonical Gospels* (Atlanta: Society of Biblical Literature, 2004).

Chapter 6

1. Kurt Aland, and Barbara Aland, *The Text of the New Testament. An Introduction to the Critical Editions and to the Theory and Practice of Modern Textual Criticism*, revised and enlarged edition (Grand Rapids: Eerdmans 1995), 29.

2. This article is a revised English version of my German paper "Labilität und Festigkeit des überlieferten Textes des Neuen Testaments und des *Pastor of Hermas*, demonstriert an wichtigen Textzeugen," *Sacra Scripta* 7.1 (2009): 65–97. For the general point made and some of the arguments set forth in this article, I am largely indebted to the unpublished paper, "The Integrity of the Early New Testament Text: A Collation-Based Comparison Utilizing the Papyri of the Second and Third Centuries" by M.A. Robinson. In addition, I want to thank Ulrich B. Schmid and Tommy Wasserman for their critical remarks and Alexander Hepher for translating the paper into English.

3. B. F. Westcott and F. J. A. Hort, *Introduction to the New Testament in the Original Greek* (London: Macmillan, 1881), 2.

4. Bart D. Ehrman, *Misquoting Jesus: The Story Behind Who Changed the Bible and Why* (San Francisco: HarperCollins, 2005), 210–11.

5. Ibid., 7.

6. Hermann Freiherr von Soden: *Die Schriften des Neuen Testamentes in ihrer ältesten erreichbaren Textgestalt*, vol. I, parts 1–3: Untersuchungen, second edition (Göttingen: Vandenhoeck & Ruprecht 1911), 712: "Die Materie des [byzantinischen] Textes bleibt durch die ganzen vielleicht 1200 Jahre intakt. Nur ganz vereinzelt tauchen bei der einen oder anderen Spielart Lesarten auf, die sich in anderen Typen finden" [The material of the Byzantine text remains intact for about 1200 years. Variants known from other texttypes may come up in the one or the other of the Byzantine subversions, but this happens very rarely].

7. See Maurice A. Robinson and W.G. Pierpont, *The New Testament in the Original Greek: Byzantine Textform* (Southborough, Mass.: Chilton, 2005).

8. Campbell Bonner, ed., *A Papyrus Codex of the Shepherd of Hermas (Similitudes 2–9) with a Fragment of the Mandates* (Ann Arbor: University of Michigan Press, 1934), 31.

9. In the New Testament manuscripts these corrections are still clearly visible; cf. the chapter "Corrections in Manuscripts" in Daniel C. Parker, *An Introduction to the New Testament Manuscripts and Their Texts* (Cambridge: Cambridge University Press, 2008), 141–48.

10. Some variants make it difficult to reconstruct a single "source text of transmission"; so that according to Parker we should perhaps in the face of these difficult variants rather speak of "source texts of transmission." This, however, would still relinquish the never-ending task of determining which of these source texts is primary (that is, the attainable source text that is most likely original) and which is secondary to us; cf. Daniel C. Parker, "Textual Criticism and Theology," *Expository Times* 118.12 (2007): 583–89.

11. Cf. Gordon D. Fee, "The Text of John in Origen and Cyril of Alexandria: A Contribution to Methodology in the Recovery and Analysis of Patristic Citations" in ed. Eldon J. Epp and Gordon D. Fee, *Studies in the Theory and Method of New Testament Textual Criticism*, (Grand Rapids: Eerdmans, 1993), 301–34; Gordon D. Fee, "Codex Sinaiticus in the Gospel of John: A Contribution to Methodology in Establishing

Textual Relationships" in *Studies in the Theory and Method of New Testament Textual Criticism*, 221–43; for an up-to-date overview of this method of qualifying a manuscript, see Eldon J. Epp, "It's All about Variants: A Variant-Conscious Approach to New Testament Textual Criticism," *Harvard Theological Review* 100 (2007): 275–308.

12. Frederic G. Kenyon, *The Chester Beatty Biblical Papyri, Fasciculus II: The Gospels and Acts* (London: Walker, 1933), xix–xx.

13. Kyoung Shik Min, *Die früheste Überlieferung des Matthäusevangeliums (bis zum 3./4. Jh.), Edition und Untersuchung* [The Earliest Tradition of Matthew's Gospel], ANTT 34 (Berlin: de Gruyter, 2005), 132ff; 151.

14. Barbara Aland, "The Significance of the Chester Beatty Biblical Papyri in Early Church History," in *The Earliest Gospels: The Origins and Transmission of the Earliest Christian Gospels—The Contribution of the Chester Beatty Gospel Codex P45*, Journal for the Study of the New Testament: Supplement Series 258, ed. Charles Horton (London: T & T Clark, 2004), 112.

15. James R. Royse, *Scribal Habits in Early Greek New Testament Papyri* (Leiden: Brill. 2008), 197.

16. Ibid., 138.

17. Kurt and Barbara Aland, *The Text of the New Testament*, 93.

18. Günther Zuntz, *The Text of the Epistles: A Disquisition upon the Corpus Paulinum* The Schweich Lectures of the British Academy 1946, (London: British Academy, 1953), 212.

19. Royse, *Scribal Habits*, 355–57.

20. Cf. Victor Martin and Rodolphe Kasser, *Papyrus Bodmer XIV: Evangile de Luc chap. 3–24* (Genève: Bibliotheca Bodmeriana, 1961), 23; Royse, *Scribal Habits*, 666 n. 278.

21. Royse, *Scribal Habits*, 704.

22. Eldon J. Epp, *The Theological Tendency of Codex Bezae Cantabrigiensis in Acts*, Society for New Testament Studies Monograph Series 3 (Cambridge: Cambridge University Press, 1966).

23. Bart D. Ehrman, *The Orthodox Corruption of Scripture: The Effect of Early Christological Controversies on the Text of the New Testament* (Oxford: Oxford University Press, 1993).

24. David C. Parker, *The Living Text of the Gospels* (Cambridge: Cambridge University Press, 1997).

25. Eldon J. Epp, "The Significance of the Papyri for determining the Nature of the New Testament Text in the Second Century: A Dynamic View of Textual Transmission," in *Studies in the Theory and Method of New Testament Textual Criticism*, 277–83.

26. Ernest Cadman Colwell, "Method in Evaluating Scribal Habits: A Study of $\mathfrak{P}^{45}$, $\mathfrak{P}^{66}$, $\mathfrak{P}^{75}$" in *Studies in Methodology in Textual Criticism of the New Testament*, New Testament Tools and Studies 9, ed. Ernest Cadman Colwell (Leiden: Brill, 1969), 117.

27. Barbara Aland, "Neutestamentliche Handschriften als Interpreten des Textes? $\mathfrak{P}^{75}$ und seine Vorlagen in Joh 10" [Are New Testament manuscripts interpreting the Text? $\mathfrak{P}^{75}$ and its *Vorlagen* in John 10] in *Jesu Rede von Gott und ihre Nachgeschichte im frühen Christentum. Beiträge zur Verkündigung Jesu und zum Kerygma der Kirche. Festschrift für*

Willi Marxsen zum 70. Geburtstag, ed. Dietrich-Alex Koch, Gerhard Sellin, and Andreas Lindemann (Gütersloh: Gütersloher Verlags-Haus Mohn, 1989), 320–23.

28. Barbara Aland,"Das Zeugnis der frühen Papyri für den Text der Evangelien, diskutiert am Matthäusevangelium," [The witness of the early papyri for the text of the Gospels: discussing the gospel of Matthew] in *The Four Gospels 1992. Festschrift Frans Neirynck*, Bibliotheca ephemeridum theologicarum lovaniensium 100, ed. F. Van Segbroeck, et. al. (Leuven: University Press), 329ff.

29. Rodolphe Kasser, Marvin Meyer, and Gregor Wurst, *The Gospel of Judas* (Washington: National Geographic, 2006).

30. Richard Bentley, *Remarks upon a late Discourse of Free-Thinking in a Letter to F.H. D.D. by Phileleutherus Lipsiensis* (London: Printed for John Morphew, 1713), 64.

31. Ibid., 64ff.

32. Kurt and Barbara Aland, *The Text of the New Testament*, 71.

33. Carl Schmidt and Wilhelm Schubart, *Altchristliche Texte* [Early Christian Texts], Berliner Klassikertexte VI (Berlin: Weidmann, 1910), 16.

34. Wilhelm Schneemelcher, *Neutestamentliche Apokryphen in deutscher Übersetzung* [New Testament Apocrypha in German Translation], 6th ed. (Tübingen: J.C.B. Mohr, 1990), 1:29.

35. Nick Gonis, *The Oxyrhynchus Papyri, Volume LXIX* (London: Egypt Exploration Society, 2005), 1.

36. Schneemelcher, *Neutestamentliche Apokryphen*, 2:538; Gianfrancesco Lusini, "Nouvelles recherches sur le texte du *Pasteur d'Hermas*" [New research regarding the text of the Shepherd of Hermas], *Apocrypha* 12 (2001), 82.

37. Bart D. Ehrman, "Textual Traditions Compared: The New Testament and the Apostolic Fathers," in *The Reception of the New Testament in the Apostolic Fathers*, ed. Andrew F. Gregory and Christopher M. Tuckett (Oxford: Oxford University Press, 2005), 10.

38. Bonner, *Papyrus Codex*, 24.

39. Fee, "The Text of John in Origen and Cyril of Alexandria," 309.

40. Colwell, "Method in Evaluating Quantitative Relationships between Text-Types of New Testament Manuscripts," in *Studies in Methodology in Textual Criticism of the New Testament*, 56–62.

41. Schmidt and Schubart, *Altchristliche Texte*, 15.

42. Lee Martin McDonald, *The Biblical Canon* (Peabody: Hendrickson, 2007), 67, 302, 304, 307.

43. Larry W. Hurtado, *The Earliest Christian Artifacts: Manuscripts and Christian Origins* (Grand Rapids: Eerdmans. 2006), 57.

44. Kim Haines-Eitzen, *Guardians of Letters: Literacy, Power, and the Transmitters of Early Christian Literature* (Oxford: Oxford University Press, 2000): 5–8, 36–40; Ehrman, *Misquoting Jesus*, 47–51.

45. Lusini, "Nouvelles recherches," 92.

46. Bonner, *Papyrus Codex*, 30.

47. Carolyn Osiek, *Shepherd of Hermas: A Commentary*, Hermeneia (Minneapolis: Fortress Press, 1999), 1.

48. Lusini, "Nouvelles recherches," 82.

49. Min, *Die früheste Überlieferung des Matthäusevangeliums* [The Earliest Tradition of Matthew's Gospel], 279ff; cf. Emanuel Tov, "A Qumran Origin for the Masada Non-Biblical Texts?" *Dead Sea Discoveries* 7.1 (2000): 61; Emanuel Tov, *Scribal Practices and Approaches Reflected in the Texts Found in the Judean Desert* (Leiden: Brill, 2004), 126–29.

50. Bonner, *Papyrus Codex*, 27.

51. Ibid., 131.

52. Ibid., 20.

53. C.H. Turner, "The *Shepherd* of Hermas and the Problem of its Text," *Journal of Theological Studies* 21 (1920): 202.

54. Antonio Carlini, *Papyrus Bodmer XXXVIII. Erma: Il Pastore (Ia-IIIa visione)* (Cologny-Genève: Fondation Martin Bodmer, 1991), 17.

55. Molly Whittaker, *Die Apostolischen Väter I: Der Hirt des Hermas* [The Apostolic Father 1: The Shepherd of Hemas], 2nd. ed. (Berlin: Akademie-Verlag, 1967), x–xi; cf. Roger Joly, *Hermas–Le Pasteur. Introduction, texte critique, traduction et notes* [Hermas, the Shepherd. Introduction, Critical Apparatus, Translation, and Notes], 2nd. ed. (Paris: Les éditions du Cerf, 1968), 61–62.

56. Michele Bandini, "Un nuovo frammento greco del Pastore di Erma" [A new Greek fragment of the Shepherd of Hermas], in *Revue d'histoire des textes* 30 (2000), 117–20.

57. Whittaker, *Die Apostolischen Väter*, xi.

58. Bart D. Ehrman, "Textual Traditions Compared," 22.

59. Ibid., 11.

60. Kirsopp Lake, *Facsimiles of the Athos fragments of the Shepherd of Hermas photographed and transcribed* (Oxford: Clarendon, 1907), iii–iv.

61. H. J. M. Milne and T.C. Skeat, *Scribes and Correctors of the Codex Sinaiticus* (London: British Museum, 1938), 16.

62. Bonner, *Papyrus Codex*, 28–29.

63. Bandini, "Un nuovo frammento greco," 120–22.

64. Johannes Tromp, "Zur Edition apokrypher Texte: Am Beispiel des griechischen *Lebens Adams und Evas*," [Editing apocryphal texts: the Greek version of *The Life of Adam and Eve*] in *Recent Developments in Textual Criticism. New Testament, Other Early Christian and Jewish Literature*, STAR 8, ed. Wim Weren and Dietrich-Alex Koch (Assen: Royal van Gorcum, 2003), 193.

65. Dietrich-Alex Koch, "Textkritik in frühchristlicher Literatur ausserhalb des Neuen Testaments: Barn 1,6 als Beispiel" [Textual criticism in early Christian literature outside the New Testament: Barnabas 1:6 as an example] in *Recent Developments in Textual Criticism*, 149.

66. Ferdinand R. Prostmeier, *Der Barnabasbrief*, KAV 8 (Göttingen: Vandenhoeck & Ruprecht 1999), 69, cf. 14.

67. H. Köster, "Überlieferung und Geschichte der nachchristlichen Evangelienliteratur" [The tradition and history of the gospels written after the initial Christian

era] in: *Aufstieg und Niedergang der römischen Welt* (ANRW) 25/2 (Berlin: de Gruyter 1984, 1463–1542), 1483.

68. Schneemelcher, *Neutestamentliche Apokryphen*, 1:334.

69. Émile de Strycker, *La forme la plus ancienne du Protévangile de Jacques* [The most ancient form of the Protevangelium of James], SH 33 (Bruxelles: Société des Bollandistes, 1961), 16.

70. The papyrus Bodmer 5 (as edited by Testuz in 1958) was collated against the Tischendorf 1876 edition (based on minuscules of the ninth through the sixteenth centuries). To get the sum total of the words, the edition of Strycker was used. M. Testuz, Papyrus *Bodmer V, Nativité de Marie*, (Genève: Bibliotheca Bodmeriana 1958); Konstantin von Tischendorf, *Evangelia apocrypha (editio altera)*, Reprint 1966 (Hildesheim: Olms 1876).

71. Strycker, *La forme la plus ancienne*, 391.

72. Kirsopp Lake, *The Apostolic Fathers*, (London: Heinemann, 1913), 2:5.

73. Bonner, *Papyrus Codex*, 31.

74. Milne and Skeat, *Scribes and Correctors*, 16.

75. A. Hilhorst, *Sémitismes et latinismes dans le Pasteur d'Hermas = Graecitas Christianorum Primaeva, Fasciculus Quintus* [Semitisms and Latinisms in the Shepherd of Hermas] (1976), 16.

76. Ehrman, "Textual Traditions Compared," 26–27.

77. The transmission of the New Testament text "ist trotz der Variantenfülle gut und zuverlässig zu nennen" [despite its numerous variants, the transmission of the New Testament text can be called good and reliable] (B. Aland, "Neutestamentliche Handschriften als Interpreten des Textes?", 396, footnote).

78. Ehrman, *The Orthodox Corruption of Scripture*, 276.

79. Cf. Klaus Wachtel, "Kinds of Variants in the Manuscript Tradition of the Greek New Testament" in *Studies in Stemmatology II*, ed. Pieter van Reenen, August den Hollander, and Margot van Mulken (Amsterdam: Benjamins, 2004), 87–98; Klaus Wachtel, "Varianten in der handschriftlichen Überlieferung des Neuen Testaments" in *Varianten-Variants-Variantes*, ed. Christa Jansohn and Bodo Plachta (Tübingen: Niemeyer, 2005), 25–38.

80. Ehrman, *Misquoting Jesus*, 7.

81. D-text; cf. Epp, *The Theological Tendency of Codex Bezae Cantabrigiensis in Acts*; Barbara Aland, "Entstehung, Charakter und Herkunft des sog. westlichen Textes, untersucht an der Apostelgeschichte" [The Emergence, Character and Provenance of the so-called Western Text, studied in the book of Acts], *Ephemerides Theologicae Lovanienses* 62 (1986): 5–65.

82. Barbara Aland, "Die Münsteraner Arbeit am Text des Neuen Testaments und ihr Beitrag für die frühe Überlieferung des 2. Jahrhunderts: Eine methodologische Betrachtung" [The work on the text of the New Testament in Muenster and its contribution for the early transmission of the second century] in *Gospel Traditions in the Second Century*, in William L. Petersen (Notre Dame: University of Notre Dame Press, 1989), 63.

83. Kurt Aland, "Der neutestamentliche Text in der vorkonstantinischen Epoche" [The New Testament text in the pre-Constantine era] in *Pléroma—Salus*

carnis, Homenaje a Antonio Orbe, ed. Eugenio S.J., Pomero-Pose (Santiago de Compostela: ed. por Eugenio Romero-Pose), 55–56.

84. Epp, *The Theological Tendency of Codex Bezae Cantabrigiensis in Acts.*

85. Heike Omerzu, "Die Darstellung der Römer in der Textüberlieferung der Apostelgeschichte" [The portrayal of the Romans in the textual tradition of the book of Acts] in *The Book of Acts as Church History—Apostelgeschichte als Kirchengeschichte*, Beihefte zur Zeitschrift für die neutestamentliche Wissenschaft 120, ed. Tobias Nicklas and Michael Tilly (Berlin: de Gruyter, 2003), 147–81.

86. Ben Witherington III, "The Anti-Feminist Tendencies of the 'Western' Text in Acts," *Journal of Biblical Literature* 103 (1984): 82–84; Richard I. Pervo "Social and Religious Aspects of the Western Text" in *The Living Text, Essays in Honor of Ernest W. Saunders*, ed. Dennis E. Groh and Robert Jewett, (Lanham: University Press of America, 1985), 235–40; Michael W. Holmes, "Women and the 'Western Text' of Acts," in *The Book of Acts as Church History*, 183–203; Dominika A. Kurek-Chomycz, "Is There an 'Anti-Priscan' Tendency in the Manuscripts? Some Textual Problems with Prisca and Aquila," *Journal of Biblical Literature* 125 (2006): 118–28.

87. Bernard P. Grenfell and Arthur S. Hunt, *The Oxyrhynchus Papyri, Volume IX* (London: Egypt Exploration Society, 1912), 12.

88. Barbara Aland, "Sind Schreiber früher neutestamentlicher Handschriften Interpreten des Textes?" [Were the scribes of the early New Testament manuscripts exegetes of the text?] in *Transmission and Reception: New Testament Text-Critical and Exegetical Studies*, Texts and Studies III/4, ed. J. W. Childers and Daniel C. Parker, D.C (Piscataway: Gorgias, 2006), 396.

89. James W. Voelz, "The Greek of Codex Vaticanus in the Second Gospel and Marcan Greek," *Novum Testamentum* 47 (2005): 209–49.

90. Aland, "Neutestamentliche Handschriften als Interpreten des Textes?" 116.

91. Westcott and Hort, *Introduction to the New Testament in the Original Greek*, 2; "substantial variation."

92. Léon Vaganay and C.B. Amphoux, *An Introduction to New Testament Textual Criticism* (Cambridge: Cambridge University Press, 1991), 2.

93. Min, *Die früheste Überlieferung des Matthäusevangeliums*, 2009.

94. Kenneth W. Clark, "Textual Criticism and Doctrine" in *Studia Paulina in honorem Johannis de Zwaan Septuagenarii*, ed. J.N. Sevenester and W.C. van Unnik (Haarlem: Bohn, 1953), 65.

95. Eldon J. Epp, "The Multivalence of the Term 'Original Text' in New Testament Textual Criticism," *Harvard Theological Review* 92 (1999): 280.

96. Ibid.

97. Kurt Aland, "Der neutestamentliche Text in der vorkonstantinischen Epoche", 57.

98. M. D. Koster, *The Peshitta of Exodus: The Development of its Text in the Course of Fifteen Centuries* (Assen: Van Gorcum 1977), 540.

99. Clark, "Textual Criticism and Doctrine," 65.

Chapter 7

1. For scholarly discussion, see Kurt Aland, "Bemerkungen zum Schluss des Markusevangeliums [Comments at the End of Mark's Gospel]," in E. Earle Ellis and Max Wilcox, eds., *Neotestamentica et Semitica: Studies in Honour of Matthew Black* (Edinburgh: T & T Clark, 1969), 157–80; William R. Farmer, *The Last Twelve Verses of Mark* (Cambridge: Cambridge University Press, 1974); Bruce. M. Metzger, *A Textual Commentary on the Greek New Testament* (London and New York: United Bible Societies, 1971), 122–26; idem, *The Text of the New Testament: Its Transmission, Corruption and Restoration*, 3rd ed. (Oxford: Oxford University Press, 1992), 226–29.

2. For scholarly discussion, see Raymond E. Brown, *The Gospel according to John I–XII* (Garden City: Doubleday, 1966), 332–38; Metzger, *A Textual Commentary on the Greek New Testament*, 219–22; Bart D. Ehrman, "Jesus and the Adulteress," *New Testament Studies* 34 (1988), 24–44; John Paul Heil, "The Story of Jesus and the Adulteress (John 7:53—8:11) Reconsidered," *Biblica* 72 (1991): 182–91; Daniel B. Wallace, "Reconsidering 'The Story of Jesus and the Adulteress Reconsidered,'" *New Testament Studies* 39 (1993): 290–96. Wallace is replying to Heil.

3. See Gary M. Burge, "A Specific Problem in the New Testament Text and Canon: The Woman Caught in Adultery (John 7:53—8:11)," *Journal of the Evangelical Theological Society* 27 (1984): 141–48.

4. For scholarly discussion, see Metzger, *A Textual Commentary on the Greek New Testament*, 177; Bart D. Ehrman and Mark A. Plunkett, "The Angel and the Agony: The Textual Problem of Luke 22:43–44," *Catholic Biblical Quarterly* 45 (1983): 401–16; Raymond E. Brown, "The Lucan Authorship of Luke 22:43–44," in E. H. Lovering Jr., ed., *Society of Biblical Literature 1992 Seminar Papers* (Atlanta: Scholars Press, 1992), 154–64. Brown argues that the longer passage may well be original to Luke.

5. For scholarly discussion, see Metzger, *A Textual Commentary on the Greek New Testament*, 209; Brown, *The Gospel according to John I–XII*, 207; Gordon D. Fee, "On the Inauthenticity of John 5:3b-4," *Evangelical Quarterly* 54 (1982): 207–18.

6. For scholarly discussion, see Asa R. Crabtree, "Translation of Romans 5:1 in the Revised Standard Version," *Review and Expositor* 43 (1946): 436–39; Metzger, *A Textual Commentary on the Greek New Testament*, 511; C. E. B. Cranfield, *A Critical and Exegetical Commentary on the Epistle to the Romans*, Vol. I: *Introduction and Commentary on Romans I–VIII* (Edinburgh: T & T Clark, 1975), 257–58; James D. G. Dunn, *Romans 1–8* (Dallas: Word, 1988) 245; Joseph A. Fitzmyer, *Romans: A New Translation with Introduction and Commentary* (New York: Doubleday, 1993), 395. For a defense of the "let us have peace with God" reading, see Robert Jewett, *Romans: A Commentary*, Hermeneia (Minneapolis: Fortress Press, 2007) 344, 348–49.

7. For scholarly discussion, see Gordon D. Fee, *The First Epistle to the Corinthians* (Grand Rapids: Eerdmans, 1987) 699–711; idem, *God's Empowering Presence: The Holy Spirit in the Letters of Paul* (Peabody: Hendrickson, 1994) 272–81; P. B. Payne, "MS. 88 as Evidence for a Text without 1 Cor 14.34–5," *New Testament Studies* 44 (1998) 152–58.

8. For discussion of the difficulties, see D. C. Allison Jr. and W. D. Davies, *A Critical and Exegetical Commentary on the Gospel according to Saint Matthew*. Volume III: *Commentary on Matthew XIX–XXVIII* (Edinburgh: T & T Clark, 1997) 628–35.

9. Early church fathers puzzled over these questions, speculating that Moses and Elijah, perhaps other Old Testament prophets and the like, were among these holy ones. Some medieval interpreters thought that these resurrected ones lived on for centuries.

10. This late textual gloss is known as the Comma Johanneum. For discussion, see Metzger, *A Textual Commentary on the Greek New Testament*, 716–18; H. J. de Jonge, "Erasmus and the Comma Johanneum," *Ephemerides Theologicae Lovanienses* 56 (1980), 381–89; Raymond E. Brown, *The Epistles of John* (Garden City: Doubleday, 1982), 775–87; Franz Posset, "John Bugenhagen and the *Comma Johanneum*," *Concordia Theological Quarterly* 49 (1985): 245–51; R. Borger, "Das Comma Johanneum in der Peschitta" [The "Comma Johanneum" in the Peshitta], *Novum Testamentum* 29 (1987): 280–84. Erasmus added the expanded form of 1 Jn. 5:7-8 to his 1522 edition of the Greek text.

11. As in Bart D. Ehrman, *Misquoting Jesus: The Story Behind Who Changed the Bible and Why* (New York: HarperSanFrancisco, 2005), 9. Ehrman's book contains several specious and misleading claims about textual variants that supposedly impinge in significant ways on important Christian teachings. For a succinct rebuttal, see J. E. Komoszewski, M. J. Sawyer, and D. B. Wallace, *Reinventing Jesus* (Grand Rapids: Kregel, 2006), 103–17, with notes on 283–95. The scholarly underpinnings of *Misquoting Jesus* are found in Ehrman's *The Orthodox Corruption of Scripture: The Effect of Early Christological Controversies on the Text of the New Testament* (New York: Oxford University Press, 1993). This work exaggerates the evidence and sometimes draws highly unwarranted conclusions. For critical reviews, see J. N. Birdsall, in *Theology* 97 (1994): 460–62; Bruce M. Metzger, in *Princeton Seminary Bulletin* 15 (1994): 210–12; and Gordon D. Fee, in *Critical Review of Books of Religion* 8 (1995): 203–6. Birdsall, Metzger, and Fee are highly regarded textual critics. In fact, Metzger is Ehrman's doctoral mentor.

12. For scholarly discussion, see M. R. Mulholland, "Abiathar," in J. B. Green, S. McKnight, and I. H. Marshall, eds., *Dictionary of Jesus and the Gospels* (Downers Grove: InterVarsity, 1992), 1–2; K. W. Whitelam, "Abiathar," in D. N. Freedman et al., eds., *The Anchor Bible Dictionary* 6 vols. (New York: Doubleday, 1992) 1:13–14; Craig A. Evans, "Abiathar," in Craig A. Evans, ed., *Encyclopedia of the Historical Jesus* (New York: Routledge, 2008), 1–2.

13. Recently this objection has been raised by Ehrman, *Misquoting Jesus*, 9–10.

14. As rightly noted by Robert A. Guelich, *Mark 1—8:26* (Dallas: Word, 1989), 249–50; Robert H. Gundry, *Mark: A Commentary on His Apology for the Cross* (Grand Rapids: Eerdmans, 1993), 229.

15. N. T. Wright makes this point in his reference to the famous episode of Ludwig Wittgenstein and the fireplace poker. October 25, 1946, Karl Popper was invited to Cambridge and for the first time met Wittgenstein face to face. At some point in the meeting Wittgenstein picked up a poker and waved it about as he made a point to Popper. He then threw down the poker and left the room. Although several learned persons, including Bertrand Russell, witnessed this remarkable event, none of then could agree as to the precise order of events and various other details. Yet, no one doubts that the event took place or doubts the principal figures and facts of the event. See Craig A. Evans and N. T. Wright, *Jesus, the Final Days: What Really Happened* (Louisville and London: Westminster John Knox, 2009), 80–81.

16. On this important point, see Richard J. Bauckham, *Jesus and the Eyewitnesses: The Gospels as Eyewitness Testimony* (Grand Rapids: Eerdmans, 2006). See also James D. G. Dunn, *Jesus Remembered*, Christianity in the Making 1 (Grand Rapids: Eerdmans, 2003).

Chapter 8

1. Bart Ehrman, *Misquoting Jesus: The Story Behind Who Changed the Bible and Why* (New York: Harper Collins, 2005), 2.

2. Dale B. Martin, "The Necessity of a Theology of Scripture," in the present volume.

3. Harry Y. Gamble, "Literacy, Liturgy, and the Shaping of the New Testament Canon," in *The Earliest Gospels*, Charles Horton, ed. (London: T & T Clark International, 2004), 28.

4. Ibid., 38.

5. Ibid., 33.

6. Larry Hurtado, "The New Testament in the Second Century: Text, Collections and Canon" in *Transmission and Reception: New Testament Text-Critical and Exegetical Studies*, J. W. Childers and D. C. Parker, eds. (Piscataway: Gorgias, 2006), 10–14. Christians also praised codices because they provided fast cross-referencing, and were easily transportable and more economical.

7. Kim Haines-Eitzen, *Guardians of Letters: Literacy, Power, and the Transmitters of Early Christian Literature* (Oxford: Oxford University Press, 2000), 104.

8. The following books on the formation of the Christian Bible explain the rapid shift from the oral transmission of Jesus' teachings to the circulation of Christian documents: Harry Y. Gamble, *Books and Readers in the Early Church: A History of Early Christian Texts* (New Haven: Yale University Press, 1995), 49–66; Frederick F. Bruce, *The Canon of Scripture* (Downers Grove: InterVarsity, 1988); Bruce M. Metzger, *The Canon of the New Testament: Its Origin, Development, and Significance* (Oxford: Clarendon, 1987); Lee McDonald, *The Formation of the Christian Biblical Canon*, 2nd ed. (Peabody: Hendrickson, 1995); Hans von Campenhausen, *The Formation of the Christian Bible* (Philadelphia: Fortress Press, 1972); E. Earle Ellis, *The Making of the New Testament Documents* (Boston: Brill Academic, 2002).

9. Gamble, *Books and Readers*, 92, 55.

10. Two types of scribes thrived: (1) the *librarii* or literary scribes functioned as stenographers, secretaries, copyists, messengers, and letter carriers; (2) the *scribae*, or bureaucratic scribes, handled public administrative tasks but could still be called upon to copy texts. Most *librarii* were slaves or freedpersons in the pay of a private person while the official scribes were men of some prestige. Even women could engage in such activities although most evidences pointed to women working for women. See Gamble, *Books and Readers*, 86–87; William H. Harris, *Ancient Literacy* (Cambridge: Harvard University Press, 1989), 196–233; Haines-Eitzen, *Guardians of Letters*, 12–47.

11. Van Der Toorn gives the example of a rabbinic tractate who priced a Torah scroll at about 100 mineh, which equaled 10,000 pieces of silver. Karel Van Der Toorn, *Scribal Culture and the Making of the Hebrew Bible* (Cambridge: Harvard University Press, 2007), 19.

12. Anthony J. Saldarini, *Pharisees, Scribes, and Sadduccees in Palestinian Society* (Grand Rapids: Eerdmans, 2001), 247.

13. Ibid., 248.

14. Josephus, *Ant.* 12.3.3. See Malachi Martin, *The Scribal Character of the Dead Sea Scrolls* (Louvain: Publications Universitaires, 1958).

15. See Josephus, *Ant.* 6.6.4, 7.14.7, 7.13.1. The Temple scribes were responsible for "teaching, record keeping, preservation of the sacred tradition and ruling on points of law and custom" (Saldarini, *Pharisees, Scribes, and Sadduccees*, 263). The Middle class scribes were imminent men, ascribed to the king (Josephus, *War* 1.26.3, 5.13.1). Finally, the village clerk knew enough to record local formalities (Josephus, *War*, 1.24.3).

16. James A. Sanders, "Text and Canon: Concepts and Method," *Journal of Biblical Literature* 98 (1979): 22.

17. Saldarini, *Pharisees, Scribes, and Sadduccees*, 273.

18. Harris, *Ancient Literacy*, 26–27; Gamble, *Books and Readers*, 10. Furthermore, Christians of the second and third centuries belonged to the same variety of social classes as the rest of Greco-Roman society. See Wayne A. Meeks, *The First Urban Christians: The Social World of the Apostle Paul* (New Haven: Yale University Press, 1983); Ekkehard W. Stegemann and Wolfgang Stegemann, *The Jesus Movement: A Social History of Its First Century*, trans. O. C. Dean, Jr. (Minneapolis: Fortress Press, 1999).

19. Gamble, *Books and Readers*, 30.

20. Haines-Eitzen, *Guardians of Letters*, 68.

21. Having found the case of an illiterate scribe, Ehrman unfairly generalizes his argument to accuse most Christian scribes of incapacity. Bart D. Ehrman, *Misquoting Jesus: The Story Behind Who Changed the Bible and Why* (New York: HarperOne, 2007), 39, 52, 55. They may have been untrained in religious matters but were not necessarily incapable of writing and reading.

22. James R. Royse, *Scribal Habits in Early Greek New Testament Papyri* (Leiden, Netherlands: Brill, 2008), 199–358. Some scholars prefer the terms "correct" and "incorrect" for the classification of textual variants.

23. Ibid., xxx.

24. Rafaella Cribiore, *Writing, Teachers, and Students in Graeco-Roman Egypt* (Atlanta: Scholars, 1996), 44, 137.

25. Ibid., 45.

26. Alan K. Bowman and Greg Woolf discussed this power issue over texts in "Literacy and Power in the Ancient World," in *Literacy and Power in the Ancient World*, ed. A. K. Bowman and G. Woolf (Cambridge: Cambridge University Press, 1994), 1–16. Consult also Robin Lane Fox, "Literacy and Power in Early Christianity," in *Literacy and Power in the Ancient World*, 126–48.

27. Gordon D. Fee, "The Use of the Greek Fathers for New Testament Textual Criticism," in *The Text of the New Testament in Contemporary Research: Essays on the Status Quaestionis*, ed. Bart D. Ehrman and Michael W. Holmes (Grand Rapids: Eerdmans, 1995), 193.

28. Hurtado, "The New Testament in the Second Century," 9.

29. In Eusebius, *Hist. Eccl.* 5.20.2.

30. J. H. Greenlee, *Scribes, Scrolls and Scriptures* (Cumbria, UK: Paternoster, 1996), 63.

31. Philip W. Comfort, *Encountering the Manuscripts: An Introduction to New Testament Paleography and Textual Criticism* (Nashville: Broadman and Holman, 2005), 262–65.

32. Van Der Toorn, *Scribal Culture*, 115.

33. Ibid., 23.

34. For a survey of this tendency in Egypt, refer to C. Wilfred Griggs, *Early Egyptian Christianity from Its Origins to 451 C.E.* (New York: Brill, 1990), 45–70.

35. Stott claims that Tacitus made a more conscious effort to consult public archives. Katherine M. Stott, *Why Did They Write This Way? Reflections on References to Written Documents in the Hebrew Bible and Ancient Literature* (New York: T. & T. Clark, 2008), 19–51, 40, 50.

36. Stott, *Why Did They Write This Way*, 15. Not only were ancient historians not as reliable as expected, but the number of their manuscripts is also limited. Stott exhibited their mistakes, biases, and limited resources (Stott, 19–51). For example, the Gospels do not show the artificiality of citations in Herodotus who used obvious sources, manipulated evidences for credibility, and searched for interest in party bias [Stott, 20–21; based on D. Fehling's thesis in *Herodotus and His "Sources:" Citation, Invention and Narrative Art*, trans. J. G. Howie, Arca Classical and Medieval Texts, Papers and Monographs 21 (Leeds: Francis Cairns, 1989)]. F. F. Bruce listed the number of manuscripts for some Roman historians in *The New Testament Documents: Are They Reliable?* 6th ed. (Downers Grove: InterVarsity, 2003), 11.

37. Division between textual authority and oral tradition was also a division between social classes in the Mediterranean world. Propagating literacy meant a more unified Christianity. William M. Schniedewind, *How the Bible Became a Book* (Cambridge: Cambridge University Press, 2004), 210.

38. Origen, *Contra Celsum*, 3.55.

39. Gamble, *Books and Readers*, 144–61.

40. Eldon Jay Epp, "The NT Papyri at Oxyrhynchus," in *Perspectives on New Testament Textual Criticism: Collected Essays, 1962–2004* (Leiden: Brill, 2005), 507.

41. To access his reconstructed text of the Synoptic Gospels, consult Sylvie Raquel, "The Text of the Synoptic Gospels in the Writings of Origen" (Ph.D. diss., New Orleans Baptist Theological Seminary), 2002.

42. Eusebius, *Hist. Eccl.*, 6.23.1.

43. See Cribiore, *Writings, Teachers, and Students* on the processes of learning.

44. Van Der Toorn, *Scribal Culture*, 31.

45. Ibid., 47.

46. As recorded in the Jewish Scriptures, Yahweh did not reveal Himself first in a written form but in a tangible and personal way; then through a series of covenants, angelic mediators, and individuals, and finally through written laws and ceremonial worship.

47. Jer. 36:32. Even if, as some scholars claim, King Hezekiah's burning of the book was a fictitious story to give credential to Jeremiah's words, the change in the original text is still notable.

48. Van Der Toorn, *Scribal Culture*, 13.

49. F. F. Bruce, "Scriptures," 42. In 2 Thess. 2:15, Paul asks his readers to stand firm in the traditions they heard by word of mouth or by letter. The Corinthians maintained the tradition Paul asserted he received from the Lord (1 Cor. 11:2, 23). In Gal. 4:20, Paul insists that not everything could be said by letter.

50. Van Der Toorn, *Scribal Culture*, 15.

51. See Gamble, "Literacy," 30.

52. Jean Duplacy, *Études de Critique textuelle du Nouveau Testament* [Studies of New Testament Textual Criticism] (Leuven: University Press, 1987), 48.

53. Eusebius, *Hist. Eccl.*, 3.39.4.

54. According to Daniel Sarefield, the Roman state did not consider Christian books a threat to the equilibrium of the society until the fourth century, probably because they had been attached to the already sanctioned corpus of Jewish Scriptures; see "The Symbolics of Book Burning," in *The Early Christian Book*, ed. William E. Klingshirn and Linda Safran (Washington, D.C.: The Catholic University of America Press, 2007), 161, 164.

55. Holmes, "Text and Transmission."

56. On the stability of the New Testament, consult K. Martin Heide, "Assessing the Stability of the Transmitted Texts of the New Testament and the *Shepherd of Hermas*," in the present volume.

57. See Frederick F. Bruce, "Scripture in Relation to Tradition and Reason," in *Scripture, Tradition, and Reason: A Study in the Criteria of Christian Doctrine*, ed. Richard J. Bauckham and Benjamin Drewery (Edinburgh: T. & T. Clark, 1988), 55.

58. Canonical recognition did not necessitate the presence of all five criteria at once. To study the unreliable characteristics of the noncanonical gospels, consult N. T. Wright, *Judas and the Gospel of Jesus: Have We Missed the Truth about Christianity?* (Grand Rapids: Baker, 2006) and J. P. Moreland, *Scaling the Secular City: A Defense of Christianity* (Grand Rapids: Baker, 1987).

59. Daniel Hoffman, "S. T. Coleridge and the Attack on Inerrancy," in *Biblical Authority and Conservative Perspectives*, ed. Douglas Moo (Grand Rapids: Kregel, 1997), 114.

60. Jesus quoted the Old Testament, declared that his words surpassed the Mosaic Law (Mt. 5–7), and asked his followers to remember and teach his commands to all nations (Mt. 28:20).

61. Richard Bauckham, "Tradition in Relation to Scripture and Reason," in *Scriptures, Tradition, and Reason*, 118.

62. Hoffman, "Coleridge and the Attack on Inerrancy," 110.

63. Rodney L. Petersen, "To Behold and Inhabit the Blessed Country: Inspiration, Scripture, and Infallability—An Introduction Guide to Augustine, 1945–1980," in *Biblical Authority and Conservative Perspectives*, 73.

64. For example, the heart of the Ezraic revival resided in the people's understanding of the Law and willingness to change (Ezra 8).

65. For a discussion on how readers of the Bible can reach understanding, consult Kevin J. Vanhoozer, *The Bible, The Reader and the Morality of Literary Knowledge: Is There a Meaning in This Text?* (Grand Rapids: Zondervan, 1998).

66. Paul D. Feinberg, "The Meaning of Inerrancy," in *Inerrancy*, Norman L. Geisler, ed. (Grand Rapids: Zondervan, 1980), 288–92.

67. Ibid., 294.

68. Kevin J. Vanhoozer, *First Theology* (Downers Grove: InterVarsity, 2002), 131.

69. Walter Brueggeman, *The Book That Breathes New Life: Spiritual Authority and Biblical Theology* (Minneapolis: Fortress Press, 2005).

70. Lee Strobel, *The Case for the Real Jesus: A Journalist Investigates Current Attacks on the Identity of Christ* (Grand Rapids: Zondervan, 2007), 75.

71. Jaroslav Pelikan, *Whose Bible Is It? A History of the Scriptures through the Ages* (New York: Viking, 2005), 23.

72. Gordon Fee, "Textual Criticism of the New Testament," 425; Royse, *Scribal Habits*, 28.

73. Carson, The *Gagging of God: Christianity Confronts Pluralism* (Grand Rapids: Zondervan, 1996), 188.

74. J. P. Moreland discussed how belief in inerrancy is rationally justifiable in "The Rationality of Belief in Inerrancy," in *Biblical Authority and Conservative Perspectives*, 155–65.

SUBJECT INDEX

SCRIPTURE INDEX